STUDIES IN
CULTURAL HISTORY

Medieval Households

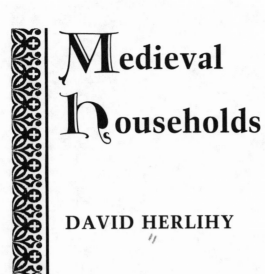

Medieval Households

DAVID HERLIHY

Harvard University Press
Cambridge, Massachusetts
London, England
1985

Library of Congress Cataloging in Publication Data
Herlihy, David.
    Medieval Households.

    (Studies in cultural history)
    Bibliography: p.
    Includes index.
    1. Family—Europe—History. 2. Households—
Europe—History. 3. Middle Ages—History. I. Title.
II. Series.
HQ611.H46 1985   306.8'5'094   85-5439
ISBN 0-674-56375-1 (alk. paper) (cloth)
ISBN 0-674-56376-x (paper)

PREFACE

Quia homines diversorum temporum diversas leges et con-
suetudines in conjugiis habuisse cognoscimus . . .

Since we know that the people of different ages have
followed different laws and customs regarding marriages . . .

—Hugh of St. Victor, *PL* 176, col. 157.

To trace in a short book the long evolution of medieval
households is hazardous, perhaps even foolhardy. For this
undertaking we need a limited agenda, a set of few but
fundamental questions to put to the sources. In the interpretation proposed here, medieval households, when compared with
those of both classical and barbarian antiquity, are shown to achieve
distinctiveness in three fundamental ways.

Ancient homes show extraordinary variety up and down the social
scale, from the huge palaces of the rich to the hovels of slaves and
the poor. I shall argue that the domestic units of antiquity were not
commensurable and comparable across society, and that the ancients lacked even the concept of family as a moral unit, common
to all levels of the social hierarchy. Put another way, the household
system of antiquity lacked symmetry, in the sense that different
sectors of society possessed fundamentally different domestic units.
Medieval families from the seventh and eighth century show much
greater commensurability. Apparently for the first time, households
could be used as standard units in censuses and surveys. Of course,
they continued to vary in size and structure, but the range of variation had become much more restricted.

From about the eleventh century, medieval families also acquire a characteristic kinship organization, initially visible among elites but eventually affecting all society. The kindred networks prevailing in the early Middle Ages were cognatic or bilineal, that is, they ran indifferently through males and females. From about the eleventh century, a new sort of descent group makes its appearance in European society—the patrilineage. Not only was it agnatic (that is, it discounted the importance of ties through women in the identification of kin), but it also tended to favor the first-born male over his younger brothers. The new lineage overlay, but it did not fully suppress, the older cognatic kin group. Elite medieval families came to follow two sets of sometimes competitive goals and rules. The good of the entire descent group was not always identical with the good of its male members. The tensions here generated helped set the social and cultural climate within families and households.

From about the same time a distinctive set of emotional ties links the members of the medieval family. It is not true, as has often been assumed, that medieval people were emotionally indifferent to their closest relatives, with whom in intimacy they passed their lives.

As they evolved from their dual heritage of barbarian society and classical antiquity, medieval households thus acquired commensurability, distinctive ties with the larger kindreds, and a tighter moral and emotional unity. Were households not also elements in a system? By system I mean the set of rules that governs entrances into and exits from households and regulates the transfer of members among them, making some large and others small, some complex and others simple. The answer to the question is assuredly yes. Unfortunately, however, the present state of knowledge allows us to inspect that system closely in only one region of medieval Europe—the province of Tuscany in Italy in the fifteenth century. This I attempt to do in Chapter 6. The analysis is an elaboration of the data and conclusions that I presented with Christiane Klapisch-Zuber in *Les Toscans et leurs familles* (1978; translated as *Tuscans and Their Families*, 1985). It remains to be seen whether or not the household system of fifteenth-century Tuscany was widely characteristic of the medieval world.

The agenda attempted here is large, though limited, and I would mislead the reader if I seemed to promise satisfactory answers to all the questions posed, for all medieval periods, in all regions. In this as in many areas of social history, the Middle Ages are a tapestry, parts of which are excellently illuminated, and parts of which remain in nearly impenetrable obscurity. I have used a great variety of sources, some statistical, many narrative and anecdotal, most of them difficult. The medieval social historian has little choice but to make use of what few records have survived, and to hazard occasionally impressionistic conclusions.

Despite these difficulties, this book does attempt a broad interpretation of the development of medieval households and the domestic system, from the period of the late Roman and barbarian antiquity until approximately 1500. The reader should be able to judge which among the proffered conclusions are well-founded, and which must be regarded as invitations to future testing. At a minimum, he or she should acquire a broad view of the evidence available (and lacking) for the study of the medieval household. May many readers be inspired (or provoked) to enlarge substantially, or interpret more persuasively, the data laid out in these pages. "If you know something more accurate than the things written here, then openly share it; if not, use these with me" (Horace, *Epistles*, 1.6.67–68).

Parts of Chapter 2, on early Irish households, appeared in somewhat different form in *Households: Comparative and Historical Studies of the Domestic Group*, ed. Robert McC. Netting, Richard R. Wilk, and Eric J. Arnould (© 1984 by the Regents of the University of California). I am grateful for permission to incorporate the material here.

D.H.

Mather House
February 1985

CONTENTS

TABLES AND FIGURES

MEDIEVAL HOUSEHOLDS

1 | THE HOUSEHOLD IN LATE CLASSICAL ANTIQUITY

Civitatem salvam esse sine matrimoniorum frequentia non posse.

The state cannot be secure without numerous marriages.

—Aulius Gelius, *Atticae Noctes*, I.66

THE STUDY of the medieval household requires an initial backward glance into the two parent societies of the Middle Ages: the classical Roman empire, and the peoples, whom the Romans called barbarians, settled to the north of the imperial frontiers. In this chapter we look at the domestic institutions of imperial Rome. The conventional date for the fall of the empire in the West is 476, but we must carry our survey a little farther, into the sixth century. One reason is that much of what we know of ancient households derives from the laws and commentaries which emperor Justinian (527–65) brought together and preserved in the *Corpus Iuris Civilis*.[1] In spite of its late redaction, the *Corpus* is the single most important source for the legal institutions of the ancient Roman empire. Then too, in things touching on the family, the sixth century seems to make a sharper break with the past than did the political collapse of the western empire, in the fifth century.

CONCEPTS OF FAMILY AND HOUSEHOLD

Historians who investigate ancient families immediately confront a perplexing question. What is the family—the primary descent group (parents and children)—called in the ancient languages?

Meanings

There are no terms, in either classical Greek or Latin, precisely corresponding to our own word "family."[2] In ancient Greek the most likely synonym is *genea*. The root meaning of *genea* is "generation," and it variously designates offspring, lineage, or a generation of time. But it seems never to have meant "family" in the modern sense. The modern Greek word for family (*oikogeneia*) sweeps away ambiguity by appending the word for house (*oikos*) to the term for generation. It thus neatly expresses the two chief aspects in the modern notion of family: primary relationship of the members through marriage and blood, and coresidency.

The lack of a precise equivalent for the modern word "family" in classical Greek is the more surprising as the ancients wrote extensively about households, meaning coresidential units of some sort.[3] The art and science of household management constituted "economics," and this was the exact counterpart to "politics," the science of city government. In their ruminations on social organization, the Greek thinkers used the word "household" (*oikos*) in two different but related ways. The educator and philosopher Xenophon wrote, about 386 B.C., probably the oldest and certainly the most influential discourse on "economics." He equated the household with its property, that is, with the material possessions of the household head: "The household looks to us to be the totality of possessions."[4] But others, including Aristotle, preferred to view the household as all those persons subject to the authority of its chief—slaves and servants as well as spouse and blood relations.[5]

In classical Latin, the word *familia* carries equivalent meanings. It designates everything and everybody under the authority (*patria potestas*) of the household head. *Familia* in classical usage is often synonymous with patrimony. "His family, that is, his patrimony," writes the jurist Gaius.[6] *Familia* could also mean persons only, specifically those persons subject to the authority of the *paterfamilias*, the household chief, usually the father. This was the more common usage in classical Latin. Thus, the jurist Ulpian, in the second century A.D., defines "family" as those persons who by nature (that is, natural offsprings) or by law (wife, adopted children, slaves) are subject to the *patria potestas*.[7] This definition still recognizes no distinction between the primary descent group and servants and slaves.

But it does retain a crucial distinction between the father and the family, the ruler and the ruled, even though by Ulpian's day the *patria potestas* had considerably weakened. Ulpian also offers a secondary definition of *familia:* slaves only.[8] But then he has no term to identify the residual members of the household, the husband, wife, and offspring. Isidore of Seville, who died in 636 and gave to the Middle Ages its favorite encyclopedia, the "Etymologies," states that *familia* derives from *femur*, and means in the strict sense "offspring."[9]

These usages yield a startling conclusion: the classical understanding of the word *familia* excluded from its membership its chief, the *paterfamilias*. He was not subject to his own authority, as Ulpian requires. Nor was he his own offspring, in Isidore's etymology. Then too, this understanding of the family was not applicable beyond the narrow range of the free and wealthy classes. The ancients, in sum, lacked a clear sense of the primary descent group as a distinct moral unit, and lacked too a concept of family or household that could be applied across all social levels.

From late antiquity into the Middle Ages, the most common meaning of *familia* continued to be the property or the dependents (sometimes only the servants) of the household head.[10] But in late Latin usage, probably under the influence of interpretations given to the Greek *genea*, *familia* assumed connotations of blood descent. It frequently appears with this meaning in Christian Latin writings. For example, around the year 200, Tertullian, the first major Christian writer to express himself in Latin, observed that "the Jewish people . . . were divided into tribes and peoples and families and houses."[11] *Familia* here means kindred or descent group. The "Itala," the oldest Latin translation of the Scriptures, uses *familia* as a rendering of the Greek *patria*, a word with the primary meaning of "lineage."[12] There is no implication in either the Christian or the pagan writings that this *familia* represented a coresidential unit, with its own moral identity.

If *familia* in ancient usage did not have the primary meaning of coresidential descent group, were there other terms in the classical vocabulary which expressed this sense? In Greek, *oikos*, which is a root of "economy," was, like the Latin *domus*, the house itself and all who dwelt within it, slaves and retainers as well as parents and children. The Roman household was a religious community, charged with maintaining the cult of the household gods, the *lares* and *penates*. These words were often used metaphorically to signify home or hearth. When Tacitus wished to say that the Germans did not herd their slaves into gangs, he observed that each slave had his own "seat" (*sedem*) and *penates*.[13] But these terms do not describe household units comparable across society. Another Latin word for hearth was *focus*. It meant the physical hearth, or, in late Latin, the fire within it, as in modern Italian, *fuoco*. Occasionally, it was used to connote all the households within the community, as in the rallying cry, *pro aris et focis*, "for altars and hearths." But it was rarely used as a metaphor for households, and it never represents a coresidential domestic unit common to all, or even one found at many social levels.[14]

The ancients failed to identify and to name the coresidential, primary descent group, the family in the modern meaning of the term. This is one indication that the ancient households varied widely across society and the homes of the rich had little in common with those of the poor. After all, the *familia* of the Roman aristocrats typically included scores, even hundreds of members.[15] These big establishments were fundamentally different from the hovels of the humble, and the secretive cohabitations of slaves.

Census Units

The conclusion that ancient households lacked uniformity across social levels gains support from the practices of census takers in ancient Mediterranean societies. This cradle of civilization nourished a long tradition of such surveys. The Bible itself records some nine censuses, made or attempted, of the Israelites.[16] According to the Book of Numbers, God instructed Moses and Aaron "to take the sum of all the congregation of the children of Israel by their families and houses, and the names of everyone, as many as are of the male sex, from twenty years old and upwards, of all the men of Israel fit for war . . ."[17] In all these Biblical surveys, the able-bodied warrior and the taxpayer, not the household or hearth, were the targets. And the word "family" used in regard to them means not so much the coresidential unit as the lineage, set within the tribe, set within the kin, and only vaguely differentiated from them.

The Romans were the great census takers in the ancient Mediterranean world. Every five years, special officers, the censors, were required to register citizens capable of bearing arms or liable to pay taxes; they also prepared an inventory of their possessions. We have fragmentary results of their scrutinies dating from 225 B.C., and the censors continued their efforts into the imperial period, apparently until the reign of Vespasian (A.D. 69–79).[18] As the empire expanded, the government took similar censuses of the newly acquired provinces and used them as the basis of tax assessments. But neither in counting its subjects nor in assessing their wealth did Rome make clear use of household units. In the period of the late empire (conventionally reckoned to last from 285 to 476), the imperial government developed an elaborate, and for historians still opaque, method of tax assessment, known as the *capitatio-iugatio*.[19] *Capitatio* involved a count of heads, presumably able-bodied workers; *iugatio* was an estimate of land area and its productivity; and in ways that are less than clear, animals too were factored into the assessment. The methods were so intricate as to cause wonder; why did not the Roman assessors simply prepare lists of hearths, and assign an assessment to each, in anticipation of the manner of medieval surveyors? The answer seems to be that domestic units were still too disparate. No common net could catch them all.

Only in one area of Roman institutions and life do households appear as equivalent units in a social array: the laying out of colonies. Since the early republic, the Roman government had rewarded veteran soldiers with grants of land. Grouped into colonies, the veterans worked their farms primarily with the aid of their families; they could have owned few or no slaves.[20] These farms were units of production as well as of residence, and this made them particularly suitable for surveys. In the late empire, as the problem of deserted fields mounted, the emperors took to settling barbarian contingents upon the land, again on the basis of families and family tenures. The emperor Aurelian (d. 277), for example, settled *familias captivas* on mountainous and wooded lands from Tuscany to the Maritime Alps; they were enjoined to plant the land in vineyards, to augment the wine supply for Rome.[21]

The appearance of commensurable household units thus seems intimately related to the extension of family-based, peasant agriculture. Perhaps this close association with peasant agriculture also explains why the ancient censors utilized hearths so rarely in their work. The unit could not be easily used to assess large, slave-run estates (or big ranches in the pastoral regions). Then too, ancient societies showed enormous variations in the range of wealth, from patricians owning thousands of slaves to the slaves themselves, pitiful chattel, most of whom were herded into barracks. Household units, with their implication of a rough equality across society, could not measure the size, wealth, and productivity of such socially cleaved communities. In sum, the households in the domestic system of antiquity were not commensurable. And the domestic array in which they were set lacked symmetry, in the sense that an observer would see vastly different types of domestic units depending on where he was looking—toward rich or poor, free or slave. Use of the household as a unit of social measurement had to await the demise of ancient slavery, and the replacement of rural slave labor in most areas of the former Roman empire by peasant agriculture.

HUSBAND AND WIFE

The expansion of the Roman republic and empire brought Roman legal institutions to all corners of the Mediterranean world and beyond: from north Britain to Mesopotamia, from the Danube valley to the Sahara desert. But the Roman law and customs of marriage were also changing profoundly in the late republican and imperial periods. We must try to recapitulate the thrust of those changes, which carried forward into the Middle Ages.

Kin and Exogamy

The Romans reckoned degrees of kinship by counting back from ego to the common ancestor, then forward to the targeted relative.[22] The number of persons touched, minus one, constituted the degrees of kinship. Accordingly, my father or mother is related to me in the first degree, my brother or sister in the second, my first cousin in the fourth, my second cousin in the sixth, and so on. Blood relationship in classical and medieval Latin is called *cognatio,* and in modern anthropological terminology a "cognate" is a blood relative whether through male or female lines. An "agnate," on the other hand, by modern convention, is one related to me only through males.

Scholars may argue as to how the early Romans reckoned kinship, but no one doubts that in the republican and imperial periods they discerned blood relationships as running through both males and females. The domain of kinship was, in sum, cognatic. There was also a legal *cognatio,* created through adoption, and the Christians would recognize even a spiritual relationship, between a baptized person and his sponsor or godparent.

About A.D. 370, a professor from Bordeaux named Ausonius (d. 395) wrote a poem which nicely illuminates consciousness of kin in fourth-century Gaul. The poem, the *Parentalia,* is in essence a celebration and commemoration of Ausonius' family tree.[23] It tells us, much better than legal texts, whom he recognized or thought important among his ancestors. In his poem he mentions by name 33 relatives, 18 men and 15 women. He clearly valued his ties through female relatives just as much as those through men. Of the 33 relatives, 21 are *cognati* or blood relatives, and 13 are affines, that is, related to him through marriage. In both groups matrilineal relatives outnumber patrilineal. Among the cognates, 9 are related to Ausonius through his father and 12 through his mother. The order in which the relatives are mentioned shows the weight given to matrilineal ties. The poet first names his father, then his mother, but the next four named are all matrilineal relatives (maternal uncle, grandfather, grandmother, and aunt). He commemorates his maternal aunt even before his paternal uncles. Likewise, the linkages to affines pass through his wife, his sister and his daughter. He fails to mention any affine through marriages of a brother or a son. His selection of relatives to commemorate shows no trace of an agnatic or patrilineal bias; rather the contrary.

In Roman custom and law, *cognatio* or blood relationship was recognized over seven degrees of kinship. The Romans did not, however, insist that this descent group with boundaries set at seven degrees practice strict exogamy.[24] To be sure, the law forbade all marriages between ego and a direct descendant. As Christian writers would later illustrate the rule, Adam could not today marry any woman in the whole human race. Initially too, the law had prohibited marriages up to six degrees (for example, between second cousins). However, perhaps in an effort to encourage marriages and births, by the second century B.C. emperors and jurists limited the prohibition to three degrees. This meant, for example, that first cousins could now marry. Emperor Claudius (d. A.D. 56) further permitted an uncle to marry a niece, if she was the daughter of a brother but not of a sister.[25] His rule might have been self-serving. But he does draw a distinction between matrilineal and patrilineal ties, and seems to suggest that the former were stronger, and presumably surer and more sacred, than the latter.

Under Roman law marriage was monogamous, "the union of a man and woman holding to a single habit of life."[26] (The phrase would be many times repeated in medieval legal codes.) The purpose of marriage was "the procreation of children."[27] Early in Roman history, only the patricians, the dominant aristocracy, could contract legal marriages (*conubium*). Quite literally, a "patrician" was someone who knew his father (*pater*) and could inherit from him. Even when plebeians were allowed to marry legally and bear legitimate children, the law continued to place impediments against numerous types of unions: between citizens and aliens, and across orders (senators, knights, and freemen) and legal categories (freemen, freedmen, slaves). The emperors gradually removed these impediments, but some remained until the reign of Justinian. Not until then, for example, could senators legally marry actresses or prostitutes.[28]

Roman law recognized an act of betrothal, or promise of future marriage, on which occasion the two families exchanged pledges or earnest money, called *arrhae*.[29] A kiss would also be exchanged, and a ring given, which in late imperial law acquired legal significance.[30] But at Rome the betrothal never acquired the solemnity and binding power it possessed among the Germans, and would retain in medieval canon law.

The bride had to have completed twelve years of age, and the groom fourteen. And both had to give their consent to the union: *nuptias consensus non concubitus facit*, "consent, not intercourse, makes the marriage."[31] (This Roman legal maxim was destined to exert a profound influence on the marriage rules of the medieval Church.)

Marriage *in Manu*

Roman law recognized two types of legal marriage.[32] The first and oldest was called *in manu*, "under the hand," or *conventio in manum*, "passing under the hand." Marriage *in manu* transferred the father's *patria potestas* over the girl into the hands of the husband. The rituals or acts by which the bride passed under the groom's authority were three: by "spelt" (a kind of wheat) bread, by purchase, and by long cohabitation.

The most solemn of these rituals, allowed only to patricians, included a sacrifice to "Jupiter Farreus," the "spelt" Jupiter. In the presence of a priest (the *flamen dialis*) and ten witnesses, the couple offered a sacrifice of spelt bread. The ceremony was called *confarreatio*, and the offspring of these solemn unions enjoyed special civil and religious privileges. They alone, for example, could aspire to enter the highest priestly colleges. But in spite of these advantages, *confarreatio* fell out of practice by the early principate (first century A.D.).

The more common ritual creating a marriage *in manu* was called *coemptio*, "a kind of imaginary sale," in Gaius' words. All Roman citizens could be married by this ceremony. In the presence of no fewer than five adult witnesses, the groom gave the bride's father a few bronze coins, and she passed under his authority. The act may once have constituted an authentic purchase of the bride, but most legal historians doubt that Roman marriages were ever truly sales (after all, the groom could not resell his wife, as he could any other purchased object). Rather, the payment may once have represented compensation to the father for his loss of authority over his daughter.

The third manner by which marriage *in manu* could be contracted was through *usus* or practice. If a nubile girl cohabited with an eligible male for a year or longer, then, in Gaius' phrase, "she passed into the family of the man and assumed the place of a daughter." But if she did not wish to do so, the Law of the Twelve Tables allowed her to return to her father's house every year for three nights (her stay was called the *trinoctium*). If this occurred, then authority over her remained with her father, but in fact was rendered largely fictional. The *trinoctium* created the possibility of marriages *sine manu*—"free" marriages, in which the wife was not subject to her husband's *patria potestas.*

Marriages *in manu* made of the old Roman household a kind of patriarchal despotism. The wife had no distinct legal position; she stood *in loco filiae,* "in the place of a daughter." She was subject to the full sweep of the *patria potestas,* which at one time gave her husband, at least in theory, the power of life and death over her. The husband holding the *manus* was free to divorce his wife, but she could not divorce him. All the property she brought into the marriage became her husband's. "When the wife comes under the *manum* of her husband," Cicero explained, "everything which had been hers becomes the husband's, under the name of the dowry."[33] She had no claim for the restitution of this property, even when the marriage was dissolved through death or divorce. On the other hand, standing "in place of a daughter," she could at her husband's death claim a share in the inheritance, alongside their children.

Marriage *in manu* fell into disuse from the period of the late republic. Under the empire, by the second century A.D., so-called free marriages (*sine manu*) become the norm.

Free Marriages

The rising popularity of free marriages in the late republic and early empire conferred singular advantages on the Roman matron. She remained, to be sure, under the technical authority of her father. But she could seek formal emancipation, and her father's death would at all events make her a person *sui iuris,* legally competent to conduct her own affairs. The law continued to insist that male tutors supervise the acts of women, but their authority remained limited (they could not, for example, prevent their remarriages) and was often entirely fictional. Moreover, under the marriage laws of emperor Augustus, the wife who bore three children was entirely freed of guardianship. Within the free marriage, the matron could now divorce her husband, and, if we can believe the contemporary satirists, many seized the chance.[34] She brought a dowry into the marriage, but the husband was now obligated to account for it; and if the marriage was dissolved by death or divorce, the wife had a legal claim to its full restitution.

Why, under the early empire, did free marriages replace marriages *in manu?* The shift reflects profound changes in Roman customs and culture, and in the Roman household. New and influential philosophical schools from Greece (for example, the Stoics) maintained that the sexes were equal; this principle was blatantly incompatible with the patriarchal despotism established by marriages *in manu.*

So too, the freer style of life, characteristic of Roman society in the early principate, doubtlessly rendered the *patria potestas* ever more intolerable for women. But probably the decisive change was in the economic arrangements accompanying the marriage. As we shall shortly see, the dowry provided by the bride (or her family) to the groom was growing larger. The new luxurious tastes and higher standards of living were rendering ever more onerous the "burdens of matrimony," until the government feared that dowry inflation would discourage marriages. To counter this, Augustus, in a *Lex iulia de fundo dotali*, made fathers legally obligated to endow any daughter who wished to marry.[35] But the families of brides were understandably reluctant to abandon all control over the inflated dowries. Under marriage *in manu* there was no assurance that the dowry would even serve the interests of the bride, her kin, or her heirs. Free marriages, on the other hand, allowed the bride to insist on an accounting from her husband as to the use of the dowry, and also on its return at the dissolution of the marriage. In sum, under the old marriage *in manu*, the husband had the power to use the household resources (even those supplied by his wife) arbitrarily. In contrast, free marriage was based on bilateral agreement, and as such was congenial with the bilineal Roman kinship group. The families of both bride and groom provided capital to the new household, and both partners retained a voice in its ultimate disposition. In shielding the wife's dowry from the husband's arbitrary power, free marriage encouraged her family to contribute still more substantial sums to the costs of establishing the new household. The return of the dowry at the husband's death also facilitated the widow's remarriage, which the government was eager to encourage.

Christian Marriage

The official toleration (A.D. 313) and then establishment of Christianity as the state religion (usually dated A.D. 380) affected, but did not substantially change, the legal and social institutions of late antiquity, including those bearing upon marriage.[36] Roman law and, later, the barbarian codes, continued to define the legal basis for marriage, and were sometimes at variance with Christian teachings. Thus, the *Corpus Iuris Civilis*, though redacted by the Christian emperor Justinian, still allowed divorce, as Roman law had always done.[37] To secure compliance with its own ethic of marriage, the Church relied exclusively on the private consciences of Christians. Not until the twelfth century did the Church develop a systematic canon law of marriage and a system of courts able to enforce it.

Still, Christian writers of late antiquity were already formulating principles of great importance for the future. Perhaps the weightiest of them was this: both men and women were equally obligated to observe chastity and fidelity.[38] In sexual ethics there could be no double standard. In contrast to the many types of marriage recognized in Roman law, there was only one Christian morality of marriage, binding for both sexes, all classes, and all nations. With some rare exceptions, Christian writers also insisted on the indissolubility of marriage—a position that from the first placed them at odds with the traditions of Roman law.

In the West, Augustine of Hippo (d. 430) was especially influential in shaping medieval views on marriage.[39] His ideas were seminal in at least three fundamental ways. Taking up a theme first expressed by St. Paul (Ephesians 5.24), he affirmed that the union of husband and wife was an analogue of Christ's union with the Church. Marriage was thus a *sacramentum,* a sacred bonding, and divorce was unthinkable. The sacramental essence of marriage is the point of departure for all subsequent theological and canonical speculation about the nature of marriage in the West.[40]

Augustine identified the three "goods" of marriage as *fides, proles, sacramentum*—fidelity, offspring, and permanent union.[41] Perhaps in opposition to the Manichees, who taught that sexual intercourse was moral only if procreation was avoided, Augustine affirmed that every sexual union had to be open to the possibility of procreation.[42] The long opposition of the Catholic Church to contraception has rested primarily upon an Augustinian analysis of sexuality and its purposes. Finally, Augustine affirmed that the love of husband and wife bound not only two persons but two lines of descent. Marriages were thus a means of bonding society together, a *seminarium civitatis,* a "seeding of the city."[43] When blood ties weakened over time, the ties of marriage intervened to knit together the human community. But the two relationships, by blood and marriage, had to be kept distinct. A man cannot take in marriage a woman whom he is already obligated to love by reason of kinship. Consanguinity and affinity are complementary, but also mutually exclusive. This idea was the point of departure for the medieval examination of incest. Here too, Augustine's influence was fundamental.

Incest

Recently, the English anthropologist Jack Goody has offered a novel interpretation of the Church's teachings on incest. From the fourth century on, the Church worked radical changes in "the ideology of marriage."[44] Specifically, it forced an alteration in the "strategies of heirship" pursued by the propertied classes. By broadening the incest prohibition (eventually to seven degrees), it prevented the great propertied families from conserving their patrimonies through endogamy—the marriages of close relatives and common heirs. Heirless owners were allegedly more likely to give their holdings to the Church. The Church struggled also to secure legal recognition for testamen-

Figure 1.1. The Mystical Marriage of St. Catherine, by Barna of Siena, fourteenth century. Courtesy Museum of Fine Arts, Boston. This depiction of the mystical marriage of Catherine of Alexandria with Christ also portrays the beneficial social effects of matrimony. Note particularly the scene of reconciliation in the center base of the painting, in which two knights exchange the kiss of peace under angelic auspices.

tary bequests, which were unknown in Germanic law. Finally, the celibacy imposed on the clergy assured that land once granted to the Church would never be lost. Church lands did indeed grow from the fourth century, and medieval society did indeed live under an incest prohibition that was remarkably extended. Neither the ancient Romans, nor the ancient Jews, nor the contemporary Muslims, applied such a sweeping prohibition against the marriages of kin.[45]

Goody thus discerns "a connection between the Church's modification of the accepted strategies of heirship and its wish to encourage bequests from the faithful."[46] He concedes that his case rests upon "deductive arguments," and in fact the hypothesis raises many problems. Were the Church's leaders unified enough, conscious enough, and shrewd enough to devise and implement this rather devious strategy of aggrandizement? It is not at all clear that the Church would have profited materially by preventing the wealthy from having heirs. Almost always, a young person entering the religious life brought with him or her some property as a kind of dowry; many of these recruits were the younger sons and daughters of the wealthy. In this way the Church stood as much to gain by facilitating as by obstructing marriages and procreation among the affluent. Furthermore, the Church lived in close alliance with the propertied elites and depended upon them for personnel as well as property. A childless magnate might grant his lands to the Church, but he could not offer a son or daughter. And the Church's need for property was no greater than its need for priests. It is not certain that the Church did indeed adopt the strategy Goody describes, or that such a strategy would have achieved its purported goals. In Chapter 3 I shall offer a different explanation for the Church's strident opposition to close marriages.[47]

Rituals

The Church was slow to develop rituals of marriage.[48] There seems to have been no Christian wedding ceremony over the first three centuries of Church history. Christian rituals of marriage appear in both East and West only toward the end of the fourth century. In the East, the most characteristic ritual was the placing of crowns upon the heads of both bride and groom; in the West, the nuptial blessing, imparted by the priest, became the central religious ceremony.

In some western communities, notably in Gaul, the priest imparted the blessing when the couple was *in thalamo*, already in the marriage bed. The story of the life of St. Amator (Lover), bishop of Autun who died in 418, tells a droll tale involving the marriage blessing. When the saint was still a young layman, his parents found him a bride named Martha, and deposited them both in the marriage bed. The bishop arrived to bless the couple. When he attempted to recite the nuptial blessing, "by divine instinct" he pronounced over the young couple prayers inducting them into the order of Levites, in which celibacy was required. Both Amator and Martha joyously accepted the divine sign and espoused lives of virginity.[49]

In Italian practice, the blessing was imparted not in the bedroom but in or at a church. This seems the earliest appearance of the common medieval practice: the blessing of the couple *in facie ec-clesie*, "at the door of the church." But the priest's blessing was not deemed necessary for a valid union. Consent alone made the marriage.

Terms of Marriage

To establish their new household and to rear their children, the young couple would normally have to face heavy expenditures—the "burdens of matrimony" in the language of Roman law. Marriage was therefore the occasion for the transfer of property, in the form of gifts exchanged between the bride and groom, or rather, their respective families. These gifts, to either bride or groom (or to both), were a principal conduit by which the old generation transferred wealth to support the enterprise (and encourage the fertility) of the young.

Under the Roman republic, and into the early empire, the most important of these marital conveyances was the *dos* or dowry.[50] Ulpian defines it as "the donation, which is given or promised by the wife or by her side to the husband or his side with the purpose, that it remain forever with him because of the burdens of matrimony."[51] In Roman law of the republican and early imperial epochs, there was no reverse dowry or *dos ex marito*. Indeed, the law forbade altogether conveyances between the spouses, except for the dowry itself.[52] The marital relationship was so close that no gift from one partner to the other could be accepted as entirely volitional.

The dimensions and direction of the marital conveyances shifted remarkably across the centuries of Roman history. Initially, the dowry provided by the girl's family was of modest size, but it shows a marked tendency to grow from the early republican era. A large dowry became essential, if the young girl was to attract a husband. "I have a big girl," laments a character in one of Plautus' comedies (c. 200 B.C.), "lacking a dowry and unmarriageable."[53] Ovid, a contemporary of Augustus Caesar, quips that a son in the army and a nubile daughter both give worry to a father.[54] Valerius Maximus, a moralist writing in mid-first century A.D., recalls the good old days when girls could be given in marriage with dowries of cheap bronze coins. He tells how the Senate, in order to keep a favored general in the field during the Punic Wars, provided his daughter with a dowry in the modest amount of 40,000 bronze coins. The gesture, he believes, showed not only the generosity of the Senate, but also the simple habits of the virtuous ancients.[55] He notes further how one Roman girl, Megulia, brought into marriage a dowry of 50,000 bronze coins, and earned for herself the nickname *dotata*, "the dowered one."[56] Valerius clearly regards the amount as trivial. In his Menippean satires, Varro (first century, B.C.) mentions a dowry consisting of the Golden Isle, a region of Latium famed for its wine, plazas in Capua, and the principal marketplace of Rome.[57] A little later, the philosopher Seneca remarks that the Senate's dowry to the general's daughter would not in his day suffice to buy a looking glass for a girl.[58] According to the satirist Juvenal, the prospect of a large dowry shot more of love's arrows than Cupid.[59]

The flow of wealth began to change course about A.D. 200 and most visibly under the Christian Roman empire, during the fourth and fifth centuries. Already from the late third century, documents mention a marital conveyance in the reverse direction, a dowry *ex marito*, from the groom (or his family) to the bride.[60] In the earliest citations, this reverse dowry is called the *sponsaliticia largitas* or "marriage gift"; it then comes to be called the *donatio ante nuptias*, or "donation before marriage." Since the law forbade gifts between the spouses, the groom had to endow his bride before the actual wedding. References to this reverse dowry become frequent in late Latin literature. Ausonius, in a poem celebrating marriage made up of lines out of Virgil, uses the gifts Aeneas gave to Dido to stand for the presents which the bride receives from the groom before her wedding.[61] In a commentary on the Song of Songs written before 410, Rufinus explains how Christ's bride, the Church, receives *sponsaliorum et dotis titulo*, "by title of dowry and marriage," "most worthy presents from [her] most noble spouse." She is "filled with gifts," accepted under this title of *dos*.[62] Rufinus' incorrect use of the word is indicative of the shifting terms of Roman marriage. *Dos* remains for him the marriage gifts, but it has now become not the true dowry but the reverse dowry, given by the bridegroom to his bride.

The inflationary trend continued, although the direction of the marital gifts was changing. By the middle of the fifth century, the groom's required *donatio* was becoming so inflated as to constitute, in the view of the imperial government, a principal obstacle to marriages. In 458, Emperor Majorian denounced the avarice of parents with marriageable daughters, and of the daughters themselves.[63] Allegedly, they were exploiting "naive youths," who were "excited by the desire of future marriage." They extracted from the young men a large *donatio*, out of which they took the bride's dowry and returned it to the groom. The bride and her family were contributing effectively nothing to support the "burdens of matrimony." Majorian branded with infamy those who entered into such deceitful contracts, declared the marriages illicit, and all ensuing offspring illegitimate.

Justinian, who legislated so frequently on nuptial matters as to earn the title *legislator uxoris*, made two changes in the laws governing these marital gifts.[64] He abrogated the old restriction on gifts between the spouses, and changed the name of the reverse dowry from *donatio ante nuptias* to *donatio propter nuptias*, "donation for reason of marriage."[65] Like the dowry itself, the *donatio* could be paid at any time. And he stipulated that the value of both conveyances had to be equal; any special pacts made in regard to one applied also to the other.[66] Both bride and groom and their respective families were obligated to contribute equal shares to the costs of setting up the new household.

We have no way of judging the success of these government efforts to keep the *donatio* from outstripping the *dos* in value. The references—oblique to be sure—outside of the jurisprudential literature, consistently imply that under the Christian empire the groom, rather than the bride, bore the principal part of the marriage burdens. Thus, in the *Vitae patrum*, a rich senator says to his wife: "Behold all my substance and that of your father I gave into your hands."[67] This seems like an allusion to both the *donatio* and the *dos*. A rich man named Cerealis tries to persuade the young widow Melany to marry him. He promises to transfer to her his riches "not as it were to a wife, but as to a daughter."[68] He intends to make her heir of all his property, but Melany contemptuously rejects the offer. "If I wished to marry," she states, "I would surely want a husband, not an inheritance."

Between approximately 300 and 500, the terms of marriage in the empire had very nearly been reversed; the earlier law had placed the chief "burdens of matrimony" on the bride and her family; later, the law shifted those same burdens in large part to the groom's side. Why had this astonishing shift occurred? Before offering some speculations, we need to consider a closely related phenomenon: the respective ages at which Roman women and men first entered marriage.

Ages at Marriage

References to ages at marriage are strewn across the great sea of ancient literature, and the evidence from inscriptions allows fairly reliable reconstruction of actual behavior.[69] Girls were very young at first marriage in the classical world, at least within the wealthier classes. Hesiod and Aristotle recommended that girls marry at 18.[70] Xenophon's ideal wife, presented in his *Economics*, was not yet 14 when she married; her husband's age is nowhere stated, but we must assume from the dialogue that he was a mature and experienced man.[71] To judge from inscriptions, pagan girls married between 12 and 15; the inscriptions commemorate literally scores of married women dead before their twentieth year. The Augustan marriage laws of A.D. 9 penalized women who had not delivered a baby by age 20.[72] Augustus forbids the betrothal of girls under the age of ten, and limits the time of betrothal to two years. His legislation assumes that many girls would join their husbands at the minimum legal age of 12 years (and clearly too, their husbands would be much older).[73]

This practice of early marriages for women long persisted. In the *Vitae patrum*, St. Melany the younger was married at age 13.[74] Euphraxia was betrothed to a senator, and received earnest money from him (the *arrhas*) when she was only five years old (this would have violated the Augustan marriage laws). While everyone waited for the girl to grow up, her fiance tried to court her mother.[75] When St. Augustine, about 384, decided to discard his concubine and marry, he chose as fiancee a ten-year old girl, and expected to wait two years until she attained the legal age of twelve before marriage.[76] The marriage never took place, as his conversion intervened; had it occurred, Augustine would have taken a bride probably twenty years younger than himself. It may of course be that Roman girls from less exalted classes were not so young at first marriage. St. Perpetua, for example, was 22 and married, with a nursing baby, when she suffered martyrdom at Carthage in 202 or 203.[77] She may have been 20 or 21 at marriage. At all events, from our earliest indications and into the fourth and even fifth century, Roman girls, at least those from families with means, were given in marriage at very tender years.

Roman males, on the other hand, were quite mature when they took a bride, and many chose not to marry at all. Aristotle recommends that males delay marriage until age 37, when their own passions had cooled and they were able to sire offspring of even temperament.[78] He thought too that husband and wife would then grow old together—evidence that he believed women lived much shorter lives than men. The Roman general P. Scipio Africanus was still unmarried at age 24.[79] The epigraphical evidence suggests an average age difference between groom and bride at marriage of nine years.[80] The Augustan marriage laws penalized males who had not become fathers by age 25.[81]

Late age at first marriage for men is almost always associated with large numbers of permanent bachelors in the population, and this is certainly true in the society of the early empire. The imperial Roman government was seeking to encourage marriages since the late second century B.C.[82] Augustus took a census of married and unmarried males within the two orders of senators and knights, and was shocked to find that the bachelors far outnumbered the husbands. According to the historian Cassius Dio, he summoned in separate groups the unmarried and the married knights.[83] He dressed down the many bachelors, calling them selfish and unpatriotic, and warmly congratulated the few married men for their willingness to assume the admitted burdens of the married state. The climax of his policy was the *Lex Papia Poppaea*, promulgated in 9 A.D.[84] It imposed numerous penalties on the unmarried (*coelibes*) and the childless (*orbi*). Ironically, the two consuls after whom the law was named were themselves unmarried.

The advanced ages at which males married in the early empire, and the reluctance of many to marry at all, correlates with the contemporaneous inflation in dowries. In order to attract reluctant grooms for their nubile daughters, families had to bid up the amount of the dowry they were offering. Their behavior corresponds well with what the economists call "decision theory." In a situation of bidding and response, the participant in a strong negotiating position is likely to reject the first offer, as his chances are good that the next offer will be even better. Conversely, the actor in a weak position is likely to accept the early offer, as the next is likely to be worse. The prospect of a still higher dowry thus persuaded Roman grooms to delay their marriages, and Roman girls to marry at the earliest opportunity.

One aspect of that picture remains difficult to comprehend. Because of attrition due to age, on the assumption that the sexes were approximately of equal number, there should have been more brides seeking grooms on the marriage market than the reverse. There should in consequence have been large numbers of unmarried adult women in Roman society. But spinster women are not often encountered in the sources. Ancient society had no institutions, comparable to the medieval convents, designed to accommodate unmarriageable girls, and classical Latin lacks even a word for spinster (but it does have one for "unplaceable," *illocabilis*). What had happened to the "unplaceable" girls? The most likely answer is that the sexes were not in balance. The widespread ancient practice of exposing or abandoning unwanted babies affected sex ratios, as little girls were more likely to be exposed than little boys.[85] A law supposedly promulgated by Rome's founder Romulus required that citizens rear all their sons, but only the first-born of their daughters.[86] Augustus himself noted a shortage of women within the nobility.[87] It is likely that families responded to the high costs of attracting husbands for their daughters in part by limiting the numbers of females they were willing to rear. However, even if exposure reduced the number of nubile girls in the early empire, the marriage market continued to impose the chief costs of forming the new household on the bride's family.

Between ca. 300 and 600, even as terms of marriage were turning against the groom, the age of marriage for males apparently was falling, while that for women climbed. Young men, facing deteriorating terms of marriage, now were eager to take brides; women, on the other hand, in a stronger negotiating position, were willing to wait for the better offer.

Our evidence is of course very scattered, but still worth reviewing. The inscriptions occasionally cite not only the age at death of the deceased, but also the years he or she spent in marriage. It is therefore possible to estimate the age at which the deceased married. (But almost never can we tell if this was a first or subsequent marriage, and most inscriptions are not precisely dated.) Table 1.1 shows for about 250 Christian inscriptions the estimated ages of marriage for men and for women.

Table 1.1. Estimated ages at first marriage, ca. 250–600

	Men		Women	
Century	Number	Age	Number	Age
Before 300	0	0	2	15.55
300–399	11 (9)[a]	30.25 (27.35)	29 (27)	18.12 (16.80)
400–499	2	22.50	8	15.95
After 500	2	25.00	6	18.23
Undated	67 (65)	27.17 (26.55)	115 (108)	19.27 (18.16)
TOTALS	82 (78)	27.43 (26.49)	160 (151)	18.81 (17.77)

Source: ILCV (data from Christian inscriptions).

a. Figures in parentheses represent results after subtracting men who marry after age 40 and women after age 30.

To reduce the complication of second marriages, we can remove from the calculations males who marry after age 40 and females after age 30, as it is doubtful that these persons were then marrying for the first time.

Table 1.1 does indicate a tendency for the age at first marriage for Christian men to fall, and that of women to rise, over the last centuries of the western empire (it can safely be assumed that most inscriptions of unknown date come from the fifth and sixth, rather than the third or fourth centuries, after the Christian population had substantially increased). The age difference between husband and wife was also dropping, from approximately 11 years in the fourth century to 7 in the sixth.

An impressionistic review of the inscriptions and saints' lives suggests a similar conclusion. A Christian inscription, probably from the fifth century, commemorates a fuller named Alexius, who joined his wife, *virgo ad virgine*, when both were sixteen.[88] In the *Vitae patrum*, St. Ammon marries, albeit unwillingly, at age 22.[89] The brother of St. Syncletica was married at twenty-five.[90] In the legend of St. Julian (supposedly martyred under Diocletian), the saint resists the demands of his parents that he marry, saying that he was not old enough. His parents answer: "You are about 18 years old; how can you excuse yourself from entering marriage?"[91]

The writings of the Gallo-Roman Ausonius also cast some light on marriages in the late empire. Ausonius himself, born in 310, was married about 334, presumably at age 24. His wife must have been nearly the same age, for she died at 28, after bearing two children. His comments imply that they were equal in age: "iuvenis iuveni quod mihi rapta viro," "young, she was taken from me, her young husband."[92]

Ausonius also introduces us to a social type rarely found in prior classical literature: the lifelong spinster. Two such *rarae aves* are mentioned in his poetry: Julia Cataphronia, his paternal aunt; and Aemilia Hilaria, his mother's sister, who lived the single life for 63 years, practicing the profession of physician.[93] The mature maiden, in no rush to marry, also appears in Ausonius' poetry. Galla is a girl "already growing old," who obviously resists the poet's warnings: "Galla, we are growing old; time is flying"; "unknown old age is creeping in, and you cannot call it back."[94] The *Vitae patrum* reveals another rarity: marriages in which the groom was apparently younger than his bride. The rich parents of St. Abraham, for example, "betrothed a girl to him while he was still in childhood."[95]

Young marriages for males are encountered also in the early Byzantine period. St. Theophanes, who died about 820, was betrothed at 12 to a girl presumably of the same age.[96] They lived in the same household for eight years. When Theophanes (and presumably also his bride) reached age 20, the father of the girl insisted that the marriage be celebrated. If this marriage is at all typical, the marriage pattern of the early empire, based on young ages for girls and mature years for men, had entirely dissolved.

The policies of the Roman government further reflect a growing reluctance of women under the Christian empire to enter marriage. In 320, doubtless under Christian influence, emperor Constantine abrogated the Augustan marriage laws.[97] But the gesture hardly eliminated, and probably worsened, the continuing threat of depopulation. Emperor Majorian (457–61) returned to a vigorous, pronatalist policy, "since it is Our wish that [children] shall be procreated in great numbers for the advancement of the Roman name."[98] But the principal targets of his legislation were not the reluctant bachelors, whom Augustus had denounced, but women and their families, girls who took vows of virginity before age 40, or widows without children who refused to remarry within five years after their husbands had died.[99]

The dramatic change in the ages of marriage is linked to the parallel change in the terms of marriage. It is not enough simply to ascribe the emergence of the *donatio ante nuptias* to the influence of eastern practices upon Roman law, as historians of law usually tend to do.[100] Even if the argument has merit, it does not explain why this foreign custom should have appealed to the inhabitants of the empire.

To explain this evolution, surely we must look to both social and cultural changes, even though it is difficult to identify, still less to measure, what they were. Perhaps for reasons of acute depopulation and shortage of labor in the late empire, women, at least in the towns, seem to have become capable of pursuing a career and supporting themselves, if they chose. Economic independence meant that they did not have to marry if they did not wish to. The physician Aemilia Hilaria, Ausonius' aunt, preferred the single life and never married.[101] The Christian inscriptions mention several older women (still, however, called "puellae") who apparently lived as single women in the world.[102] The inscriptions also mention female physicians.[103] Aemilia Hilaria was not unique. We meet in the *Vitae patrum* a woman named Piamon, who spent "all the years of her age," "continuously working linen."[104] She lived with her mother and never married. And the emperor Majorian condemns the presumably many widows who refuse to remarry and "choose a lascivious freedom of living."[105] If we can believe the hagiography, the cities of late antiquity abounded in virgins—10,000 of them in Ancyra alone.[106]

Then too, the changing perspectives and values of late ancient culture were reducing the prestige accorded marriage and procreation. Stoicism, Neo-Pythagorianism, and above all, Neo-Platonism, contained a strong ascetic element.[107] So also, on a popular level, did many of the new mystery religions emanating from the East, including Christianity. With the exception of the Stoics, who regarded marriage as natural, these philosophical schools recommended the celibate life, as it offered freedom to reflect upon the supersensory verities. The various Christian sects developed a range of attitudes toward marriage, some totally opposing it and others recommending it for all.[108] Ultimately, the orthodox position affirmed that marriage was a dignified state, but inferior to virginity and even widowhood. St. Jerome rates the three states on a numeric scale, scoring virginity at 100, widowhood at 60, and marriage at a poor 30.[109] "I praise weddings," he says, "I praise marriage, but only because they generate virgins."[110]

A life of virginity was considered especially appropriate for women. Christian writings on the subject could be read as a feminist critique of marriage. To be sure, among the pagans marriage also had its critics, but they denounced its inconveniences specifically for males who wished to pursue the contemplative life.[111] Apparently for the first time marriage is criticized from the perspective of women. Thus, St. Jerome claims that widowhood was for the woman an "occasion of freedom."[112] At last she gained control of her own body; she was no longer the slave of her husband.

In the seventh century, St. Leander, brother of Isidore of Seville, in a letter to their sister rehearses the "worries and dangers" of marriage for women. He points out the discomfort of carrying babies, the pains of childbirth, the dangers to both mother and child, the oppressiveness of subjugation to a husband. "[Wives], along with modesty, lose freedom."[113] Numerous saints' lives, particularly those of female virgins, contain similar passages. Thus, the life of the martyr Flavia Domitilla contains a particular biting denunciation of the vices of husbands. Two servants, both eunuchs, tell her that she should not allow a "strange man" power over her body—power that even her parents did not exercise. A husband would surely abuse her "with most vile authority." He would be jealous and would beat her. "All husbands," they claim, "before the marriage, pretend to be humble and most gentle; afterwards, they display what they have concealed; if they are lecherous, they make love to slave girls, despising their wives and treating them like dirt."[114]

In the cultural climate of late antiquity, both Christian and pagan women, and their families of origin, attached surprisingly low value to marriage and to procreation. And single women appeared able to support themselves, inside and outside religious communities. Marriage was not the only possible career for women of that era, or the dominant value in their lives.

PARENTS AND CHILDREN

Ancient attitudes toward children are singularly paradoxical. Parents in classical antiquity undoubtedly loved their children. The huge body of gravestone inscriptions preserved from both pagan and Christian antiquity overflow with expressions of parental, or filial, devotion. The great eighteenth-century scholar, Lodovico Muratori, even classified the ancient inscriptions he collected according to the form of *affectus* (affection) they expressed: between husband and wife, parents and children, brothers and sisters.[115] The inscriptions also record the age of deceased children with surprising accuracy, measuring the duration of their brief stay on earth in months and days, sometimes even hours.[116] Perhaps astrological interests explain their precision, but even this would indicate that parents were deeply concerned with the fortunes of their offspring.

And yet the treatment accorded children in ancient society was often severe, even brutal. The exposure of unwanted babies was commonplace. The pedagogy practiced in ancient schools was notoriously harsh. "Who would not shudder," Augustine exclaims in the *City of God*, "if he were given the choice of eternal death or life again as a child? Who would not choose to die?"[117]

And yet this odd mixture of dedication and discipline is understandable, given certain fundamental assumptions of ancient society about the state of the world and the nature and goals of education.

The Sense of Limits

From the late republican era through the age of the Christian empire, writers express the conviction that the world was already crowded with people, more even than its exhausted resources could support. In the late republic, the Roman poet and Epicurean philosopher Lucretius, in his essay "On the Nature of Things," gave eloquent expression to this theory of cosmic senility:

> Furthermore of her own accord [earth] first created the shining grain and smiling vineyards for mankind. She herself produced sweet fruits and fertile pastures, which now can scarce grow anything, for all our toil. And we exhaust our oxen and our farmers' strength, we wear out plowshares in the fields that barely feed us, so much do they begrudge their fruits and increase our labor. And now the aged plowman shakes his head and sighs and sighs again, to see his labors come to naught, and he compares the present age to days gone by . . . and groans to think of

> the good old days, when . . . life was easily supported on smaller
> farms . . . The gloomy grower of the old and withered vines sadly
> curses the times he lives in, and wearies heaven, not realizing
> that all is gradually decaying, nearing the end, worn out by the
> long span of years.[118]

This theory of cosmic senescence proved marvelously congenial
to Christian writers, who saw in it proof that the despised earth was
nearing its end. It also justified the high praise they rendered to
virginity. This is how the crowded earth appeared to Tertullian about
A.D. 200:

> Everything has been visited, everything known, everything
> exploited. Now pleasant estates obliterate the famous wilder-
> ness areas of the past. Plowed fields have replaced the forests;
> domesticated animals have dispersed wild life. Beaches are plowed,
> mountains smoothed and swamps drained. There are as many
> cities as, in former years, there were dwellings. Islands do not
> frighten, nor cliffs deter. Everywhere there are buildings, every-
> where people, everywhere communities, everywhere life.[119]

Tertullian takes no satisfaction in the human conquests he describes. Rather, in phrases that anticipate the grim ruminations of
the English clergyman Thomas Malthus, he lists the penalties of
excess population:

> Proof [of this crowding] is the density of human beings. We
> weigh upon the world; its resources hardly suffice to support
> us. As our needs grow larger, so do our protests, that already
> nature does not sustain us. In truth, plague, famine, wars and
> earthquakes must be regarded as a blessing to civilization, since
> they prune away the luxuriant growth of the human race.[120]

St. Augustine, the most prolific of the Latin fathers, reiterates all
these themes. The world is saturated with people, there is no more
space to fill; nature has grown old, and human history approaches
its term.[121]

With these assumptions, the Christian writers faced an evident
difficulty in the Biblical injunction: "increase and multiply, and fill
the earth." The command, in their exegesis, was once applicable to
Adam and Eve and to their immediate descendants—a single couple,
then a small family and tribe set within an empty earth. But now,
the command had been changed, indeed abrogated, by what Augustine calls "the mystery of time." As the world was already crowded
with people, "no duty of human society"—the phrase is again St.
Augustine's—required marriage and procreation.[122] "There is not the
need of procreation," he writes, "that there once was." "The coming
of Christ," he argues elsewhere, "is not served by the begetting of

children."[123] Even within the Christian community, marriage was a concession grudgingly conceded to the morally weak; in Augustine's words, "marriage is not expedient, except for those who do not have self-control."[124]

But would not the growth of the Christian community at least increase the number of saints in heaven? No, reply the Christian fathers, for the number of saints had been fixed from eternity, and could not be altered by human behavior. "The number of saints," says Augustine, "will be perfect, none fewer, and none greater."[125] In a widely shared view, the saints would exactly replace the numbers of the fallen angels.[126]

In lauding virginity over marriage, and childlessness over parenthood, the Christian fathers had to face an evident consequence; if all men adhered to their counsels, the human race would not last a generation. This would be, Augustine responds, entirely a good thing. It would indicate that the number of saints had reached its predestined size, and the City of God had become perfectly populated. The Christian fathers refused to concede that there was any social or religious value in sheer numbers of people.

The fathers thus agreed completely with the pagans in denying the value of vigorous procreation, though of course they recommended opposite means to the same end. For pagans, the presumed density of human settlement justified both the avoidance of marriage and the limitation of children within it, including abortion, exposure, and infanticide. The many who did not marry were free, in the common pagan ethos, to satisfy their appetites through nonreproductive sexual activities, including homosexuality and pederasty. The Christians condemned extramarital sexual indulgence and praised virginity and continence, hoping for few marriages and small families. Pagan sensuality and Christian asceticism, contrary as values, in fact bore the same demographic consequences: few children and a stable or declining population.

Apaideia

Convinced that the world was already crowded, ancient communities exerted powerful and effective control over their own numbers. As early as the second century B.C., the Greek historian Polybius warned that this policy of childlessness, of "apaideia," was threatening the survival of Hellas:

> In our own time the whole of Greece has been subject to a low birth rate and a general decrease of the population, owing to which cities have been deserted and the land has ceased to yield fruit, although there have been neither continuous wars nor epidemics . . . [People] either do not wish to marry, or if they

marry, to rear the children born to them, or at least they rear only one or two of them, so as to leave them in affluence.[127]

The few estimates of population size in classical antiquity indicate an extraordinary stability over centuries. The population of Italy, for example, may have grown from 5 to 7 million, between 225 B.C. and the Augustan age, but imported slaves seem to account for all the increment; the free population probably declined.[128] Stable populations and small families seem thus to have been an abiding characteristic of ancient communities, and remained so even in the era of the Christian empire.

Strategies of Child Rearing

While they did not welcome or choose to rear many children, the parents of antiquity still invested heavily in the education of the young. Ancient civilization depended for its survival on the preservation over generations of elaborate traditions of thought and skill. Ancient society would be inconceivable in the absence of formal instruction, professional teachers, and numerous schools. Even in the troubled fourth century, Ausonius, himself a poet, rhetorician, and teacher, composed a collective elegy in memory of the professors he had known in his school days at Bordeaux.[129] He names 32 teachers who had presided over his cultural formation. But the economy was poorly productive, and strained to support a huge educational establishment.

The ancients thus adopted an understandable strategy: they reared comparatively few children, but invested heavily in their training. Given their slim resources, they were reluctant to invest in children with evident bodily or mental weaknesses. And the surviving children were subject to close supervision and discipline. Good returns on the resources invested in them had to be assured. St. Augustine, truly a child of his times, tells in his *Confessions* how his father, Patricius, and even his pious mother, Monica, urged him to high performance at school, "that I might get on in the world and excel in the handling of words, to gain honor among men and deceitful riches."[130] "If I proved idle in learning," he says of his schooling, "I was soundly beaten. For this procedure seemed wise to our ancestors; and many, passing the same way in the days past, had built a sorrowful road, by which we too must go, with multiplication of grief and toil upon the sons of Adam."[131]

Christianity and Childhood

The Christian religion powerfully influenced the treatment of children in many complex ways. Christianity, like Judaism before it, unequivocally condemned the exposure of infants or infanticide. To be sure, the abandonment of unwanted babies remained common social practice in the Middle Ages, but was always regarded as a sin. The abandonment or killing of babies in medieval society was the characteristic resort of the fallen, the poor, the desperate. In the ancient world, exposure of babies had been accepted practice, even among the social elites.

Christian teachings also informed and softened attitudes toward children. Christian scriptures held out several examples of children who enjoyed or earned God's special favor: in the Old Testament, the young Samuel and the young Daniel; in the New, the Holy Innocents and the Christ child himself. According to the evangelists, Jesus welcomed the company of children, and he instructed his disciples in the well-known words: "Unless you become as little children, you will never enter the Kingdom of Heaven" (Matt. 18:15). This partiality toward children evoked many echoes among patristic and medieval writers. In a poem attributed to St. Clement of Alexandria, Jesus is called the "king of children."[132] Pope Leo the Great writes in the fourth century: "Christ loves childhood, for it is the teacher of humility, the rule of innocence, the model of sweetness."[133]

But alongside this positive assessment of the very young, Christian tradition supported a much harsher appraisal of the nature of the child. In Christian belief, all persons, when they entered the world, bore the stain of Adam's sin and with it concupiscence, an irrepressible appetite for evil. Moreover, if God had predestined some persons to salvation and some to damnation, his judgments touched even the very young, even those who died before they knew their eternal options. The father of the Church who most forcefully and effectively explored the implications of original sin for children was again St. Augustine. Voluminous in his writings, clear in his logic, and ruthless in his conclusions, Augustine finally decided, after some early doubts, that the baby who died without baptism was damned to eternal fires.[134] There was heaven and there was hell, and no place in between. "If you admit that the little one cannot enter heaven," he argued, "then you concede that he will be in everlasting fire."[135]

The great African was, moreover, impressed by how early evil establishes its dominion over the growing child. The suckling infant cries unreasonably for nourishment, wails and throws tantrums, and strikes with feeble but malicious blows those who would care for him. "The innocence of children," he concludes, "is in the helplessness of their bodies, rather than any quality of soul."[136] "Who does not know," he asks elsewhere, "with what ignorance of the truth (already manifest in babies), with what plentitude of vain desire (initially apparent in children), man enters this life? If he is allowed to live as he wishes . . . he will fall into all or many kinds of crimes and atrocities."[137]

The suppression of concupiscence thus becomes a central goal of Augustine's educational philosophy and justifies hard and frequent punishments inflicted on the child. While supposedly rejecting the values of pagan antiquity, he advocates the classical methods of education. Augustine prepared the way for retaining under Christian auspices that "sorrowful road" of schooling which he, as a child, had so much hated.

This strategy of child rearing—to have few offspring, but to train them well—seems understandable, given the literate culture of ancient society, given its poorly productive economy. But this strategy placed the Roman world at a critical disadvantage in the face of the barbarian peoples settled beyond the *limes*. With no literary culture or system of formal education to maintain, the barbarians invested little in their offspring, and were under no cultural compulsion to limit fertility. Isidore of Seville thinks that the name "Germany" derives from the land's ability to generate (*gignere*) peoples.[138] In the opening pages of his *History of the Lombards* (written shortly before 800), Paul the Deacon affirms that *populosa Germania* is much more suited for multiplying the human race than Mediterranean regions, and he sees in this dire consequences. "For the reason that [Germany] produces so many human beings that she cannot feed them all, many tribes have issued forth from her, and these have afflicted both parts of Asia and especially neighboring Europe."[139] These opinions are naive, but not without truth: the barbarians from populous Germany did eventually overwhelm the Roman frontiers.

2 | THE HOUSEHOLD IN LATE BARBARIAN ANTIQUITY

For a mother is a venerable treasure, a mother is a goodly treasure, the mother of saints and bishops and righteous men, an increase of the kingdom of heaven, a propagation on earth.

—*Cáin Adamnáin*, an Old-Irish treatise, on the Law of Adamnan, c. ninth century

MEDIEVAL SOCIETY was formed not only out of the institutions and customs of the classical Mediterranean world, but also of the northern, barbarian peoples settled beyond its frontiers. It is, to be sure, difficult to investigate the barbarian family and household. To begin with, there was no single barbarian nation and culture, but many. We ought not assume that households were the same in all the tribes, or that they retained the same structure over time. Moreover, we have little direct information about these northern peoples. Classical authors offer scattered comment on their customs, but it is hard to judge how clearly these distant observers saw, or how accurately they reported. The barbarians themselves did not have writing before they were converted to Christianity. Thus, the national laws of the Germanic peoples, one of the chief sources for their social history, were not written down until the sixth and subsequent centuries. They are late texts, already subject to strong Christian and Roman influence. Even archeology, the one true frontier of early medieval history, does little to illuminate the softer aspects of culture, such as human relations or domestic ties.

But despite these difficulties, in this general history of the me-

dieval household we cannot fail to look hard at its barbarian antecedents. More even than the heritage of classical Rome, barbarian
traditions and customs shaped the domestic system of early medieval Europe.

IRELAND

The region of northern Europe that has the most abundant literary
materials illuminating early households is Ireland. And among the
several genres of surviving records (penitentials, laws, sagas, lyric
poetry) the most revealing for our purposes are the lives of Irish
saints. Some few have survived in Old Irish, and many more in Latin.
I must use the Old-Irish lives in English translation, but they follow
closely their Latin counterparts, and these latter unquestionably
represent the older tradition. The following reconstruction of the
household system of early medieval Ireland draws principally from
these hagiographical sources.

Saints' Lives

Early Irish hagiography is an exceptional source for social history.
The named saints of Ireland for the period before 800 are nearly a
hundred in number, remarkable for a region never part of the Roman
empire and not converted to Christianity until the fifth century.[1]
This small land, set on the margins of the world, merits the title it
is given in one of the lives, the *insula sanctorum*, the "isle of saints."[2]

But these were saints of a special sort, more nearly heroes than
holy men. To the Bollandist fathers who first subjected them to
close study, the lives often seemed to provoke ridicule rather than
edification.[3] But this only gives tribute to the rich ethnographic
materials they have preserved.

The principal setting is of course Ireland, but the saints in their
famous peregrinations wandered widely, and allusions to Scotland,
Britanny, Britain, Gaul, Germany, and Italy are frequent. The range
of geographic references gives assurance that the lives reflect not an
insular but a maritime Celtic culture, concentrated along the northwest coasts of Europe.

The tradition by which these stories have reached us is very obscure. The numerous Latin lives are principally preserved in three
great manuscripts, all of them apparently written in the fourteenth
century.[4] Internal evidence (references, for example, to the Norman
conquest of England) indicates that they were composed in the late
eleventh and twelfth centuries.[5] But all of them pretend to recount
the lives of saints who flourished in early Christian Ireland, soon
after the times of St. Patrick, in the sixth and seventh centuries.

These lives thus hover like a mist over some 800 years of Irish and European history, without firm moorings. The precise events they describe can rarely be dated and accepted as historical. But the pious legends they contain display, in marvelous fashion, culture as well as cult.

Unlike the lawgiver, the hagiographer of early Ireland did not seek to direct future behavior by establishing rules and norms, which may or may not have been respected. He pretended to describe concrete realities and living people. And he looked out onto a society still in large part heathen, still only lightly touched by a crude Christianity. The saints repeatedly contend with pagan kinglets, chiefs, and magicians. No other set of sources known to me offers so detailed a view of an early medieval social system, still drifting on the border between heathenism and Christian belief.

Then too, Irish lives lack the rhetorical bombast which obscures many continental lives of comparable age. They are rich in homely allusions—to the tending of flocks and herds, to the making of cheese and butter, to the daily activities of peasants, shepherds, craftsmen, and bards. Most important for our purposes, they populate the landscape with living families and households, and describe domestic arrangements in vivid detail.

Many scholars have commented on the aura of archaism that permeates these lives, as it does other Irish sources.[6] Works written in Old Irish, it is claimed, constitute Europe's oldest vernacular literature.[7] The saints, for example, ride about in chariots, driven by an *auriga* or charioteer. One of the three great collections of Latin lives, the Salamanca Codex, formerly the property of the Irish College of Salamanca in Spain and now at Brussels, is especially noteworthy for its archaic flavor.[8] In the fourteenth century, copyists and editors tried to rid all three collections of incidents or events thought to be unedifying, but the censors of the Salamanca Codex proved especially inept. *Felix culpa!* The Codex, for example, contains a rare reference in medieval hagiography to delousing. The young saint Molua is depicted picking lice from the hair of an elderly friend.[9] The service must have been frequently performed in medieval society, but it is not the usual stuff of pious legend.

The Codex also treats in startling fashion an act of abortion. In the life of St. Kieran, according to the version preserved in the Salamanca Codex, a petty king named Dimma abducts a "noble and beautiful girl" from a convent founded by Kieran's mother, and takes her to wife. The enraged saint seeks him out, and through his miraculous powers forces him to relinquish the girl. The story continues: "When the man of God returned with the girl to the monastery, the girl confessed that she had conceived in the womb. Then the man of God, prompted by zeal for justice, not wishing that the seed of vipers should quicken, making the sign of the cross on the womb, caused it to empty."[10]

The text is unambiguous: the saint miraculously aborts the fetus. The act is closely analogous to the curses, which the saints frequently utter against an enemy and his *semen*, which typically cause the ruin or even the extirpation of the lineage.[11] However, both the Irish penitentials and the legal collection known as the brehon laws, themselves archaic sources, forbid induced abortions, even of illegitimate fetuses, even before they quicken.[12] The Salamanca Codex thus hearkens back to a more ancient epoch. In the expurgated Latin versions of the same life, the saint causes the fetus conveniently to vanish, and the Old-Irish accounts are similarly bowdlerized.[13] The reference to abortion is suppressed, and this doubtlessly reflects the refined morality of a later age.

Early Irish hagiography carries us to a strange, occasionally savage world. We shall here draw out from the lives what they purport to show: social life in late iron age, Celtic society, at the origins of the Middle Ages.

Septs

Irish society was divided into tribes (*tuath*) and the tribes into kindreds called septs, although the sources do not always differentiate with clarity one from the other. The sept is exactly equivalent to the Germanic or Indo-European sib, *Sippe* or *Geschlecht*. The sept appears frequently in the lives as the *gens*, a kin group stemming from a named ancestor or founder. Its members are usually referred to as the "sons" or "grandsons" (*nepotes*) of the same forefather. It is also called *cognatio* or simply *natio*.[14]

The sources occasionally identify the founder of the sept and inform us how distant he was in generational count from the present. Thus, in the Old-Irish life of St. Abban, the head of the sept that produced the saint was Brian son of Eochaid, seven generations back; the founder of the sept of St. Mochua, named Lugo, was his *abavus* or great-great-grandfather, four generations into the past.[15] It should be noted, however, that these short genealogies did not exhaust the lineage memory of the Irish. They were capable of pushing pedigrees back fifteen and more generations.[16] The extended pedigrees showed the relationships of septs within the same territory and gave structure to tribes and nations, but did not define the functional kindred, that is, the sept itself.

Thus, within their seemingly interminable lineages, the sources identify some prominent figures as those who established existing kindreds. "This Lugo," reads the life of St. Mochua, "was the founder of the Lugic sept, which is not at all obscure among the Irish."[17] The clear reference to the founding of a sept within human memory suggests that the septs within society were constantly dividing and reforming. Presumably, a member of an established sept, if he became wealthy, powerful, and prolific, could become the *auctor* of a new *gens*. If we assume that Lugo and his descendants all reared four children to adulthood (those marrying out would be replaced by those marrying in), then by Mochua's generation the sept would have included 32 households, about 160 persons. Abban's kindred would have had 256 households, more than 1250 persons—probably as large as the sept could be. These admittedly crude estimates at least give us a range of magnitude which the Irish septs probably attained.

Many historians of early law have maintained that the primitive Germanic and Indo-European *Sippe* or descent group was agnatic, that is, it recognized relationships only through males.[18] Although all the founders of the Irish septs were indeed men, nonetheless the kin association was emphatically not restricted to patrilineal relatives. King Echach tells St. Patrick that he hoped "to extend my lineage (*prosapia*) from the body of my daughter, by the procreation of grandchildren, for the strengthening of my kingdom."[19] His wish would make no sense if matrilineal relationships were ignored. Descent through women was very important in Irish society. Among the works of the eighth-century Irish monk, poet, and hagiographer, Oengus, there are maternal genealogies of some 210 Irish saints; it is not known whether he ever traced the paternal lines of these holy people.[20]

The Irish septs practiced exogamy, but not exclusively of women. Clearly, king Echach, mentioned above, expected his future son-in-law to join his household, and his grandchildren to remain with him, "for the strengthening of my kingdom."

Septs inhabited and controlled a particular territory with recognized boundaries. The territory of a sept seems to have had a ceremonial center. Once, St. Daverca goes to visit her *cognati* in the north. She arrives "at the field called Murthanna, which was the particular habitation of her sept."[21] Both the field and the *habitatio* have a special relation to her sept, although we are not informed of its exact nature.

Members of the sept meet together to discuss common issues and make collective decisions. Thus, the sept of Arad "one time came together and took counsel, in order that they might drive out wolves from their borders."[22] The life of St. Brigid by Cogitosus, which is perhaps the oldest of all Irish lives, mentions how the task of building a road was divided "among septs and families," "so that each sept and family should build the part assigned to it."[23] The sept defended its members against outsiders, kept the peace among them, and more than likely adjudicated disputes. The brothers of St. Aedh, in his absence, divided their father's inheritance immediately after his death, and left Aedh "no share." His biographer observes: "But this displeased his relatives."[24] We are not, however, told what his *cognati* did to help him.

Although the sept's territory had fixed and recognized boundaries, the members did not own fields or flocks in common, and did not participate in common economic enterprises, other than building roads and expelling wolves. The lives leave no doubt that fields and flocks were privately owned, and that differences in wealth among the sept members were pronounced.[25] Probably, the sept retained some residual rights over the property of its members. Its permission, for example, might have been required if a member wished to alienate property. Perhaps too, it could claim and assign unsettled lands, or take possession of properties for which there was no direct heir. On these legal issues, the lives offer no enlightenment. But unmistakably, individual ownership of property and marked gradations of wealth were characteristic of early Irish society.

Within the community, the septs differed one from the others in numbers, in territory controlled, in prestige, power, and even skills. The sept of St. Daverca "in former times was imbued with skills in the magical arts above other neighboring septs, but by the grace of God working through St. Patrick it became Christian."[26]

Households

The sept was comprised of individual households, which, we have guessed, might number between 120 and 256. At the head of the household was the chief and his wife (or wives).

Most of the marriages in the lives are monogamous. But we hear of a "very rich man" who had two wives, "according to the law of that time."[27] The life's unknown author finds no blame in such polygamy: "This man walked in the commandments of God, giving gifts and tithes in His honor."[28] But his wives quarreled so much, that he eventually fled the household and entered the monastic life. And the apparent prevalence of monogamy did not, as we shall shortly see, preclude the formation of other forms of sexual liaison, with concubines and slaves.

The legal wife is the *domus domina*, the mistress of the household, as she is called in the life of St. Brigid.[29] According to the *Cáin Adamnáin* or Law of Adamnan, all wives were at one time slaves.[30] They were even forced to go to war, to slay and be slain, while their husbands, standing safely behind them, whipped them onward into the fray.[31] St. Adamnan allegedly freed them; his was "the first law made in heaven and on earth for women." Moreover, ". . . ever since Adamnan's time, one-half of your house is yours, and there is a place for your chair in the other half."[32] It is hard to know what to make of this bizarre text, but clearly it celebrates the freedom of women and their authority within the Irish household.

The wife also performs certain critical services for her male kin. When the four half-brothers of Brigid try to force her into marriage, they complain that through her vow of virginity, "she avoids that for which God made her, and in her obstinacy so lives, and is determined to live, so as not to want to make her father a grandfather and her brothers uncles."[33] She thus causes them "great shame and expense." Here, I believe, is an important insight. Brigid is the half-sister of these males, and indeed her mother is a slave. But their own mother—Brigid's stepmother—has become cursed with sterility and cannot produce another sister. Brigid offers her half-brothers their one possible link through a sister to the coming generation. (She also offers her father his last chance to have grandchildren through a daughter, and this may be the reason that he comes to regret his initially bad treatment of her.) Brigid's brothers seem to be unmarried, and no one of them is bothered by the celibacy of the others. Yet they strongly insist that Brigid marry. Their behavior highlights the capital importance of the relation of brother to sister's son (the "avunculate") in the early Irish kinship system, and indeed of all relationships running through women. To be sure, Irish chiefs certainly wanted male descendants, to uphold in a violent world the status of their lineages.[34] But they also wanted the pedigree of male descendants certified through matrilineal connections.

In urging her to marry, Brigid's brothers further argue that her husband, who will surely be noble, will be for brothers and for father a *propugnator et amicus*, a champion and friend. The wife was thus of critical importance in defining the relations of her family of origin to other powerful persons and septs in the vicinity.

In keeping with the important services she renders, the legal wife seems also to have controlled important wealth.[35] The brehon laws imposed strict limits on a woman's power to hold and to alienate property, especially land, but these restrictions leave no trace in the hagiography. A woman named Flandnait holds from her father an "inheritance" in the town called Feic, along the banks of the Nem (Blackwater) river.[36] And women often give themselves and their property to the saints.[37]

One source of the wife's wealth was the dowry system. The groom, or his family, conveyed property to the bride, which she personally controlled. The reverse dowry, probably best called bridewealth, included even land. In the life of St. Mochteus, for example, a widow bestowed on the holy man a field she received as part of her dower, an *agrum dotalem*.[38] Apparently some women accumulated wealth through gifts from their husbands, and even from other males, over the course of their marriages. In the life of St. Fursa, a nobleman of Gaul reminds his wife of the "riches I have given you." She had accumulated wealth "since youth."[39] In the life of St. Aedh, a king gives a gold and silver brooch to a woman who is clearly not his wife.[40] Other wealthy women are mentioned in the tales. St. Fursa, when passing through Arras in Gaul, seeks hospitality from a lady named Ermenfleda, who owns "many possessions and moneys."[41] After the saint's death, his merits cure the illness of another rich lady, who holds "many riches and possessions."[42] To be sure, some of these rich ladies live in Gaul and bear Germanic names (Leuti-sinda, Ermenfleda), but the lives give no hint that this in an Irish perspective was at all exceptional. As the Old-Irish life of Berarch states, what valor is to the warrior, and learning to the clerk, so is prosperity or abundance to a woman.[43]

The wives are likely to have wielded considerable influence, power even, over decisions made within the household. They had the right to divorce their husbands and depart their households, taking their wealth with them. The stepmother of St. Brigid threatens to leave her husband Dubthach, if he does not sell his slave concubine, Brigid's mother, then pregnant with the saint.[44] Her threat carries real force, as she bends her reluctant husband to her will, and later gains his acquiescence in her persecution of the young saint. So also, in Gaul, the lady Leutisinda berates her husband and threatens to abandon their marriage if he continues to bestow their properties on St. Fursa.[45]

The legal wife in these elite households is rich and powerful, but her presence does not stop her husband from forming other sexual alliances. Concubines are frequently mentioned in the lives, and clearly not all of them are slaves.[46] The life of St. Brigid offers a particularly lively picture of sexual relations, inside and outside of legal marriage. Dubthach, Brigid's father, is evidently a rich man, possessing large flocks and herds and extending the hospitality of his table to numerous guests. Perhaps he is also a Christian; at least he welcomes bishops to his table, with exultation and a smiling face, in the language of the life.[47] Besides his legal wife, he cohabits with a slave girl, called *concubina* in the text. When the story of Brigid's life begins, Dubthach has made both women pregnant. The life utters not a hint of reproach against Dubthach for this violation of Christian marriage. On the contrary, the anonymous author rather reproaches the legal wife, for forcing her husband with threats of divorce to get rid of his concubine. The wife is depicted as stupid and mad;

she lacks matronly modesty and fails to show proper respect for her husband; she has an evil mind, and she behaves like a raging beast.[48] She draws all this abuse because she objects to the presence of a concubine in her household. Dubthach is exonerated from all guilt, even for driving his pregnant concubine from his home. "My wife prevents me," he explains, "from being liberal and humane toward my concubine."[49]

The lives consistently show a tolerant attitude, not only toward bigamy, but toward all sexual relations outside of legal marriage. They describe, for example, again without a suggestion of reproach, the illegitimate births of several other saints. The noble father-to-be of St. Ailbe secretly sleeps with a slave girl, the concubine of king Cronan of Artaige.[50] The girl becomes pregnant, and her lover, fearing the wrath of the king for impregnating one of his women, takes to flight. King Cronan assumes that the father of the baby was, like the mother, a slave, and in his fury orders that the child be exposed. Servants leave the baby in the wilderness, where a she-wolf finds him and suckles him together with her cubs. In spite of these inauspicious origins, the boy grows up to become a renowned bishop and, according to this account, a second Patrick. In another story, king Echach has three beautiful daughters. One of them falls in love with a noble warrior in her father's service, apparently seduces him, and bears a son by him, without benefit of legal matrimony. She delivers the baby in secret, and his father spirits him away to his own country. The child, called Tigernach, also grows up to become a holy bishop and a famous saint.[51] The abbot Nemanus, successor of St. Boecius, was conceived when a monk slept with a nun, who had come to do his laundry.[52] The father of St. Barr is born of an incestuous union of father and daughter, is exposed at birth, and is also suckled by a wolf.[53] The holy bishop Dimma was conceived in adultery and abandoned at a church door, where St. Carthach found him and reared him.[54]

Incest as well as adultery is commonly encountered in these biographies. Three Irish princes, sons of king Echach, sleep with their sister, and she conceives a child "from their three mixed conceptions."[55] One Irish king, after the death of his wife, wishes to marry the most beautiful girl in the land; he dispatches a delegation to find her. The delegation reports that the most beautiful girl in the land is his own daughter, Dympna.[56] The king determines to marry his daughter and makes preparations for the wedding. The distraught girl flees to Brabant, but the king eventually searches her down and kills her.

Although only monogamous marriage was legal after the abrogation of the "old" law, these Irish aristocrats sometimes cohabited with two or more free women simultaneously. The Irish laws in fact recognize a form of "free marriage," a union achieved between free persons without benefit of dowry or formal agreement. It seems analogous with the *Friedelehe* (from *fidila*, "beloved") of Germanic law.[57] Dimma, the petty king who, according to the life of St. Kieran, abducted the girl from the convent, made her his wife. But clearly, no agreement had been struck with her kin and no dowry provided. And Dimma seems already to have been married; at least, he has had two children by another woman, one of whom, at the time of this incident, was still being nursed.[58]

Polygyny

If these scattered references to early Irish households can be interpreted in terms of a single, coherent domestic system, it must be one that incorporates polygyny. According to the lives, the maintenance of several sexual liaisons is unmistakably the prerogative of the wealthy and the powerful. The man who lived with two wives "according to the old law" is expressly described as "very rich."[59] Another rich man, Dubthach, Brigid's father, can afford to purchase a slave girl for a concubine and to support her in his household. The traffic in slave girls was so brisk that the word *cumalach* (female slave) serves as a standard measure of value in early Ireland. A petty king, such as Dimma, has the power to abduct the girl that he desires, and only a wonder-worker can retrieve her. The rescue of abducted girls gives frequent employment to the saints.[60]

Those males who possess wealth and power use it to acquire women too. In anthropological terminology, the common name for such a system is "resource polygyny." Even in societies where polygyny is legal, only the richest and most powerful males will usually command the resources needed for the support of several sexual partners; this was the case in early Christian Ireland. But if some men claim several wives or concubines, then others will have none. The Irish lives do not reveal a great deal about the lower levels of society, which had to be marked by a shortage of women. Doubtlessly many males, unable to marry, worked as servants in the households of the powerful. Dubthach's own household employed shepherds, swineherds, cowherds, and cultivators. The lives give the further impression that the surrounding forests and wastes were infested with brigands; they waylay travelers, rustle sheep and cattle, and attack homesteads.[61] Their ranks were doubtlessly filled by poor males unable to find mates.

The anthropological model of resource polygyny, applied to early Irish society, is suggestive, but still requires further refinements. Women were gathered into the households of the powerful not exclusively for sexual purposes. Even the households of the early Irish bishops, who were celebrated for their chastity, seem to have accumulated women. There is a curious passage on the "three orders of the saints of Ireland."[62] The first, and indeed the holiest of the orders, flourished from the days of St. Patrick. It numbered some 350 bishops, founders of churches. "They did not," reads the passage, "spurn the administration of women, and their company."[63] Presumably, these women directed the celibate bishops' households. Women were also involved in many productive activities. St. Brigid, when she labored under her stepmother's cruel dominance, was a jack of all trades, or a jill of all chores: she tended the sheep and pigs, milked the cows, and helped in the harvest; she cooked, baked, made butter and cheese, and brewed beer; she waited at table, and nursed the sick.[64] Women dominated all phases of cloth manufacture, from spinning, to weaving, to dyeing, to the sewing of cloth.[65] In the words of the *Cáin Adamnáin*, the woman "carries the spindle and . . . clothes everyone."[66] The close association of women with cooking, brewing, and dyeing, with arts that men did not understand, may have given them prominence too in the practice of magic.[67] The divorced wife of duke Colman murdered through incantations his offspring by his new wife, as soon as they were born; only the intervention of St. Coemghen finally broke her magic.[68]

Among the arts considered appropriate for women—for religious women surely but perhaps lay as well—was reading. St. Ite was an extraordinarily learned woman. She tells her sister to send her son Mochoemog, Ite's nephew, known also by his Latin name Pulcherius. "Bring him here," she orders, "for it is fitting that I should nourish him." "And for twenty years the most blessed abbess Ite instructed him in honest morals and a knowledge of letters . . . so that he could become a priest and build a place for God."[69] We should note the special relation here between a woman and her sister's son—an interesting variation of the avunculate tie.

Women thus tended to gather in the households of rich and powerful males, both for reasons of their sexual attraction and for reasons of service. A modified form of resource polygyny seems to have been a common model of aristocratic marriages and households in early Christian Ireland. The model allows us to draw certain inferences concerning the social life of the epoch. We can then judge whether such inferences find support in the period's scattered documentation.

One implication of resource polygyny is that it tends to raise the incidence of sexual promiscuity within the community, on the part of women as well as men. The rich man cohabiting with several women seeks to guard them from other men, but the task is difficult. Men without sexual partners will seek to overcome their deprivation through the purchase of a concubine, if they have the money; through abduction, if they have the power; or through seduction, if they have the charm. Moreover, the woman, like Dubthach's wife, may resent the fact that she shares her husband's attentions and look for satisfaction, or even retribution, in her own extramarital affairs. And the disgruntled wife will have no trouble finding willing paramours.

Indeed, the women who appear in the Irish lives are not passive sexual objects, moved about without acquiescence or resistance among powerful males. Women sometimes initiate sexual liaisons. They repeatedly tempt the saints, although this may be only a hagiographical topos.[70] St. Carthach was so handsome that "at various times during his youth thirty young women fell in love with him with great carnal passion, and did not conceal it."[71] The beautiful daughter of king Echach seduces a soldier in her father's retinue, and becomes the mother of the great St. Tigernach.[72] According to the life of St. Kieran, a queen named Ethnea, wife of Engus, comes with her husband to a feast sponsored by another king named Concraid. She falls in love with her host, and tries to seduce him. She is unable to consummate the adultery, but her failure does not indicate any lack, on her part, of desire and effort.[73] One day, St. Columba asks a young monk whether his mother is a religious woman.[74] The surprised young monk replies that his mother is certainly of good morals and reputation. The saint instructs him to inquire from her about a certain grave sin—unnamed, but surely sexual. The abashed mother admits her guilt. In the same story, a layman expresses the fear that his wife, out of love for a younger man, may murder him.[75] Still another layman complains that his wife refuses to sleep with him, and only the saint's admonitions and power succeed in persuading her to fulfill her conjugal duties.[76] In the life of St. Kentigern, bishop of Glasgow, a queen cultivates an adulterous relationship with one of her husband's knights, and gives him a ring, through which the affair is discovered.[77] These are not passive women.

Even limited sexual promiscuity has the result of obscuring lines of descent through males. The issue of uncertain paternity emerges in the lives, and is a frequent occasion for miraculous enlightenment. St. Dimma is born out of an adulterous union, and no one knows what to call him.[78] But St. Carthach has a vision of the past: "This baby is called Dimma, and he is the son of Cormac of the seed of Eathach." All present praise the saint, "who revealed the lineage of the holy baby Dimma, no one telling him except the Holy Spirit." In another incident, a woman commits adultery, bears a child, but refuses to identify the father; St. Ailbe summons all the men of her village, as if all were equally suspect.[79] The baby at the saint's command names the father. In one of St. Brigid's miracles, the saint in comparable fashion instructs a three-year-old to identify its father;

Brigid thereby refutes the allegations of his lying mother, who claims that a bishop is the father.[80] A recently converted petty king named Brendan "begged St. Patrick that he should bless a certain pregnant woman, as he believed that his blessing would benefit her and her offspring."[81] The saint was about to do so when, "the spirit revealing it to him," he recognized that the baby's father was of a lineage he had previously cursed, out of which, he had predicted, no king would come. Apparently, the woman—was she Brendan's wife?—was concealing the true paternity of her baby. The mother of St. Kentigern of Glasgow cannot tell him who his father is. "That which was born in her, she received by human intercourse. But she many times affirmed, and swore, that she did not have awareness by whom, or when, or how, she had conceived."[82] Were it not for miracles, the paternity of all these babies would have remained uncertain.

Under such conditions, the male is likely to develop the most steadfast ties with persons related to him through women. He has good reason too for favoring them in the distribution of his properties through gifts and inheritance. The children of his sister are without doubt members of his kin and representatives of his stock—his *semen* in the terminology of the Irish lives. Indeed, they will usually be the sole members of the younger generation who can be so identified. And he can be more certain that his grandchildren through a daughter are his blood relatives than the grandchildren through a son.

The Irish lives make frequent mention of the avunculate tie, and of other forms of relationship running through women. In the life of St Patrick written by the English Cistercian Jocelin of Furness (after about 1180), Patrick is represented as the great-nephew of St. Martin of Tours; his mother Conquessa is Martin's niece.[83] Jocelin is the first to claim that the two saints were related, and significantly, he runs their blood tie through two women. Still according to Jocelin, to his *cognatus* Patrick, Martin gives the monastic habit and his rule.[84] As a boy, Patrick had been reared in his aunt's house in a town called Nemphtor (presumably Clyde) in northern Britain.[85] The aunt was his mother's sister. Patrick himself had three sisters, one of whom, Lupita. had seventeen sons and five daughters. They all become priests and nuns, and all come to help Patrick on his Irish mission; so also did his other nephews, sons of sisters. "Truly the offspring of these [sisters] appears blessed . . . and a holy inheritance was the nephews of St. Patrick."[86] The embellishments, which Jocelin added to the ancient legends of Patrick, are extraordinarily rich in matrilineal allusions.

The maternal uncle of St. Alban, the bishop Ybar, is present at his birth, and blesses both mother and baby.[87] At age twelve, the nephew joins his uncle and remains with him "many years." The nephew of St. Braccan, again the son of a sister, is a thief.[88] He accidentally kills his uncle, and the crime is represented as especially heinous. The three Irish saints, Cronan, Mobai, and Machonna, are parallel cousins whose mothers are sisters.[89] Their spiritual relationship replicates the kinship tie running through women. In the life of St. Ruadanus, a man named Odo Guori flees for protection against an angered king to the bishop Senachus; the two are cousins, sons of sisters.[90] Fraech, uncle of St. Berarch, takes the latter as a baby from his sister. The life in Old Irish relates: "And Berarch was the one person in all the world who was dearest to Presbyter Fraech of all who ever received human nature, save Christ alone."[91] The Latin version adds a quaint touch: the uncle suckles his little nephew on his right ear.[92]

The bond joins uncle and niece as well as nephew, but always through a woman. In the Old-Irish life of Brendan of Clonfert, "Brig, daughter of Findlug his sister, was with him there, and great was his love for her."[93]

Under the system of Irish kinship, not only matrilineal relatives, but the women who served as linkages, and women generally, were held in high esteem. To St. Brendan, the face of his sister Briga, "whom he warmly loved," at times takes on "the look of the splendid moon."[94] St. Cainnech finds "great joy" in visiting his sister Columba.[95] And the *Cáin Adamnáin* is lyrical in its praise of mothers.[96]

This modified form of resource polygyny also affected practices of child rearing. In the households of the powerful, the presence of several mothers and several sets of children inevitably invited jealousy and dispute. Dubthach's legal wife, herself pregnant, is incensed when she hears the bishop prophesy that the offspring of her husband's concubine is destined to be mistress over her sons, and indeed over all Ireland.[97] Later she subjects the young Brigid to cruel persecutions. The wife of the king of Laigin, "like a faithless stepmother," tries to kill her husband's son, "for she feared that he would prevail over her own offspring."[98] In part for their own protection, young children were frequently, even usually, sent to be reared in different, often distant households. The foster mother is called in the lives the *nutrix*, as she assumes the duty of nursing the young child. The foster father is the *nutritor*. The bonds linking foster child and parents were often close. In the life of St. Fintanus, a monk named Sinkellus tries to convert to the ways of righteousness both his natural father and his *nutritor*. He brings the two men to St. Fintanus. The saint utters the gloomy prophecy that the natural father will be numbered among the goats at the Last Judgment, and adds, rather anticlimactically, that kings will also confiscate his property.[99] But the foster father will be saved, suggesting that the services of the foster father were more meritorious than those of the natural parent.

The household system of early Christian Ireland, in summary, was based on the descent groups, kindreds or septs, which traced their origins back to a named ancestor. The sept's founder was always male, but matrilineal ties retained a special importance. The sept's fortunes, especially in battle, depended upon men, but relations through women certified their membership and kindled their loyalties. The sept controlled a particular territory, and was in turn divided into households. The households were not, however, very similar or commensurable. Polygyny, concubinage, and a need for the services of women gathered females into the households of the rich and the powerful. At the other end of the social scale, bands of robbers—predominantly male, as far as we can judge—lurked in the forests and mountains and preyed upon the households of the *divites*, *duces*, and little kings, in quest of food, cattle, booty, and women. Between these two extremes, Irish households doubtless differed considerably in their size and the sex ratio of their members. And violence reigned, as some men sought to protect, and others to steal, these treasures.

The skewed distribution of women doubtlessly subjected them to high risks of rape and abduction. But the system also favored women, in marked ways. They played a major role in the administration of the great households, even those of the celibate bishops. They participated in, even dominated, many types of economic production, especially the manufacture of clothing. In religious life and perhaps in the secular world as well, women were repositories of literacy. The learned St. Ite "reared many of the saints of Ireland from their infancy."[100] Within the kinship network, women served as signposts, indicating to ego his surest relatives. This function made them important conduits for the flow of property, in the form of marital gifts and inheritances, down the generations. To pass on property through female relatives offered the best assurance that the wealth would benefit one's own lineage, one's *prosapia* and *semen*.

The hagiography of early Christian Ireland displays Irish septs and households with remarkable clarity, and shows a coherent system. How closely does this Celtic model resemble the domestic arrangements of the continental, Germanic barbarians?

THE CONTINENT

The early sources illuminating the ethnography of the continental barbarians, the Germanic tribes which overwhelmed the Roman empire, are far less detailed and vivid than those surviving for Ireland. Tacitus' famed *Germania* presents an unquestionably idealized portrait of Germanic life.[101] The national laws of the Germanic peoples, redacted between ca. 500 and 900, contain frequent references to marriages, dowries, and inheritances, but are often obscure and have elicited from the experts contrary interpretations. Collections of charters, numerous after ca. 750, similarly make references to families, but they are typically terse and again hard to interpret. Saints' lives have survived in considerable numbers from the Continent in the early Middle Ages, but are not as rich as their Irish equivalents in ethnographic materials.

Over many years, many scholars have investigated the family system of the early Germans.[102] Many of them have been concerned with the history of law, and they freely incorporated much later texts into their analysis. Among these sources is the fourth book of Adam of Bremen's *Deeds of the Bishops of the Hamburg Church*, the capital text for the study of north German society.[103] It dates from the late eleventh century. The Icelandic sagas from the late twelfth century and after similarly provide much information on Norse domestic institutions, though centuries later than the Viking period.[104] Late medieval German "mirrors" or collections of local legal customs and of legal wisdom are also exploited, in the effort to reconstruct the family system. Even the practices of the northern German province of Diethmarsch, in which in modern times family clans held a particular prominence, have served as materials in this difficult research.[105]

The *Sippe*

The main focus in this research on the Germanic kinship and family system has been the *Sippe* or *Geschlecht*, the descent group common in Indo-European social organization and equivalent to the Irish sept. The legal historians to whom we owe much of the relevant literature have tried to envision an orderly pattern of social development, and have tended to draw upon widely scattered sources to buttress their arguments. Many of their assumptions are today not convincing. They have maintained, for example, that the primitive *Sippe* was based exclusively on agnatic or patrilineal descent lines, and only at a later stage in its development were matrilineal ties recognized.

In spite of its importance, the *Sippe* is rarely encountered in the early sources, and it remains very hard to investigate its size, structure, and internal organization. According to Tacitus, "parents and relatives," that is, members of the *Sippe*, were present at the wedding ceremony and received and approved the gifts given the bride.[106] Presumably, the *Sippe* had some voice in arranging the marriages of its members. The most explicit early references to this kin group come from the laws and charters of three Germanic peoples: the Lombards, Alamanni, and Bavarians. All these surviving allusions are terse, and all have evoked much scholarly comment and dispute.

The Lombard sources make sporadic mention of a particular group of persons called *fara*.[107] The Bavarian law also cites the term *far-amanni*, which would seem to identify the members of a *fara*.[108] Like other terms designating groups, the word also identifies the territory which the group settled, and becomes a synonym for *curtis*, court or estate. Thus, according to a chronicler named Leo, some time not long after 862 a man called Maio donated to the Benedictine abbey of Monte Cassino a *fara*, called also in the passage *curtis*, named after himself.[109] It was big, measuring 5,800 modia of land.[110]

Many place names, in both Italy and France, incorporate *fara* or one of its variants; this suggests that the places were in origin the villages or lands where the groups known as *farae* settled or controlled.[111]

In one interpretation of the *fara*, Alexander Callander Murray, supported by Walter Goffart, argues that in its earliest appearances the group represents the "following" or retinue of a chief, "an artificial, mainly military grouping." They point out that etymologically the term suggests movement and accompaniment, as in modern German, *fahren*, "to go, to travel."[112] Murray cites the text of an early chronicler, Maurius Aventicensis, who says of the arrival of the Lombards in Italy in 569: "This year, Alboinus king of the Lombards with all his whole army leaving and burning his homeland Pannonia with women or all his people *in fara* occupied Italy."[113] This must mean, he argues, "in his expedition." The usage is obscure, but the interpretation Murray offers is not convincing. Would women have ever been considered part of the company, the following, the *comitatus* of a king? Would not the king be traveling with his own *fara*, his own family? Further along, the chronicler reports that Alboinus was killed "by his own," with the connivance of his wife.[114] Who were "his own"? Surely not the entire Lombard nation, but most likely his *fara*, with whom he had entered Italy.

There are cogent reasons for believing that *fara* is not the chief's retinue, but the elusive *Sippe*. The Lombard laws known as the Edict of Rothar, in chapter 177, declare that, with the king's permission, "the free man has the right to migrate with his *fara* wherever he wants."[115] Now, only the richest and most powerful Lombards would have had a following. But this text leaves the impression that every free Lombard has a *fara*. "*Parentes, parentilla*," rather than "following," makes the better sense here. Finally, the crucial text supporting this interpretation comes from the historian of the Lombards, Paul the Deacon. Writing in the late eighth century, Paul offers an explicit definition of the *fara*. "The *farae* of the Lombards," he writes, "that is, *generationes* or *lineas*."[116] He goes on to equate the term with *prosapia*. *Generatio, linea,* and *prosapia* are all common terms in medieval Latin for descent group, kin group, and *Sippe*. This is the clearest contemporary definition of the term we possess. (Indeed, how could Paul, in citing three synonyms, have been clearer?) His definition must prevail over the necessarily vague inferences drawn from etymological associations. It is gratuitous to assume that he did not know its real meaning. In supplying three synonyms, he (or whoever is glossing him) assures us that he does. Murray is certainly correct in arguing that these texts do not prove that Germanic society was organized on the basis of extensive unilineal (that is, agnatic) kindreds. But he goes too far in denying to the word *fara* its basic sense of *prosapia*, or bilineal descent group.

And the word long preserves the sense that Paul attributes to it. An imperial charter, dated 1027, refers to "the *fara* of the sons of Guarnerius," unmistakably in the sense of *genealogia*.[117]

The laws of the Alamanni mention a dispute arising between two *genealogiae* in regard to their respective territories, and lay down the mechanisms by which the dispute should be adjudicated.[118] The most likely explication of the text is that, among the Alamanni, the descent group or *Sippe* held its own territory with recognized boundaries. From Freising in Bavaria, in a donation dated 750, members of two *genealogiae,* identified as the Ferings and Fagana, give an uncultivated piece of land called Eriching to the church.[119] Moreover, among the Bavarians, as among the Alamanni and the Irish, the name of the kin group or *Sippe* is applied to the territory, especially forests and wastes, it controlled. The *Sippe* seems also to have had a voice in approving transfers of common or undeveloped lands; in a donation from Freising dated 821, *conmarcani* (neighbors) and *coheredes* (fellow heirs, surely members of the *Sippe*) are present and presumably approve of the gift (offered by a woman).[120]

References to the early Germanic *Sippe* are few and obscure, but perhaps they are enough to conclude that the Germanic peoples, in their movements into the empire, settled the lands they occupied on the basis of descent groups. This does not mean—and the point cannot be too much emphasized—that the members of the *Sippe* practiced some form of primitive communism, that they held or worked the land in common. Charters surviving from the late eighth century assign clear boundaries to fields and identify contiguous owners, who are almost always named individuals or a saint, patron of a monastery or church.[121] The *Sippe* and its claims are all but invisible within them, save for the rare references just now examined. Doubtless too, gradations in wealth were pronounced among the *faramanni*. The Germanic *Sippe*, like the Irish sept, probably exerted a kind of overlordship over its territory, held some residual rights to the lands of its members, kept the peace, and adjudicated disputes among them. But this did not compromise the prevalent rule of individual landownership and enterprise, and it did not erase gradations of wealth.

The sources tell us almost nothing about the internal organization of the *Sippe*. It seems, however, incontrovertible that its basic structure was cognatic and not agnatic, that is, that membership was based on both matrilineal and patrilineal linkages. Conclusive evidence for this comes from the use of matronymics in the early charters. Most valuable are the charters of Amalfi in southern Italy, unique in Europe, in that the principals and witnesses frequently identify themselves by giving their genealogies back to the prominent person regarded as the founder of the kin group.[122] The earliest of these charters, dated 12 January 860, mentions "lord Lupus the count, son of the lady Drosu of blessed memory, [daughter of] Lupus the count."[123] Lupus the count is founder of the *Sippe*, and his grandson traces his connection to him through a woman. This seems to be the only instance in the Amalfitan charters in which a woman appears in intermediate position in a genealogical sequence, but women are often cited at the head of the line. There is no patriarchy here, in the literal sense of the word: a male at the origins.

In the late eighth and ninth centuries, always a few (but always some) of the persons appearing in the European charters identify themselves with a mother rather than a father.[124] The use of matronymics suggests further that exogamy did not involve women exclusively. Occasionally, even if rarely, the groom must have joined the *Sippe* of his bride.[125] Their offspring remain within the *Sippe* of the mother, and proclaim this through the use of a matronymic.

The size of the *Sippe* is again difficult to judge. Germanic custom, and the canon law of the early medieval Church, extended the degrees of kinship over seven degrees.[126] But it seems likely that only the most exalted kin groups could have preserved the long generational memory needed to define such extensive boundaries. Paul the Deacon can count his genealogy back four generations, to his *abavus* Leupchis; he is singularly well informed about the doings of his ancestors.[127] In the early charters of Amalfi, in those antedating the year 1100, the maximum number of remembered generations reaching back to the founder of the line is seven, but about 80 percent of the signers mention only three or four.[128] If these numbers are typical, then the *Sippe* could rarely have included more than 50 families. Presumably too, these descent groups were continuously splitting and reforming.

If the *Sippe* was the foundation of the kinship system of the early Germans, why does it appear so rarely in the sources? One reason might be that very early on the Continent (much later in Ireland), the *Sippe* was losing many of its functions to other social groups, based on territory rather than on blood: villages, manors, lordships, and the state itself.[129] But even more fundamentally, the *Sippe* never did fulfill the many functions which legal historians have sometimes assigned to it.[130] There is an assumption broadcast in the literature that the monogamous family, the *Kleinfamilie*, gradually replaced the *Sippe* as the basic social unit in early medieval society. In fact the larger kin group and households of some type had existed side by side since time immemorial. Moreover, the *Sippe* always played a secondary role in production and reproduction, the two functions which households have classically assumed. And these basic functions, often mentioned in the documentation, lend to households a special visibility. It was not the small household that replaced the Sippe; rather, larger social groupings, based on territory, edged it into the shadows. And the households continued to be centers of production and reproduction, even as the larger society was changing.

Households

The Germanic *Sippe*, again like the Irish sept, was made up of separate households. The national laws of the Germanic peoples give us a detailed view of the internal organization of the household, and of its formation through marriage. The authority which the father exercised over all his dependents—wife, children, and slaves—was called *munt*, or *munduburdium* in Frankish law.[131] It was analogous to the Roman *manus*, but was not as absolute or permanent. The father had the right to discipline his dependents, and they needed his concurrence if they wished to enter into any legal agreement. But sons who reached the age of majority, which differed across the various legal traditions, became persons *sui iuris*.

Distinct from *munt* was a special authority which in Lombard law fathers exerted over their daughters, and husbands over their wives. It was called *mundius*, and the male who held it was the woman's *mundualdus*.[132] (The term was also applied to the sum of money the groom paid to the bride's father.) Among the Lombards, women never achieved full autonomy, but were always subject to some *mundualdus*, if not the father or husband, then a close male relative, or finally the king. Of all the national codes, Lombard law placed the most restrictions on the juridical capacities of women.

At the center of the household was the chief and his wife—or wives. Tacitus claims that "almost alone among the barbarians," the Germans were monogamous, but he concedes that "a few . . . because of their high position rather than out of lust enter into more than one marriage engagement."[133] Polygyny was probably more common among the Germans than Tacitus admits. Even after their conversion to Christianity, the Merovingian kings often kept several wives, and numerous concubines.[134] In an anecdote related by Gregory of Tours, queen Ingund, wife of Clothar I, asks her spouse to find a rich husband for her sister Aregund.[135] The king inspects his sister-in-law and finds her so much to his liking that he marries her himself, without of course divorcing her sister. King Dagobert, "like Solomon," enjoyed three wives and numerous concubines.[136]

Much later, in the eleventh century, Adam of Bremen comments on the marital customs of the north German Swedes. "Each one," he reports, "has according to the extent of his powers two or three wives or more at the same time; the rich and the nobles have uncounted numbers."[137] It would be hard to find a better description of a system of resource polygyny.

The Germans recognized two forms of marriage, which were roughly analogous to Roman marriages *in manu* and *sine manu*, with or without a transference of authority to the husband. Formal marriage involved three separate acts: betrothal or *sponsalia*; the payment by the groom of the dowry or *pretium nuptiale*; and the delivery of the bride to the groom.

The betrothal was the promise of a future marriage and an agreement as to its terms. It was much more solemn than its Roman equivalent.[138] The betrothal was often celebrated at a joint family feast. Under Roman and ecclesiastical influence, the heads of the two families came to draw up a formal written contract in which the terms of the marriage were exactly stated.

Marriage was the occasion for the conveyance of several types of payments or gifts. Both the bride's father and the bride herself received payments and gifts. The payment to the father may have been the survival of an older brideprice or, more likely, compensation given to him for the loss of authority over his daughter. The Lombards first called it *mundius*, then *meta*.[139] The term *meta* comes subsequently to be applied to all the gifts the wife receives from the husband or his family. Whatever the origins of the payments given the bride's father, in the period of the national laws the sum had become only symbolic. For example, among the Franks it consisted of one solidus and one denarius, and among the Lombards from the time of King Liutprand it was also a token payment.[140]

The chief beneficiary of the flow of marital payments and gifts was now the bride. The conveyances she received were of three types: the dowry itself; the *Morgangabe* or "morning gift" received after the consumption of the marriage; and gifts from her own family. These latter were called in Lombard law the *faderfio*.[141] In a Merovingian life, the bride's father says: "give him [the groom] to me, and I shall give to him my daughter Hebrelda, and I shall enrich them copiously with riches."[142]

Tacitus in A.D. 98 observes that among the Germans the groom brings a dowry to the bride, not the bride to the groom, as was the Roman custom of his times.[143] This reverse dowry or bridewealth is the universal rule of marriage throughout the early Middle Ages. Frankish law uses (or, in a strict sense, misuses) the word *dos* to designate this counterdowry. Moreover, the payment to the bride seems to have grown during this period. At least, several lawgivers tried to limit its size, even as Roman emperors from Majorian to Justinian had tried to hold back the inflation of the *donatio*. The Visigothic king Reccessuindus set the maximum *dos* at one-tenth the groom's property, but nobles could add 10 slave boys, 10 slave girls, 20 horses, and ornaments up to a value of 1000 solidi.[144] The Lombard laws set the *dos legitima* at 400 solidi.[145] Frankish custom came to limit the size of the *dos* to one-third the husband's possessions, the so-called *tertia*.[146] In 711 king Liuprand of the Lombards forbade the assignment to the bride of more than one-fourth the groom's properties, a share called the *quarta*.[147]

The *Morgangabe* was paid to the wife after the consummation of the wedding. She too may have given gifts to her husband—Tacitus mentions a "gift of arms"—but was not legally required to do so.[148] With time, the *dos* given to the wife and the morning gift came to be conflated, and *Morgangabe, morgancap,* or *antefactum* applied to the total property conveyed to the wife. The properties assigned to the bride at marriage could be substantial. According to Gregory of Tours, Gallesuinda, the sister of Brunhilde, received as her bridewealth the cities of Bordeaux, Limoges, Cahors and others, "whether in dowry, or in *Morgangabe,* that is, the morning gift."[149] The lives of Merovingian saints sometimes describe in detail the dowries offered to young women, who usually refuse them, as they are vowed to virginity. Thus, a suitor offers to St. Bertilia of Artois (seventh century) "numerous dresses, woven gold and gems . . . many fields and a great number of slaves."[150] Bertilia rejects his suit, but clearly marriage could make the fortune of the barbarian woman.

The Germans also recognized a type of informal marriage, called *Friedelehe,* from *fidila,* "beloved."[151] It did not involve the transfer of authority over the woman and did not require a dowry. It was a kind of abduction, to which the bride consented. She was more than a concubine, for the union was public and recognized, and she also received a morning gift. Still, the Church objected to these free unions, as they were often clandestine and not readily enforceable. In 524 the Council of Arles decreed that there should be "no marriage without a dowry," and further required that "no one presume to marry without a public wedding."[152] Pepin the Short in a capitulary of 755 similarly ordered "that all men both noble and non-noble should marry in public."[153] Still, "free" or clandestine marriages remained common, and constituted a major problem for the Church over the entire Middle Ages.

The Germanic laws, like the Roman, continued to allow husbands to divorce their wives, but not wives their husbands.[154] The husband had only to draw up a *libellum repudii*, or document of repudiation, in which he formally renounced the obligations he had assumed in the original marriage contract.

Kinship and Inheritance

Like the Irish sept, the German *Sippe* was bilineal, but it also laid great importance on relationships traced through women. Men were favored, but women indicated who among them should be preferred. The most striking example of this are the provisions of the *Pactus legis salicae* concerning the *reipus*.[155] The *reipus* was a fee of three solidi one denarius (or 62.5 solidi if the proper procedures were not followed), which a man who married a widow had to pay to the members of her kin group. In order of priority, the first five relatives to receive the *reipus* were: (1) the son of her sister, (2) the son of a niece, (3) the first cousin through an aunt, (4) the son of a female first cousin, "who comes from the maternal kin," or (5) the maternal uncle. Only in the absence of these relatives did the fee pass to the kin of the deceased husband who had not been his heirs. The provisions direct the payment to males, but they also assume that the surest relatives of the widow were those related to her through women. In commenting on this capital text, one historian of early law, Joseph Balon, goes so far as to state: "It well appears that we can deduce from these texts that according to the Salic law the tie which wove together the family group was matriarchy."[156]

In all the Germanic laws, sons and daughters had rights to the property of their parents, but those rights differed from people to people and depended on the nature of the property, whether real or movable.[157] The Visigothic laws contain the most liberal provisions concerning women. They explicitly state "that sisters should enter equally with brothers into the inheritance of their parents."[158] Regarding women, Salic law is the most restrictive. In the famous fifty-ninth chapter of the *Pactus legis salicae*, women are excluded from the inheritance of "Salic" land.[159]

Exemptions existed: the Merovingian king Chilperich (561–584) allowed women to inherit even Salic land, in the absence of male heirs.[160] Thus, even under the most unfavorable legal tradition, sisters were postponed in regard to brothers in the inheritance of land, but not excluded. Women were not postponed in the inheritance of movables, and in certain traditions, as we have seen, were even favored. Acquiring property whether through inheritance or marriage conveyances, women appear frequently and prominently as property owners in early medieval society.[161]

The system of kinship and marriage among the Germans bears many similarities to that of the Celtic Irish. Concubinage and polygyny tended to concentrate women into the households of the powerful, and created an apparent shortage of women in the middle and lower levels of society. The laws of the Alamanni mention women "in the service of the duke"; they are protected by a *wergeld* three times that of ordinary women.[162] This demand for women guaranteed them favorable terms on the marriage market. To gain a wife the suitor had to outbid his rivals in the amount of dowry and gifts he offered. But the maldistribution of women across society doubtless also increased the incidents of abduction, to which the Germanic laws make frequent reference. In the laws of the Alamanni, for example, the fine for abducting and selling a free woman outside the province, 80 solidi, is twice as high as that for a free man, and becomes 400 solidi if she cannot be reclaimed.[163]

Muliebria Opera

Among both the Germans and the Celts, women were valued not only for their sexual attractiveness but also for their many skills. On the highest levels of society, they often appear as administrators—of households, of estates, and even of the royal palace.[164] The ninth-century life of the German saint Liutberg enumerates some of "the various skills which suit women," or the *muliebria opera*, "feminine labors."[165] A lady of the high Frankish nobility named Gisla encounters the young Liutberg in a convent, admires her skills and virtues, and takes her into her household. Liutberg assumes a major role in the direction of household affairs, first for the lady Gisla, then for her son Bernard. Her biographer relates: "So completely did she assume the management of affairs, that the governance of the household rested almost entirely with her."[166] Not only was she cook and nurse, but she wove cloth and ran a dye works.[167]

Women were actively engaged in many productive activities. They participated in the agricultural labors, especially with tasks associated with the household's "inner economy," such as gardening and the care of courtyard animals. They cooked and brewed. Above all, they dominated cloth production in all its phases. The great estates of the early Middle Ages characteristically contained a *gynecaeum*, a "women's workshop," where female servants and the wives of peasants made cloth.

Remarkably, after the Germans were converted to Christianity, even a knowledge of letters was considered appropriate to women, at least within the upper classes and in the religious life. The Merovingian queen St. Radegundis was taught letters as a girl "along with other skills, which suited her sex."[168] The nun St. Astrudis, sister of St. Baldwin, archdeacon of Laudon, "[learned] letters in the days of her tender youth . . . she learned to sing praises to the son of the virgin. By divine mercy she acquired a strong memory by speaking and reading, exercising herself also in the teaching of doctrine . . . She was full of eloquence and even more of wisdom."[169] The lives of two eight-century saints, Herlindis and Renildis, show the kinds of skills most religious women acquired. The two girls were trained: "in reading, modulation of the singing voice, chanting the psalms, and . . . writing and painting. In like manner they were honestly instructed in skills of every sort, which are usually done by the hands of women, that is, spinning, weaving, stitching and sewing; they were perfect workers in the wondrous ways of working with gold and pearls and silk."[170] The young women produced a richly embroidered cloth for a holy priest. And they copied out the four gospels, the psalms, and "other writings."[171] Lay noble women too were often literate. In the eleventh century the countess Hedwig read the psalter so continuously that her neglected husband Eppo seized it one day and threw it into the fire.[172]

Children

Tacitus claims that the Germans, unlike the Romans, did not practice infanticide.[173] Here again, he wishes to shame the Romans by exaggerating the strict morality of Germanic society. Merovingian saints' lives do in fact give several examples of attempted infanticide. The mother of St. Germain of Paris tries to abort him by taking a poison, "because she had conceived in a short space of time after another pregnancy."[174] Even barbarian women, or some of them, wanted to space their children. The father of St. Odilia determines to kill her, because she is born blind.[175] St. Bathildis tells her husband, king Clodovic, "that that most evil and impious institution ought to be ended, according to which many men seek to kill their offspring and not to rear them."[176]

The life of the bishop St. Ludger tells us how, among the pagan Frisians, a baby might be killed. Ludger's mother Liafburg, "when she was born, had a pagan grandmother, the mother, that is, of her father, who renounced altogether the Christian faith. This woman, whose name is unmentionable, became enraged that [her daughter-in-law] gave birth only to daughters, and did not produce a living son. She sent *lictores* who were to seize the then delivered girl from the breast of the mother, and kill her, before she took milk. For this was the custom of the pagans: if they wished to kill a son or daughter, they did so before they took material food."[177] Liafburg was rescued and fed some honey, which gave her immunity from the evil machinations of the grandmother. The authority of the grandmother is worth noting: she orders the baby to be killed without considering the parents.

Although infanticide was known among the Germans, it seems never to have been systematically practiced. As Tacitus implies, the Germans reared many children, but did not invest heavily in their upbringing, whether psychologically or materially.[178] The education of a nobleman's son was indistinguishable from the rearing of a slave. Here, the nature of preliterate Germanic culture had crucial importance. The survival of that culture did not require, as with the Romans, the support of expensive educational institutions and numerous professional teachers. And the training of the young did not demand that parents monitor their progress closely, and impose a stern discipline over growing children. Barbarian children grew up in an atmosphere of benign neglect.

AVUNCULATE TIES AND FOSTERING

Polygyny and concubinage among the Germans might be expected to increase sexual promiscuity, obscure lines of descent through males, and make matrilineal ties the surest indication of kinship. And the issue of uncertain paternity does appear in Merovingian sources. According to Gregory of Tours, king Gunthram refuses to believe that the child of his sister-in-law Fredegundis is truly the son of his deceased brother Chilperic and his own nephew.[179] (Had Fredegundis been his sister, he would have had no cause for doubt.) "I think that he is the son of some member of our following."[180] Gunthram had evidently little confidence in the fidelity of his sister-in-law. Fredegundis must solemnly swear before three bishops and 300 great men of the realm that Chilperic really was the father. "And so doubt was removed from the mind of the king."

The avunculate tie, and other forms of relationship through women, also appear in the records. So also does the practice of fostering, the rearing of young children outside the household, often by a matrilineal relative. Tacitus had already recognized the special relationship among the Germans between brother and sister's child.[181] In the seventh century, St. Walaric enters a monastery in Picardy, "where he followed the footsteps of a certain uncle," and succeeds him as abbot.[182] St. Aldetrude is entrusted to her maternal aunt, "to be educated and taught the rule."[183] The avunculate tie, it again should be noted, was not limited to men.

Duke Ludwin, who died ca. 713, "embraced with love" his maternal uncle St. Basinus, bishop of Trier, followed his counsel, gave up wife and rank to enter the religious life, and succeeded his uncle as bishop.[184]

In Search of System

The Germans, like the Irish Celts, settled the land on the basis of tribes and kindreds. The households and marriages of these two barbarian peoples also show resemblances. Resource polygyny resulted in widespread concubinage, the gathering of women in the households of the powerful, and a shortage of brides, especially on the lower levels of society. The high prestige which the Church accorded to a life of virginity probably also contributed to the shortage of women willing to marry. The dearth of women assured them favorable marriage terms, but had as counterpart frequent abductions. Considerable promiscuity, obscuring lines of descent through males, enhanced the importance of matrilineal ties, the avunculate, and similar relations through women. The inclusion (if sometimes also the postponement) of women in all inheritance laws is another salient characteristic of early Germanic and Irish societies. But differences too must be noted. References to all the elements mentioned above permeate the Irish sources, but they are rare and scattered in the documents of early medieval, continental Europe. It may of course be that our sources are deficient. Certainly, no set of continental records matches Irish hagiography in clarity of ethnographic materials. But more likely, the Germanic *Sippe* itself was weakening and losing functions and visibility on the Continent very early in the Middle Ages, as P. D. King concludes.[185] Ireland, in contrast, was socially conservative, and long clung to its archaic institutions. In other words, the glimpses we perceive of early medieval kindreds and households on the Continent are of a society that is already changing.

3 | THE EMERGENCE OF THE EARLY MEDIEVAL HOUSEHOLD

> Tanatos insula non modica, id est, magnitududinis juxta consuetudinem aestimationis Anglorum, familiarum sexcentarum.
>
> The isle of Thanet, not small in size, that is, according to the method of estimation of the English, 600 families.
>
> —Bede the Venerable, 731

FROM APPROXIMATELY 750, the extant sources illuminating medieval society become, if not exactly abundant, at least considerably more numerous and more yielding than in any previous period. In particular, there survive for the first time an unprecedented number of "documents of practice" administrative records chiefly, which reveal not only the aspirations of lawgivers and the exhortations of pastors, but the actual workings of the social system. They are of two general types: serial records, or runs of charters over time (mainly land conveyances), most of them generated by the administrative activities of great monastic landlords; and surveys of particular manors at particular times. Of the latter, deservedly the most famous is the polyptych of the abbot Irminon, redacted probably between 809 and 839 and describing the estates of the abbey of St. Germain des Prés near Paris.[1] It names the persons resident on the dependent farms—nearly 8,000 persons on 1,378 farms—and offers the first large view of households in medieval history.

COMMENSURABLE UNITS

Both the charters and the surveys make use of a new unit for measuring land and counting the households settled upon it: the peasant farm. Even though obligated to labor services on the demesne of the lord, most serfs lived with their families on their own farms, which they worked for their own benefit (except for payment of customary rents) and which they could pass on to their heirs. To identify and to count this new unit of settlement, the surveyors utilized old terms in a new way: *familia*, not in the classical sense of those subject to the *paterfamilias*, but the entire family, including the chief; *sors*, meaning share or inheritance; *colonia*, the land worked by the free tenant, the *colonus*, of late Roman law; even *casa* or "house."[2] They also adopted neologisms; *hide* in England; *hobanna*, *hoba*, *Hufe* in German lands; *res masseritia*, or "household possession" in Italian records; and most common of all, *mansus*. As I have elsewhere argued, it carries the sense of "permanent possession" or "inheritance."[3] "Inheritances," says the Edict of Pfistes (864) of Charles the Bald, "that is, mansa."[4]

The earliest references to these family farms date from the late seventh century, and the use of these terms is generalized in the Frankish empire in the eighth century.[5] In his *Ecclesiastical History*, finished in 731, Bede the Venerable uses the classical *familia* (though he was doubtless thinking "hide") to estimate the size of both individual estates and entire regions of England.[6] He explicitly states that he was following "the custom of the English," but in fact, at the time he was writing, it had become the custom of the continental peoples too.

As units in a survey, these family farms must have been roughly comparable one to the other in extent, in the size of the families settled upon them, and in their overall productive powers. There is further evidence that these peasant families were viewed as moral as well as fiscal units. The German "books of tradition" from the late eighth, ninth, and tenth centuries occasionally ascribe a proper name to the family working the land. Thus, the *Traditiones corbeienses*, from the great Carolingian monastery of Corvey in Westphalia records a donation: "Folcberth gave for the soul of Gherberga one family in *Altungunhus*, by the name of *Unuan*, and XXX *jugera* [of land]."[7] Or again: "Albmer, Pumi, Magenhard and the sisters Adallog, Fastred and Hildiburg gave one mansus in *Aldberteshusen* with the family *Weinwed* and another mansus in *Boffeshusen* with the family *Hun*."[8] We cannot tell whether these are true family names, stable over generations. But even if they are not, they clearly encompass all the family members and proclaim its moral unity.

The shared labors of these peasant cultivators probably helped cement that unity. We have hints that this was so, but in a somewhat different context. St. Severus of Ravenna lived in the fourth century, but acquired a biographer, a priest named Luidolph, only about 850.[9] Presumably, the values reflected in the life are those of the ninth, not the fifth century. Severus is married to a woman named Vincentia, and they have a daughter called Innocentia. They all work together at weaving wool. "With them, to earn his food, [Severus] performed women's labors. For he was accustomed to stitch and weave wool, after the manner of women, and for this reason was popularly called *lanarius*."[10] Later in life, this humble worker is miraculously summoned to become bishop of Ravenna. But he does not forget his wife and daughter and their life together. Both women die before him, and he builds for them a family sepulcher. At the end of his own life, he opens the grave, and the bodies move over to make room for him. "We who lived a common life in this world," he says, "should also have a common burial."[11] He enters the tomb, lies down, and falls to eternal sleep at their side. Severus' family of workers was a moral unit, in life and in death.

Traces of the solidarity of a small family unit can be found even in the terse Latin of the *Libri traditiones*. In the books of the Westphalian monastery of Corvey, for example, the donations are usually given for the benefit of a named relative, although only rarely are we told whether the relative is living or dead.[12] Many donations accompanied the oblation of a son or brother to this male monastery, and sons and brothers are therefore the relatives most commonly remembered in the entries (the former, 86 times; the latter, 54). But the donors are very much aware of women; mothers are remembered 24 times (nearly as often as fathers, 30 times); wives 43 times; but sisters only three times and daughters only five. The donors' view of women was thus oriented toward the past, probably because most sisters and daughters had married outside the family and were no longer part of the domestic group. The commemorations rarely mention relatives beyond the direct line of descent; there are two male uncles, one nephew through a brother, three nephews through a sister, two mothers-in-law, and one son-in-law. Even unnamed relatives are not often cited (*proximi*, 13 times; *propinqui*, 3 times); and ancestors beyond the parents, never. The sense of spiritual obligation to kin, except for oblates, seems very much limited to those who would normally be living within the same household.

Family Farms

As I argued in the previous chapters, households in Mediterranean antiquity and among the barbarian peoples were not comparable and commensurable across society. In classical society, mass slavery alone assured that some households might include scores or even hundreds of persons, while many slaves and poor freemen were denied any sort of independent domestic life. Moreover, Roman law recognized several forms of marriage, and this also undermined the comparability of domestic units. Barbarian customs likewise admitted several types of legal marriage, and, as Roman law did not, countenanced both polygyny and concubinage. The polygynous practices of the northern barbarians, the concentration of women in the households of the rich, also accentuated the differences in domestic organization up and down the social scale.

Given these antecedents, the formation of commensurable household units in early medieval society requires an explanation. Surely the most important single factor was the demise of ancient slavery, and the effort to resettle and reclaim the land on the basis of family farms, which is to say, on the basis of peasant agriculture. In the period of the late Roman empire, great landowners faced a critical problem: the supply of slaves was drying up as Rome's frontiers were stable or retreating, since war had traditionally supplied large numbers of slaves to the victorious Roman commanders. The diminishing numbers of field hands raised the problem of the *agri deserti*, "abandoned fields," which threatened to cripple agriculture. To offset this baneful trend, landlords allowed some slaves to marry and to settle on the empty lands. These "housed" slaves at once acquired certain privileges. Their families, for example, could not be divided—wife taken from husband, or children from parents.[13] Although they paid some form of rent to their lords and patrons, the lands they cleared and the houses they built came to be regarded as their own *peculium*.[14] This was a special form of property under Roman law over which slaves exerted a moral claim, even though the master remained, in a strict sense, the *dominus*.

The institution of the Roman colonate worked in similar fashion to encourage resettlement on the basis of family farms.[15] The *colonus* in Roman legal terminology was a free person settled on another's land. The imperial legislation of the fourth and fifth centuries imposed numerous restrictions on the *colonus*. He could not leave the land without permission, and his children were similarly bound to his place of origin. He could not sue his lord in the public courts; at least in respect to the *dominus* of the land he worked, he was stripped of the rights of a free Roman citizen. He was viewed as a *servus terrae*, a slave of the soil.[16]

But the imperial legislation presents an incomplete and in many respects a distorted picture of the *colonus'* social and legal position. In 1928 archeologists discovered in Algeria forty-five wooden tablets, containing some thirty-four private acts dating from 493 to 496, during the period of Vandal rule in North Africa. They are called the *Tablettes Albertini*, after the then curator of antiquities in French Algeria.[17] Although Roman law still prevailed in the Vandal kingdom, the *Tablettes* show us a Roman colonate much different from the one outlined in the imperial decrees. These records frequently refer to settlers called "Mancian" cultivators. The name derives from a law of the first century A.D. that intended to promote land reclamations in North Africa by extending to those who improved the soil a claim to its permanent possession.[18] As set forth in the *Tablettes Albertini*, the terms under which the Mancian cultivators held their fields were extraordinarily liberal. They could sell the lands without apparently seeking or obtaining the permission of the one who holds *dominium* over it, although his name is mentioned. The imperial legislation binding *coloni* to the soil exerted no visible constraints on these free cultivators. Peasants able to sell their property must have been free to leave it. The contracts show clearly the formation of a hierarchy of rights over the soil, shared by its lords, shared by its workers. The *dominus* remains the owner of the land, and claims a rent from those who labor on it. But the cultivator too now enjoys, according to the custom or "vulgar law" of late antiquity, a moral right to profit from the labor he has invested in land clearing and cultivation.[19]

In a desperate effort to shore up the sinking economy, the Roman government settled even barbarian contingents upon the land, again on the basis of family farms, presumably too with guarantees that the cultivators and their heirs would benefit from the sweat they invested.[20] The slave economy of antiquity, an economy of coercion, was giving away to an agriculture based, at least in part, on incentives.

The barbarian kings and their warrior elites also favored extending cultivated lands (and thus their own rents and services) by means of peasant farms.[21] In sum, the customs of early medieval Europe, constituting a vulgar law and prevailing both within and without the borders of the vanished empire, extended to those who would improve the land a right to hold it permanently, to claim the chief part of its fruits, and to pass it on to their heirs. Numerous donors in the Carolingian records, especially in the newly settled German lands, give serf families to the great monasteries and churches, together with their *elaboratus*, sometimes with their *labor*.[22] The terms signify the lands they have settled and improved, and those lands have become inseparable from the families that rendered them productive. These serfs might have told their lords, as Russian serfs are alleged to have done in the nineteenth century: "We are yours, but the land is ours." Work in early medieval Europe conferred a title to permanent tenure. The canons attributed to Theodore, Archbishop of Canterbury, but probably dating from northern France in the ninth century, echo this moral principle: "it is not allowed for a man to take from his slave the *pecunia* he has acquired with his own labor."[23]

Religion

The appearance in early medieval Europe of commensurate household units thus seems intimately associated with the resettlement of the land on the basis of family farms, with the full emergence, in other words, of the European peasantry as a historic class. But other factors also were lending uniformity to these households, and chief among them were the ethical teachings of the Christian Church. It sought to impose a common rule of marriage upon all the faithful, in all social classes. Two of its commands had a powerful impact upon marriages and the formation of households: exogamy and monogamy.[24]

The two chief legal traditions, the Roman and the Mosaic, which were the foundations of medieval canon law, were comparatively indifferent to the marriage of kin. Roman law calculated blood relations up to seven degrees, but allowed marriages from the fourth; thus, even first cousins could marry without the taint of incest. In the West, between the council of Agde in 506 and that of Rome in 721, the Church extended the domain of prohibited marriages over the full seven degrees. In 726 Pope Gregory II, in a letter to St. Boniface, affirmed: "We say that it should be followed, that as long as they recognize that they are relatives, they ought not to enter this marital association."[25] At the same time, the Church adopted the Germanic method of reckoning degrees of kinship, which had the effect of expanding still further the kin group, within which intermarriage was prohibited.[26] Finally, the Church extended the incest prohibitions over those related through marriage (the *cognatio legalis*) as well as by blood.[27] A man was prohibited from marrying his stepmother, the widow of a brother, a stepdaughter, or his daughter-in-law.[28]

Legal historians have found the Church's preoccupation with incest in the early Middle Ages surprising, as it finds no precedent in either Roman or Mosaic law.[29] One reason for this policy may have been the concentration of women in the households of the rich and powerful, to the deprivation of other sectors of society. The Church's insistence on exogamy must have forced a freer, wider circulation of women through society. The poorer, less powerful male improved his chance of finding a mate. The breaking of the monopoly of the powerful over women, their fairer distribution across social classes, also promoted the comparability of household units.

The Church's insistence that marriages be monogamous would have had a similar effect. King Chlothar could not claim as his sexual partners both the lady Ingund and her sister Aregund, not at once and not in succession.[30] To be sure, it is difficult to know how effectively the rule of monogamy was respected. The European elites long resisted it, and not until the ninth, perhaps even the eleventh and twelfth centuries, did they finally bow.[31] On the other hand, even in the earlier centuries, can we assume that the Church's continuing insistence on monogamy was entirely without an impact on behavior? European society was relentlessly directed toward a common rule of marriage, based on exogamy and monogamy, and these principles helped establish the uniformity of early medieval households.

The appearance of commensurable domestic units in the early Middle Ages, the formation of a symmetrical array of households encompassing the entire community, mark an epoch in the history of the European family. Of course, the households of the rich continued to differ from those of the poor; they were generally larger and invariably included servants. Family members moved in and out of them at different ages and for different reasons. These contrasts did not, however, break the bonds of comparability; the terms for humble hearths also applied to the rich ones. The early charters and surveys account for the farm of the lowly slave, the *mansus servilis*, along with the lord's manor house, the *mansus indominicatus*.[32] The same word identifies both. Later in the Middle Ages, from the twelfth and thirteenth centuries, counts of hearths were made among urban populations as well. Urban households continued to serve as units of production and consumption, and this undoubtedly explains their continuing uniformity. In the cities of the later Middle Ages, as at Florence in 1427, the big and bursting patrician families, and destitute, solitary widows, still live in units which the government treats as comparable.[33] Rather than being simply a matter of administrative convenience, I would argue that this usage signals the continuing existence of a fundamentally symmetrical array of households, based on commensurable units. And uniformity is necessary, of course, if we are to make any general statement concerning medieval families.

THE HOUSEHOLDS OF ST. GERMAIN

The swelling documentation from the middle of the eighth century makes available, for the first time in medieval history, actual surveys of households, which in turn allow us to measure their size and examine, if always partially, their internal structures. These surveys are in the main inventories of monastic estates, carried out by ecclesiastical lords to clarify and enforce their claims to rents and services. The largest and most famous of these surveys, the polyptych of the abbot Irminon, was redacted in the opening decades of the ninth century and surveys the lands of the monastery of St. Germain des Prés.[34]

Many scholars have studied the families of St. Germain, and some have concluded that the data are too lacunose and intractable to yield much certain information about their size and structure.[35] Skeptics point especially to the large disparity in the sex ratio of this population, seemingly 135 men for every 100 women. They suspect that either the surveyors were failing to count many women, or women were indeed mysteriously absent or removed from the population. Whatever the explanation, the households which emerge from Irminon's polyptych appear strangely distorted.

But clearly, in any effort to trace the evolution of the medieval household, this largest and most detailed of the Carolingian surveys cannot be discarded. To use it well, we must inquire into the technical character of this extremely complex record, and attempt to find an explanation for its notorious distortions.

The Survey

The polyptych contains twenty-five surveys of particular estates, called *brevia* or "briefs." B. Guérard, who first edited the polyptych in 1844, added two fragments of surveys that he discovered in a separate manuscript. For convenience, we shall refer to all twenty-seven sections of the edited polyptych as *brevia*. Folios are missing from the beginning of the manuscript, and Guérard himself recognized that the estates surveyed represented only a part of the abbey's domains; in particular, it lacked a full description of the lands which the abbey had given in benefice.[36] On the other hand, it seems to include nearly all the dependent farms directly serving the monastery.

Each *breve* contains separate paragraphs or entries, the first letter of which is written in majuscule or uncial script and set out in the margin. This is important, as it shows that the surveyors intended each entry to be a "logical unit," in the jargon of contemporary information technology. In addition, the surveyors sometimes numbered the paragraphs, sometimes not. Guérard added numbers to the paragraphs that did not originally show them. The total number of paragraphs or entries—"logical units"—is 1,981.

In order to analyze this complex record more efficiently, Larry

Poos prepared some years ago, under my supervision, a machine-readable edition of the entire survey. The coding of the 1,981 entries in a manner compatible with the strict demands of computer logic proved to be a valuable exercise. The computer works only with rigorously consistent data; it balks at ambiguity. We had therefore to look very closely at the nature and content of the survey's logical units.

It was evident from the start that both the *brevia* and the entries themselves were of different kinds. One *breve*, the twelfth, is in its entirety a register of fifty-one donations made to the abbey. It might seem appropriate to study each *breve* separately, but even this tactic would not overcome the considerable differences among the entries. We therefore chose the separate entries as the principal target of analysis.

The entries variously describe the *mansus indominicatus*, the demesnal lands (but unfortunately not the staff resident in the manor house), churches, mills, and properties given in benefice. Others give lists of persons subject to particular charges, without mention of land. While these types of entries occasionally mention dependent families, that is not their principal purpose, and they do not do so systematically. We concluded that persons mentioned in entries of this type ought not to be included in the statistical recapitulations of St. Germain's households.

Of the 1,981 entries, those which describe true tenurial units—tenants, land, rents, and services—number 1,742, and these contain data on which an examination of households must be based. But here too, problems of consistency arise. The difficulties are best illustrated in a consideration of the sex ratio. A crude count of persons listed in the 1,742 household entries yields 4,188 males, 3,556 females, and 939 unspecified. All of this last set are unnamed *infantes* appearing in the survey; the fifth, sixth, and seventh *brevia* give the number, but not the sex, of children present in the homes.

If we exclude those of undifferentiated gender, then the ratio is 135 males per 100 females (4,857 men to 3,601 women). This ratio breaks the bounds of credibility. Scholars have assumed that the surveyors were simply failing to report women; but the entries themselves show that they were interested in listing children and in establishing whether or not they were dependents of St. Germain.[37] Spectacular negligence in counting little girls would seem to defeat the evident purpose of the survey—to define the monastery's rights. Others have concluded that infanticide of baby girls was being practiced on a massive scale.[38] But the assumption finds no support in other records. The substantial fines levied for the injury or murder of females—even of aborted female fetuses—also points to a high value given women, even little ones, in this society.[39]

A different approach to the interpretation of the document is required. Perhaps the question scholars should be asking is not "where are the missing women?", but "who are the supernumerary men?" In other words, are some males inappropriately included in the survey, or even counted twice?

There seems little doubt that some males are counted twice. Thus, in *breve* 22, entry 92, Adricus, a *colonus*, his wife Leodramma, and their four children, appear with another family, settled on two *mansi*. Further on in survey, entry 96 states "Adricus with his children [and] heirs holds nine *jornales, de proprietate.*"[40] Surely this Adricus with his small plot of land is the same as Adricus settled on the dependent farm mentioned four entries earlier. He appears in the survey twice, apparently because he holds the small plot by a difrent title *(de proprietate)* from the two *mansi*. But in his second appearance, his wife is not mentioned nor his children named. Now, if Adricus was not a dependent of St. Germain, if his family had not been earlier described, he would be counted without a wife on the basis of entry 96, and his presence would swell the sex ratio.

Among the entries are a great many in which the resident family consists of a solitary person, almost always male, but sometimes female. An example of this frequent type is the following, from *breve* 1: "Ermentildis, a *colona* of St. Germain, holds of arable land one *antsinga*; for which she does one day [of labor] every week; one chicken, five eggs."[41] Was Ermentildis a single woman living alone, on this tiny plot of land which, for all we can tell, did not contain a house? Was she capable of fulfilling the labor obligation, which consisted of driving a heavy plow across the demesnal fields? Or did this little field represent for her a tenure separate from her family farm, her *mansus*? There is a *colona* named Ermentildis in a neighboring manor, living with a husband and family; although we cannot make the identification certain, she may well be the same person, listed once with her family on her homestead, and again without her family on a plot of outlying land she had somehow acquired.[42] Others among the many solitary tenants may not have been dependents of St. Germain, even though they leased land from the monastery, so their families are not mentioned.

It should be recalled that the surveyors wished to provide the abbey with a list of revenues. The polyptych was not primarily a census, although personal charges made up an important part of the sums collected. Besides these dues, the abbey collected numerous rents from pieces of leased land or from *mansi*. In listing these, the survey gives the name of the individual responsible for the rent, but not the names of his or her dependents. Either the individual and his or her family are listed elsewhere in the polyptych, or they are outsiders, not personal dependents of the manor.

Most of these solitaries appear in separate entries in the survey. But occasionally they figure alongside listed families. Thus, entry 19 of *breve* 2 reads as follows:

> Teutbertus a *colonus* and his wife a *colona* by name of Rat-gundis, men of St. Germain, have with them three children, with these names: Rantgarius, Rantgis, Teutberta; Ebreharius, a *colonus* of St. Germain. These two hold one free *mansus*, having of arable land three *bunuaria* and one-half *antsinga*, of vineyard three *aripenni*, of meadow 3 *aripenni*. They pay the same [as in the preceding entry].

Was Ebreharius really a solitary bachelor? It is possible that he is an adult, unmarried brother of Teutbertus. But it is more likely that he, like Adricus, lives elsewhere with his family and retains, perhaps through the play of inheritances, some rights and responsibilities for the farm.

Of these solitaries, 616 are men and 44 are women, yielding a staggering sex ratio of 1,400 men per 100 women. Now this alone proves that the solitaries found in the survey are not a random sample of the total population. They are responsible for rents, but the surveyors do not describe their families, either because they are outsiders or because the families are listed elsewhere.

It is then our contention that these solitaries, who appear exclusively as rent payers, ought to be excluded from the statistical analysis of household composition. The exclusion of the 616 solitary males and 44 females reduces the sex ratio of the community as a whole to 119 (4,244 males and 3,557 females). The value remains high, but now it falls within the range of other known populations. The sex ratio for the city of Florence in 1427 was 119.[43]

The high sex ratio is not uniform across the community. It is particularly elevated among children, 141 for those children of stated sex. Perhaps the surveyors were not rigorously precise in identifying sex. Out of a grand total of 4,740 children, 939, or 20 percent, are not identified by sex. This suggests a certain indifference on the part of the surveyors to the sex of children, and perhaps a tendency, evident in other surveys also, to treat all children as males.[44] Then too, women are missing in the ranks of slaves.

The survey classifies the personal status of persons according to three juridic categories. Those with the heaviest obligations are the *servi*, and those with the lightest are the *coloni*. An intermediate group is the *lidi*, who may be distantly connected with the barbarian contingents, which, centuries earlier, the Roman government had settled upon abandoned lands. The sex ratio of the *coloni* is 119 (2,017 males and 1,701 females), as it is for the entire population. For the *lidi*, it is 159 (94 males and 59 females). And for *servi* it soars to 266 (250 males and 94 females). Women, in sum, are conspicuously missing from the less favored juridical categories. Where are the missing *lidae* and *ancillae*?

The polyptych omits (or at least, it does not clearly identify) one important segment of the population: the residents of the manor house who served the monks directly. For example, the typical manor would contain a *gynecaeum* or women's workshop. In the capitulary *De Villis*, an unknown Carolingian king, probably Charlemagne himself, directs his steward to provide to the women working therein "linen, wool, woad, red dye, madder, carding implements, combs, soap, soil, containers, and other small things which are needed there."[45] Irminon's polyptych echoes these provisions. In one place (xiii.109) it gives a list of fourteen *ancillae*, and says of them: "These women, if linen and supplies are given to them, make shirts (*camsilos*)." It supplies another list of nineteen *lidae* (xiii.110) and reports: "All these women either make shirts of eight *alne* or they pay four pennies."

Since women were skilled in cooking, cloth manufacture, and similar domestic work, most of the servants residing in the manor houses would be female. For example, Adelard, abbot of Corbie in France who helped found Corvei in Westphalia, settled upon his estates "widows and single men"; presumably he kept the younger unmarried women in his direct service.[46] A partial survey from the monastery of Farfa in central Italy, redacted between 789 and 822, describes 299 dependent households, and also the "slaves" attached to a manor house at a place called Forcone.[47] The sex ratio for the entire population shows a typical dearth of women. Males outnumber females by a ratio of 122 to 100. But among the servants in the manor house, women outnumber men by 73 to 23, for a sex ratio of only 32. Women tended to congregate in the households of the powerful, even on monastic estates. It seems likely that the monks of St. Germain similarly recruited women into their direct service, and likely also that the women were taken from the ranks of the *lidae* and *ancillae*, over whom they exercised full authority. It is probable too that the monastery took young and single girls into its *minesterium*, returning them to the farms when they reached marriage age. This would explain the shortage of female children.

Irminon's polyptych does contain ten lists of persons who seem to be unattached to any tenure and were most likely directly serving the monks. Nothing is said about their families, and they are presumably unmarried. Some are expressly identified as *lidae,* and the fact that the others are subject to the head tax (*capaticum*) indicates that they are of servile status. Two of the lists contain *homines votivi:* persons who seem to have dedicated themselves to the service of the monastery, while the monastery held the *mainbourg* or *mundium,* the power of a father or household head, over them. Table 3.1 shows the number of men and women among these landless serfs.

Probably the male *servi* brought into the direct service of the monastery were young and still unmarried. This would help explain the smaller size of servile households. At all events, girls predominate in the lists of the servants in the manor houses; this surely was an important factor in producing the high sex ratios within the general population.

Size and Structure

To recapitulate: individuals who appear without a family on the farms of St. Germain had some sort of association with the land, but probably were not resident upon it. If these solitaries are removed, the population of St. Germain loses the severe distortion in

Table 3.1. Landless Persons on the Estates of St. Germain-des-Prés

Survey entry	Capaticum list		Votivi list	
	Men	Women	Men	Women
ii.118	14	12		
iv.33	9	11		
iv.34			7	14
v.86	2	7		
vii.81	15	14		
xiii.108	30	14[a]		
		19[b]		
xiv.90	13	9		
xx.45	27	11		
xx.46	0	32		
xx.47			5	7
TOTALS	110	129	12	21

Grand totals: Men = 122, Women = 150, Sex Ratio = 81.

Source: St. Germain, 1886–95.
a. *servae.*
b. *lidae.*

its sex ratio derived from a raw count of persons. And the remaining imbalance between the sexes can be imparted to a known factor, the recruitment of girls, *lidae* and *ancillae* in particular, into the direct service of the monks. The survey, thus balanced, provides a realistic picture of the organization of peasant households in the region of Paris, in the early ninth century.

In calculating the size and examining the structure of households, we again stay close to the logical organization of the survey. We assume that the family or families (but not the solitaries) listed in each entry or logical unit are coresidential. (The basic meaning of the *mansus* is the farm of a single household.) When the resident families had in fact divided the farm, then the surveyors with full consistency place them in distinct entries and assign them a fraction of the *mansus*. The surveyors, in other words, distinguish through the form of the entries integral farms (and the households living on them), and those which have been divided.

Irminon's polyptych also provides much information on the size and kinds of land the dependent families worked. We thus have a good picture of the resources supporting the households. Here, we shall take as a measure of those resources the extent of the arable land each family worked, divided in *bunaria*. According to Guérard, the *bunarium* was about 120 *ares* in size.[48] To avoid unnecessary complexities, we suppress all fractional values and also measurements in *antsingae*, a smaller unit than the *bunaria*.

Table 3.2 shows the number, membership and average size of the households of St. Germain, arranged according to the number of integral *bunaria* of plowland they worked.

The average size of the households on the lands of St. Germain is 5.79 persons, and the median size is 6. Table 3.2 also illustrates a correlation that is frequently encountered in medieval household lists—one that is so strong as to constitute, it would appear, a general rule of household organization. Households controlling the larger amount of resources appear with the greater number of persons. Peasant families acquire members in proportion either to the numbers that they can support or the work required of them. However, the relation between lands worked and household size shows a distinct break between groups of households with fewer than ten *bunaria*, and those with ten or more. This suggests that the household system was two-tiered. The richer households—and, if the data existed, we should include here the manor houses of the monks—presumably were taking the older children, boys but especially girls, and returning them at marriage age to their families. This pattern of collecting older childen into richer households, and returning them at marriage age, will recur.[49]

Table 3.2. Household size on the estates of St. Germain-des-Prés according to amount of arable land

Land in *bunaria*	Number of households	Men	Women	No sex given	Total	Average household size
1	34	77	66	7	150	4.41
2	75	173	139	19	331	4.41
3	110	229	184	51	464	4.21
4	206	463	397	90	950	4.61
5	153	403	348	41	792	5.17
6	169	422	378	72	872	5.15
7	111	354	289	21	664	5.98
8	96	248	204	40	492	5.12
9	55	162	127	20	309	5.61
10	60	238	165	15	418	6.96
11	42	155	137	7	299	7.11
12	80	305	268	12	585	7.31
13	38	175	141	6	322	8.47
14	32	132	119	12	363	8.21
>14	151	605	508	101	1214	8.03
Totals	1378	4064	3404	507	7975	5.79

Source: St. Germain, 1886–95.

In contrast to size, the sex ratio (as previously adjusted to 119) shows no certain tendency to vary with wealth within this community of dependent peasants. Identifiable women, at least among the peasantry, remain evenly distributed across the wealth categories. However, it is worth noting that persons of undetermined sex, almost all of them *infantes,* tend to congregate in the richest households. The wealthiest 10 percent of households contain 20 percent of these unnamed children. It is easy to speculate that the failure to give them precise names means that they were temporary transfers into the household and not the natural offspring of the head.

The internal structure of these households is quite distinctive. There is very little evidence of vertical extension, that is, over generations. There are only 26 grandmothers among the 3,404 women, and no grandfathers. The absence of grandfathers could mean that the male chiefs held on to their authority until death, but if they did, we should expect to find married sons and grandchildren among the household members. Clearly identified grandchildren are only two. The absense of vertical extension, of three generational families, and of grandfathers, grandmothers, and grandchildren, is thus striking. The classical stem family was not present on the estates of St. Germain.[50]

On the other hand, lateral extension is very pronounced. To be sure, the survey rarely identifies the exact relationships of those who appear as joint heads of households in the same entries, and it may be that some are fathers together with married sons. However, if the failure to identify relationships really did conceal large numbers of generationally extended families, then we should expect to find many widowed parents—relics of the once ruling older generation. But even widowed mothers of the chiefs are very few. The joint chiefs of households must belong in their great majority to the same generation. Probably they are brothers, but some may be brothers and sisters. The mention in the survey of husbands who do not belong to St. Germain indicates that marriages were not exclusively virilocal.[51] Occasionally, the husband must have joined the household of his bride.

If we consider only those households headed by male chiefs, then an astonishing 43 percent (601 out of 1,401) contain more than a single male head, and 11 percent (155) more than two. The households look quite flat in a generational sense, with an overwhelming proportion of the population within the central generations of parents and children.

With an average size of nearly six persons, the households look large, but the number of children is relatively few. If we calculate the balance between male adults and male children, which would be roughly equivalent to a male replacement ratio, then we count 2,006 adults and 2,200 children, for a ratio of 1.11 boys per adult man. This stands above unity, but as the generation of male children would experience further attrition, it becomes unlikely that the visible population was even replacing its own numbers. For women, the comparable rate is below unity (1,975 female adults to 1,569 girls, or 0.79 female children per adult woman). Again, the best explanation for these low replacement ratios is the transfer of children from poor into rich peasant households and into the manor houses, the membership of which is largely lost to us for St. Germain, though not for Farfa. The children of the least advantaged class, the *servi* and *lidi*, were especially subject to these transfers. Slavery died slowly in Europe, and it weighed the longest on the young. The household system at St. Germain seems to have been founded not only upon births and deaths, but also upon the transfer of children as they grew. These movements among households can only be dimly ascertained in the polyptych of St. Germain, but we shall encounter a similar pattern, in another community, later in the Middle Ages.[52]

What kinship and marriage pattern produced these large, generationally flattened households? The naming conventions followed by the families of St. Germain betray an awareness of descent and a sense of kin. The Germanic names, by far the most numerous in the polyptych, are composed of two elements. For example, "Sigi," meaning "victory," is combined with "bercht," "brilliant," to produce "Sigiberchtus," "brilliant in victory." Frequently the names of sons and daughters combine elements taken from the names of both parents. Thus, Ragenildis is the daughter of Rainordus and Agenildis. Elements borrowed from the parents' names can also identify siblings. The children of Godelhardus are Godelharius, Godelhildis, and Godelberga.[53] It is important to note that the name elements are taken indifferently from the mother and the father. The name-giving indicates a spirit of family cohesiveness that may have worked to keep the members of the same descent group together on the same farm, even in adulthood.

Doubtless too, manorial discipline helped preserve the unity of these households and resisted divisions of their farms. The peasants were, after all, the *homines* of St. Germain, and could not leave the soil with the abbey's permission. Perhaps too, their own desire for enhanced security, and fear of the wilderness, kept them ensconced upon the ancestral lands.

The preponderance of laterally extended households on the estates of St. Germain further implies that marriages were comparatively late for both men and women, and were not exclusively "neolocal," that is, they did not always result in the establishment of a new and independent household. Late marriages for both sexes would have lengthened the distance between the generations and diminished the chances that three or four generations would be found within the same house.

The high percentage of laterally extended households and the division of many *mansi* into fractions seem to indicate that there was considerable crowding upon the lands of St. Germain.[54] The cultivators were packed into "population islands," and unable or unwilling to launch a concerted attack on the surrounding forests and wastes. The community experienced high population pressures but, rather paradoxically, could achieve little absolute growth. But the community also possessed considerable capacity for expansion, if the marriage age dropped and the increasing numbers of its members were directed toward the colonization of virgin lands.

This is the most likely pattern of marriage which the peasants of St. Germain followed. But there should be other evidence to confirm that ages of first marriage were indeed high for both men and women in early medieval society.

PATTERNS OF MARRIAGE

Illuminated by numerous inscriptions and by literary sources, patterns of marriage in classical times are reasonably clear, at least for the elite segments of society, and quite distinctive. As we have seen, girls were young at first marriage (typically in their middle or late teens) and men rather mature (usually in their middle or late twenties).[55] Many men chose not to marry at all. The age difference between bride and groom at first marriage was about nine years. The institution of the classical dowry imposed the chief costs of establishing the new household upon the bride or her family. However, in the period of the late empire, ages of first marriage for males apparently were falling, even as the terms of marriage were turning against them. Women, on the other hand, were coming to delay marriage, and they entered it on ever improving terms. The wide difference in ages separating the spouses consequently collapsed.

Among the barbarian Germans, according to Tacitus' famous depiction, "The young men marry late and their vigor is thereby unimpaired. The girls, too, are not hurried into marriage. As old and full-grown as the men, they match their mates in age and strength, and the children reproduce the might of their parents."[56]

If Tacitus is to be believed, the Germanic groom and bride were both mature and nearly the same age at marriage. And the groom brought the dowry to the bride, not the bride to the groom, as in classical Rome. Remarkably, over the centuries of the late empire, by measure of both marital terms and ages, the Roman marriage was converging toward the barbarian model.

Terms of Marriage

References to the classical *dos* or dowry, in a sense of a conveyance of property from the bride's side to the husband, vanish from early medieval texts; the word itself comes to signify the groom's gifts to the bride. About 600, St. Leander, brother of Isidore of Seville, in typical usage explains that "those men who take wives are accustomed to provide dowries and confer gifts, and in exchange for [her] lost chastity convey patrimonies, so that wives seem to be solicited rather than led."[57] A letter of Pope Nicholas to the Bulgarians, dated November 13, 866, offers a full description of the wedding ceremony according to the Latin rite. The letter was subsequently included in Gratian's *Decretum* (ca. 1140), the first officially recognized collection of authoritative canons:

> Our people, both men and women, when they make the marriage contracts (*nuptualia foedera*) do not wear on their heads bands of gold, of silver, or of any metal. After the betrothals,

which are a promise of future marriage, with the consent of those who have made them and of those under whose authority they stand, certain agreements are struck. After the groom has betrothed the bride through a ring of fidelity which he puts as a pledge on her finger, and after the groom has given to her the dowry upon which both have agreed together with the written instrument containing the agreement, in the presence of persons invited from both sides, then, immediately or after a suitable interval, lest it be presumed that such an act was done before the legal age, both are brought to the marriage vows. And first the vows are taken in the church of the Lord with offerings, which they ought to offer to God through the hands of the priest. Thus finally they are given the blessing and the celestial veil.[58]

Nicholas makes no mention at all of any dowry or gift made by the bride to the groom; the classical dowry has disappeared. The groom and his family have assumed all the burdens of matrimony. Apparently too, the bridewealth assigned by the groom to his bride was inflating in the early Middle Ages. The Visigothic Codex Euricianus (681) and several subsequent codes set limits on the amount of dowry the groom could give his bride.[59]

The text also implies that bride and groom were often young when betrothed. The agreement of those "in whose authority they are" must be sought, implying that they were often minors; and a suitable time must elapse before the actual marriage, in other words, until they attained legal age. Papal letters of the twelfth century give several examples of young betrothals.[60] A letter written sometime between 1159 and 1181 mentions a boy age 6 pledged to a girl of 7; another from 1185–1187 describes a girl of 12 engaged to a boy of 9 or 10. In these unions, when the vows were finally exchanged, the husband and wife would have been nearly equal in age.

Ages at First Marriage

The evidence for marriage ages during the early Middle Ages is spotty, but there is enough to suggest that grooms were not as mature as their Roman predecessors, and that they married brides not much younger than themselves.

Marriage was ideally to take place at the *aetas perfecta*, or "perfect age." In both antiquity and the Middle Ages, moral counselors recommended that men delay marriage until they had attained this perfect age. Thus, the Frankish noblewoman Dhuoda, who wrote a tract for the education of her son sometime between 841 and 843, assumes that he will marry and father children when he reaches the *perfectum tempus*.[61] Specifically, the perfect age is attained at the end of the stage of life known as *adolescentia*, at the time of *iuventus*, the full bloom of youth. If the course of life is conceived as an overarching span, this is its highest point. In the words of Thomas Aquinas, this is the moment "at which the movement of growth ends, and from which the movement of decline begins."[62]

In the ancient world, Aristotle had set the prime of life at 37 for men and at 18 for women, and urges both to marry at that point.[63] But most ancient philosophers favored 30 years as the perfect age. In the Christian New Testament, Luke (3.23) states that Jesus was about thirty when he began to preach in public, and this impressed Christian authors.[64] No one younger, no *adolescens*, could have preached with authority. Augustine in his *Confessions* declares that at age 30 "my adolescence was dead." Elsewhere, he specifically identifies age 30 as the moment when "men begin to decline."[65] Appropriately too, he then decides that he should marry. This assumption of the ancients that age 30 was the prime moment of life long persists. In the sixth century, the life of St. Eutychus, patriarch of Constantinople, observes that the saint attained "perfect height as he reached the perfect age [of 30]," and that "Christ God was seen to honor this age more than any other, as he was baptized at 30 years."[66] Isidore of Seville, whose *Etymologiae* is a storehouse of ancient lore, identifies age 30 as the perfect age for men; he was writing in the early seventh century.[67]

But new definitions of the perfect age appear in early medieval sources, and they are characteristically younger than 30. The Visigothic law from the late seventh century defines the *aetas perfecta* as age 20 for men and for women, which implies that both would marry soon after.[68] Also in the Visigothic law, boys obtain their highest *wergild*, the money to be paid in case of their injury or death, when they turn 20. (Girls obtain their highest *wergild* at age 15, which indicates that the Visigoths believed that girls reached sexual maturity earlier than boys, even though the "perfect age" was 20 for both.) In 731 Liutprand, king of the Lombards, set the *legetima etas* at 18 (it was 25 among the Romans), and this too suggests that men achieved full adult status at a younger age than before.[69] Both the Visigothic and Lombard codes complain of marriages in which the brides are older than the grooms.[70] These older women were taking as husbands boys who had yet to reach the perfect or legal age.

In 796–97, a council held at Fréjus explicitly states that the groom and bride should be "not of dissimilar age but of the same age."[71] Many abuses take place, it warns, when the groom is adult and the bride immature, or *vice versa*. If the bride is mature and the groom a child, she is often sexually exploited by the father or elder brother of the groom. The council strongly advocated that marriage unite mature partners of equal age.

Both the barbarian codes and the early medieval councils thus imply that grooms were not much older than their brides at marriage and were on occasion even younger. To be sure, the evidence is ambiguous and some girls were young at first marriage. St. Austrudis, sister of St. Baldwin, was sought in marriage when she was in her twelfth year.[72] But she was a member of the high aristocracy, among whom young ages at first marriage for women were often the rule.

The Carolingian surveys offer further evidence that relative equality in ages at first marriage, for men and for women, was characteristic of early medieval society—at least within the communities surveyed. Thus, among the serfs of St. Germain des Prés, widowers number 86 and widows 133.[73] If the men were significantly older than women when they first married, then there should have been a larger preponderance of widows in the population. For example, at Florence in 1427, when the age difference between bride and groom was over 12 years, widows outnumbered widowers by a factor of 5.6.[74] The near equality of the two groups at St. Germain suggests that brides at first marriage were only slightly younger than their spouses.

The Carolingian survey which offers the best data about marriages in the ninth century comes from the Church of St. Victor of Marseilles.[75] The survey was redacted probably between 813 and 814, and includes 128 households, for which the names of the members are stated. It not only names the household members, but classifies them by age category: infants at the breast; children between 2 and 15 years, for whom exact ages are given; unmarried adults, called *baccularii* and *baccularie* for males and females respectively; and mature adults, otherwise undifferentiated, who were married or widowed. Table 3.3 shows the breakdown of the peasant population of St. Victor by ages.

Among the peasants of St. Victor, both girls and boys were considered marriageable from age 16, when they passed out of the category of children into that of bachelor men and women. Still, they could have entered marriage only slowly, as the number of bachelors—127 men and 120 women—is quite large, constituting 24 percent of the population. In the city of Florence in 1427, 24 percent of the males were bachelors over age 15, and the mean age of first marriage for males was nearly 30. While the age distributions of the two populations were undoubtedly very different, nonetheless it appears incontrovertible that the peasants of St. Victor, both men

Table 3.3. The peasants of St. Victor of Marseilles by age.

	Men	Women	No sex stated[a]	Totals
Nurslings			29	29
Children	99	106	126	331
Bachelors	127	120		247
Adults	212	203	5	420
TOTALS	438	429	160	1027

Source: St. Victor, 1857, II, 633–56.

a. Children described only by the plural *filii* with no names or ages given are counted as two children of uncertain sex.

and women, were postponing marriage until their late twenties. Moreover, given the nearly equal number of bachelor men and women, the males in this peasant community could have been only slightly older than their brides at first marriage. Then too, if a wide age difference separated bride and groom, we would again expect to find many more widows than widowers in the population. But in this community of Carolingian peasants, the number of widows is small— only 43—and it is not strikingly greater than the number of widowers, 31.[76]

Chroniclers and hagiographers also cast some light on early medieval marriage patterns. They leave no doubt that payments from groom to bride were the predominant, even the only form, of nuptial conveyance. Merovingian queens received entire cities "in dowry and in *morgangabe,* that is, the gift of the morning."[77] The sources are less explicit concerning ages. However, the Anglo-Saxon saint Guthlac, who lived in the days of king Ethelred (675–704) and who attracted a contemporary biographer, chose "from the ranks of noble girls" a bride expressly said to be "of the same age" (*coaetana*).[78] He himself had to be twenty-four or younger, as at that moment in his life he gave up worldly pomp to become a hermit.[79]

Marriages in the early Middle Ages thus seem closely to resemble the barbarian model described by Tacitus. Men and women were roughly equal in ages at first marriage, and they married in their middle or late twenties. At the same time, all across the continent, the bridewealth of the barbarians became the standard. Legal historians have certainly argued with much ingenuity that traces of Roman practices survived in central and southern Italy and in other areas under strong Byzantine influence.[80] But beyond question, the dominant form of marital conveyance in western Europe during the early Middle Ages, from the barbarian migrations until the twelfth century, was the reverse dowry. In regard to both marital ages and marital terms, barbarian or late ancient practices, rather than the customs of classical Rome, provided the basic models of marriages in the early medieval West.

In early medieval Europe, the decline of ancient slavery, the spread of peasant agriculture, the rules of monogamy and exogamy which the Church enforced with slow success, lent unprecedented uniformity to households across society. From roughly 700, apparently for the first time in the West, households are used as units in surveys, intended to measure the population and productivity of communities. Commensurable households also meant a more even distribution of the sexes across society, and this surely reduced abductions and rapes of women and probably calmed the endemic violence of early medieval life. The prohibition of polygyny and concubinage and the rule of exogamy prevented men of the elites from accumulating or retaining many women in their houses and gave non-elite males a better chance of gaining a mate.

Comparatively late ages at first marriage for both sexes seem understandable, from what we know of the crowded conditions within the Carolingian population islands. The practice would have slowed or halted further growth of already crowded and impacted communities. But the custom also gave the population a powerful potential for growth, if changing conditions persuaded or allowed men and women to marry at younger ages.

And Europe was to witness dramatic changes in its economy and society, and in its households, from about the year 1000.

4 | THE TRANSFORMATIONS OF THE CENTRAL AND LATE MIDDLE AGES

Knights who covet honor, my lord, must not stay home with their parents when they are young and able to bear arms, and especially if they are the youngest and still more if their fathers ignore them. Were I you, I would sooner eat grass in the mountains than spend one more day at this court. Be mindful of that old saying: with a change of age comes a change of fortune. And consider whether you might not find better fortune elsewhere.

—Advice to a young prince, from *Tirant lo Blanc*, cap. 100.

THE DOMESTIC institutions of medieval society were profoundly transformed after the year 1000. In a great reform movement, the Church reorganized itself and tried with unprecedented vigor to shape and direct secular society. It developed a systematic theology and canon law of marriage, and successfully claimed the right to judge marriage cases within its own courts. The new era brought a new form of kin organization— the agnatic lineage or the patrilineage. Both the ages of marriages and the terms of marriage shifted. The new arrangements are most visible in Italy, but evidence of their presence can be found widely across Europe. After the turn of the millennium, in sum, Europeans find new ways to recognize their kin, to view marriage, to enter and to leave it, and to organize their households.

THE SOCIAL AND CULTURAL ENVIRONMENT

From probably the late tenth century, the European population was expanding rapidly, and its growth continues until about 1250; it then stabilizes but stays at very high levels for another hundred years. The evidence for this is largely indirect but nonetheless convincing.[1] New place names proliferate in the records, indicating a dramatic multiplication of settlements. Towns gird themselves with bigger circles of walls. To judge from the great Domesday survey, England in 1086 contained a population of some 1.1 million; at the peak of this demographic surge about 1300, it may have held as many as 7 million people.[2] Many historians now affirm that Europe in the fourteenth century had become overpopulated; the terrible plagues, famines, and wars which then wracked the land were rooted in a true Malthusian crisis.[3] Whatever the truth of this controverted thesis, population pressures certainly intensified between the eleventh and thirteenth centuries. Europe's multiplying households had to find new resources, and to develop new methods of managing and conserving those they already possessed.

The achievements of the eleventh and twelfth centuries were cultural and intellectual as well as social.[4] Theologians and canonists defined with new specificity what marriage was, who could marry, and what impediments were "diriment" (that is, nullifying the marriage) and what only prohibitive (forbidding the marriage, but not nullifying the union once it was made). Canon law largely replaced the secular codes which had governed questions of marriage during the early Middle Ages. The Church's rules, in other words, formed the legal environment within which kindreds and marriages assumed new forms.[5]

Consensus non Concubitus

In the schools of the twelfth century, theologians and canonists elaborated two differing definitions of valid marriage.[6] The first of them was advanced in Italy and was given its most influential expression in Gratian's *Decretum* (ca. 1141).[7] Even in classical antiquity, Roman lawyers had discussed whether consent or sexual intercourse, or both, were necessary for a valid marriage. The most common opinion was that consent alone was sufficient, but some experts continued to affirm that physical union perfected the marriage and rendered it binding. Christian writers found the issue especially delicate, as they were loath to affirm that the marriage of Jesus' parents, Joseph and Mary, which was never sexually consummated, was in any respect imperfect.

Gratian attempted to resolve the difficulty by distinguishing two stages in the contracting of a marriage. When the partners expressed their consent, the couple entered into a *matrimonium initiatum*, an "initiated marriage." Their subsequent sexual union validated or confirmed their marriage, rendering it a *matrimonium ratum*. Joseph and Mary had entered upon the first, but not the second, of these stages leading to full union. But Gratian's analysis failed to command universal assent, as it still implied that the marital union of Jesus' parents was incomplete.

Beyond the Alps, the flourishing theological schools of France offered a different interpretation. Its chief proponent was the bishop of Paris, Peter Lombard, author of the *Sentences*, the most popular theological textbook of the Middle Ages. In his view, to achieve a valid marriage, the bride and groom, otherwise eligible to marry, needed only to express their consent *per verba de presenti*, "in words of the present tense." A promise "through words of the future tense" was a betrothal, and, though a serious commitment, was not yet a marriage and might under certain conditions be annulled. Because they had expressed consent in words of the present tense, Joseph and Mary were joined in a fully realized union, even in the absence of sexual intercourse; "the contract was already rendered perfect through consent alone."[8]

Peter Lombard's interpretation eventually became the standard doctrine of the Church, the foundation of its law as well as theology of marriage. In a series of decretals, pope Alexander III (1159–1189) endorsed Lombard's analysis and affirmed that the spoken consent of the eligible partners alone rendered the marriage valid and binding.[9]

This principle had extraordinary social consequences. The Church, in effect, affirmed that no one and no institution could interfere with the right of a man and a woman, otherwise eligible, to marry or not to marry. The manorial or feudal lord lost control over the marriages of his serfs or vassals. The doctrine even limited the authority of the Church. The Church had long insisted that the couple seek the blessing of a priest.[10] In the north of Europe the endowment of the bride "in the face of the church" was a principal proof that a legal marriage had been contracted.[11] Failure to obtain the nuptial blessing, to endow the bride, or to publish the banns of marriage (after this was required by the Fourth Lateran Council in 1215), were prohibitive impediments; they rendered the marriage illicit but not invalid. The offending couple were liable to reprimand and penances, but their marriage stood.

Perhaps most decisively, the principle undermined the authority of the parents, fathers in particular, who might seek to arrange, or prevent, the marriages of their offspring. The father, for example, could neither force a son or daughter into an unwanted marriage, nor prevent him or her from marrying. He was helpless in the face of an elopement. The Church's doctrine was a damaging blow to paternal authority within the medieval household, and by itself assured that the medieval family could never develop into a true patriarchy. The Church had been traditionally wary of the claims of the family over its offspring, which might well conflict with the claims of God. Its teaching on marriage gave practical, powerful expression to this ancient suspicion.

THE PATRILINEAGE

It is possible that the Church's denial of a parental (meaning paternal) veto over marriages of the children was meant to counteract a contemporary resurgence of the father's authority within the medieval kindred. As many historians have noted, aristocratic kindreds (or many of them) were transformed in Europe from the eleventh and twelfth centuries.[12] The great novelty is the appearance within these elite circles of the agnatic lineage or patrilineage.

Kin Organizations

The agnatic lineage differs from the old bilateral kindred (the *cognatio*) in several significant ways. It is organized around the agnatic line of descent, and becomes a kind of fellowship of males, stretching backwards and forwards over time. Women no longer serve as the nodules through which pass the surest kinship ties. The daughter is treated as a marginal member of her father's lineage, and after her marriage, her children will leave it entirely; their allegiance passes to her husband's line. Women also lose the claim to a full (or at least a fair) share with their brothers in the family patrimony. Their fathers and brothers arrange for their marriages and provide the dowries that the changing terms of marriage now require (see below). The dowry usually marks the limit of the material support that women receive from their families of origin.[13]

The patrilineage is ancestor-focused, in the sense that it traces its descent through the male line back to a known founder. The *cognatio*, on the other hand, is ego-focused; the lines of relationship run forth from ego in both directions, through males and females, to the accepted limits of kinship, whether the Roman four degrees, or the Germanic-canonical seven. The domain of kinship is thus unique to every ego, and is also redefined with every generation. As an ancestor-focused system, the agnate lineage tends to acquire new members over time and also typically comes to include several or many parallel lines of descent. Like a great cable, it holds multiple strands; the members of the lineage look back to the same ancestor, and they see around them relatives in equivalent positions.

Anchored in the past and in a fixed genealogy, the agnate lineage is encompassed by relatively stable boundaries and enjoys a rather clear sense of its own origins and history. Its members can therefore cultivate a sense of solidarity and of pride in their ancestry and in their blood. Almost always in the literature of feudal society, allusions to ancestry have the ring of boasting.[14] The members exalt their lineage through adoption of a family name, often formed from that of the revered ancestor or of the ancestral castle. They devise an identifying coat of arms, subject to the strict rules of heraldry but still distinguishing the lineage and advertising its accomplishments.[15] The great houses commission (or inspire) the recording of genealogies and the composition of family histories.[16] Again, pride of ancestry underlies all these exercises.

The importance of the lineage in the social history of elite European society is manifest, but we should not exaggerate its dominance. According to David Nicholas, the patrician kindreds in Ghent in Flanders in the late Middle Ages remained primarily bilateral in their organization.[17] Nowhere did the lineage truly replace the old, bilateral kindred; rather, it was superimposed upon it. As Jack Goody observes, patrilineal, matrilineal, and bilateral kindreds can exist simultaneously in the same society, usually organized for different purposes.[18] The goal of the patrilineage was to preserve the wealth and status of its male members over time, by limiting the number of claimants upon its resources or by reducing the size of some shares. The traditional purpose of the *cognatio* was the enlargement of the kindred, which would assure its biological survival. It continued to define the domain of blood relationships, within which marriages were forbidden but inheritances allowed.[19] And the *cognatio* surely defined a domain of affective ties as well. The simultaneous existence of these two kindred groups raised contentious questions. The conservation of wealth in the interest of male members was not entirely compatible with the proliferation of the kindred. How large a dowry should be offered to facilitate the marriage of a daughter? How many resources should be expended to further the career of a younger son? How assiduously should matrilineal relatives and affines be cultivated? These difficult questions heightened tensions within the households and kindreds. But they also extended the range of choices in the families' efforts to preserve their wealth and numbers.

Origins

Cultural, social, economic, and political changes contributed to the emergence of the patrilineage. One prerequisite to it was the long-delayed success, always limited but still substantial, of the Church's protracted struggle to impose upon society a rule of monogamy and to suppress all manner of extramarital sexual liaisons. Sexual promiscuity inevitably obscures patrilineal relationships, and the sexual behavior of the men and women who formed the early medieval

Figures 4.1., 4.2. Trees of Consanguinity (*left*) and Affinity (*right*). Manuscript illuminations from the Gautier Lebaude Atelier, Paris, thirteenth century. Courtesy of the Pierpont Morgan Library, New York.

These two elegant illustrations of consanguinous relationships (with the

degrees numbered) and of relations through marriage illustrate the elaborate incest prohibitions developed by the medieval Church. The prohibitions obstructed close marriages and forced a circulation of marriage partners, women in particular, across households.

elites was singularly loose.[20] As long as the European elites strayed from strict monogamy, any effort to organize a descent group along patrilineal lines would be frustrated. The Gregorian reform of the eleventh century carried forward with new force the old effort to impose the Christian ethic of marriage upon the reluctant ruling circles.[21] Lapses may have remained frequent, but since then monogamy emerges as the unquestioned rule of Western marriage.

Georges Duby has recently contrasted what he calls the lay and ecclesiastical models of marriage in northern France in the eleventh and twelfth centuries.[22] While he offers a close and helpful reading of several critical texts, the terminology he proposes is problematic. Did the efforts of powerful laymen to bend in their interest long-standing ethical principles really constitute a "model of marriage" parallel to the Church's own? No one, after all, was proposing that the rules be rewritten, only that they not be applied in particular instances. Disputes over aristocratic marriages are frequent in ecclesiastical annals from at least the ninth century. How often did they involve rival "models," rather than simple misbehavior?[23] Moreover, sexual promiscuity obscures relationships in the male line, whereas the Church's insistence on monogamy (and fidelity) supported the new agnatic dynasties.

The triumph of monogamy was a precondition, but surely not the principal cause, of this realignment of descent groups around the male line. The crucial factor seems to have been diminishing opportunities and resources for the support of elite households. The aristocracies of the early Middle Ages lived from pillage, gifts, and rents. From the eleventh century, the stabilization of feudal principalities and the partial pacification of European life reduced the chances of collecting plunder, except along distant frontiers. Many great families now looked for support primarily to their landed properties; they struggled to increase the rents they collected through better management and through expanding the cultivated area. They also protected the integrity of their patrimonies from destructive partitions among heirs.

Indeed, in the eleventh century, the entire patrimonial base of the European aristocracies was changing. Typically, in the earlier Middle Ages, patrimonial lands were widely dispersed with few recognized centers and were loosely managed.[24] Tenures were remarkably fluid. The play of inheritances, marriage settlements, benefices given and received, donations to the Church, and land exchanges generated repeated transfers of property.[25] The distinction between lay and ecclesiastical properties was especially blurred. The great family typically possessed its own monastery or church, endowed this religious establishment, and named or proposed the presiding abbot or priest. But it also made free use of the landed endowment for its own purposes. Through benefices, favorable leases, or fraudulent exchanges, the monastery or church returned land to its patrons or delivered it to relatives or followers, as directed. Abbots who enriched their relatives through the lands of their monasteries are a social commonplace in the early Middle Ages. The great family and its monastery or church were joined together in a kind of economic symbiosis.[26] Given the general fluidity of tenures, partitions of lands among many heirs did not mount a major threat to the wealth and status of the family.

The reform movement of the eleventh century radically altered the tenurial base of aristocratic power. The reformers took as their principal goal the "liberty of the Church"—its offices and its lands—from lay domination. Lay control of ecclesiastical lands and offices, they believed, forced the clergy into the sin of simony, the buying and selling of spiritual services and appointments. In an instructive letter to the clergy and people of Lucca (of which city he was simultaneously the bishop), pope Alexander II (1061–1073) forbade all sales, leases, investitures, or any form of alienation of Church property to laymen (except to cultivators) for the following reasons:

> For before our times our predecessors, who presided over the said church, whether out of affection for their blood relatives, or drawn by the love of money, or overcome by the excessive press of petitioners, gave away the castles, lands and possessions of this church indiscriminately, with such excessive generosity that [the endowment] could not serve them or their administrators in their needs, as was fitting. There thus arose such poverty, that they conferred for money or for remunerations holy orders or ecclesiastical offices on profane and unworthy men. These ought to be granted without venality and with consideration given only to eternal life. They sustained the life of the body by the death of the soul. This, all Catholics must despise and condemn.[27]

The reform of the clergy thus required the recovery and stabilization of the Church's landed endowment, and the program worked a revolution in its relationship with the lay world. Deprived of easy access to the Church's properties, the great families also had to devise new strategies of preserving and augmenting their resources.

One tactic they adopted was to exclude some offspring—typically daughters and younger sons—from a full share in the inheritance. Daughters (all or some) received from their fathers or brothers the dowries they now needed for marriage, but barring unusual circumstances, neither they nor their offspring could advance any further claim upon the patrimony. Daughters were pushed to the margins of the agnate lineage, and their children passed entirely out of the *generatio* of their maternal ancestors.

Although lineage is recognizable everywhere by its agnatic bias, it took on a variety of forms. We shall consider here two types, which are not truly distinct but make up, as it were, the opposite ends of a continuum over which many intermediate forms are found: the "consortial" and the "dynastic." "Consortial" derives from *sors*, "inheritance," and means a group sharing an inheritance. This lineage was organized to call male heirs to a partible patrimony, and also to prevent ancestral lands from escaping altogether from the kindred's control. The "dynastic" lineage called a single candidate to a indivisible inheritance or office. The *consorteria* usually contained several descent lines, but no one of them was singled out as senior to the others. The dynastic lineage, on the other hand, included both a preferred and postponed, or senior and cadet, branches.

The *Consorteria*

Northern Italy, a land rich in documentation, offers perhaps the clearest examples of the *consorteria* or consortial lineage. There are at least three reasons for this. The traditional legal systems—Roman, Lombard, and Frankish—all envisioned that sons would share equally in the inheritance. There were no powerful overlords in Italy; families were not under pressure from above to keep fiefs and offices undivided. Finally, the early growth of towns and a commercial economy favored this form of kin organization. The principle of equal support of all male heirs was, as we shall see, congenial to merchant families.

The earliest evidence of consortial lineages in Italy comes from references to collectively owned property. Italian charters, which have survived by the thousands, characteristically locate pieces of land by naming those who own the bordering properties. From about the year 1000, there are references such as *terra Sifredisca* (1032, from Farfa in Lazio), *terra Gherardinga* (1010, from Lucca in Tuscany), *terra Garibaldisca* (975, from Bobbio near Pavia in Lombardy), and many others.[28] All these names refer to the lands of a *consorteria*. It is obviously a descent group, and its name evokes the memory of a founder, undoubtedly the one who established the wealth of the line. To hold property in common must mean that the members of the group formed some kind of corporation, and made collective decisions concerning the management of its properties.

References to unnamed "heirs" as collective owners also multiply; their frequency among the contiguous owners rises from 7 percent in the eighth century to 10 percent in the ninth; to remain at 10 percent during the first three quarters of the tenth; and then to soar to 22 in the last quarter of the tenth and into the early eleventh century.[29]

By the twelfth century similar associations have become common in the towns, where they are known as "tower societies," as they characteristically possess a fortified tower.[30]

That *consorterie* began to be mentioned only from about the year 1000 is not an accident of source survivals. Charters of the ninth and early tenth centuries are abundant in Italy, and they yield thousands of references to property owners. Rather, it points to changing strategies of land management, and to the growing tendency of heirs to keep at least part of their patrimony undivided.

The more abundant records of the twelfth and thirteenth centuries give us a good idea of the organization of these consortial lineages. There are surviving statutes of one such *domus*, the Corbolani of Lucca, dated December 14, 1287.[31] That *consorteria* consisted of at least sixteen households (to judge from the number who signed the statutes) and had its own elected consul; members were supposed to join forces in periods of civic disturbance. All resided in three of Lucca's urban parishes. These records make clear that the *consorteria*, at least from the twelfth century, included inner and outer circles of members. For example, according to the Corbolani statutes, an inner circle of members regulated their relationship by formal contract. The group was recruited primarily but not exclusively from the larger circle of agnate relatives. A formal contract defined the membership of the inner circle, which could and did include individuals who were not by blood Corbolani. (Only three of the signers of the statutes bear the name.) In analogous fashion, at Genoa the great houses known as *alberghi* brought together persons who were not blood relatives into artificial kindreds.[32]

The contract defining the inner group was periodically renewed, and the membership therefore changed over time. The *consorteria* continued to own some property in common—typically a castle in the countryside or a tower in the town; and often too an urban compound, consisting of a chapel, warehouse, even baths. But each member retained his own properties. According to the Corbolani statutes, a member who learned that land was offered for sale in the three urban parishes had at once to inform the consul. He in turn would summon the membership, to determine what action should be taken. So also, if a member purchased property in the parishes, he was obligated to extend to his fellows the option of purchasing shares if they so desired.[33]

In Italy the *consorterie* in the great commercial cities are of special interest, as the banks and companies they founded led the commercial revolution of the central Middle Ages. The Bardi house of

Florence offers a clear example of the growth and organization of a great mercantile lineage. Though magnate in status, the Bardi formed a comparatively new *casata* at Florence. In his description of the great houses of the city in the early thirteenth century, the chronicler Giovanni Villani notes their presence, but says that they were of "small beginnings."[34] The founder of the family's fortunes appears to have been Ricco di Bardo, or Riccus Bardi, who appears in the records of the guild of wool merchants, the Calimala, from 1234 to 1254.[35] In what may be a typical pattern, the lineage took its name not from the one who established its fortunes, but from his father— from the patronymic by which he too had been identified. Ricco had at least eight sons, most of whom were similarly prolific.[36] In 1342, members of the house appeared before a notary, to swear to preserve peace with their traditional enemies, the Buondelmonti.[37] The adult Bardi males, actual or potential heads of household, who took the oath, whether in person or by proxy, numbered 120, and even this large group did not represent all living members. By 1342, only three generations after Ricco, they were probably the largest *consorteria* in Florence, a distinction they still retained in the Catasto survey of 1427.[38] Even then, in a radically depopulated city, some 60 collateral branches made up this great *consorteria*. There was and remained no distinction between a senior and cadet lines. Leadership shifted among the component branches. For example, the directorship of the Bardi bank, which was tantamount to leadership within the *consorteria*, passed from Cino di messer Iacopo, its chief in ca. 1300, to his brother, ser Lapo di messer Iacopo, and his nephew, son of another brother, Doffo di Bartolo, who later calls himself messer Ridolfo.[39] Doffo or messer Ridolfo ruled the bank for more than 40 years, and after his death, in a reorganization of 1357, the directorship passed to another brother, Filippo di Bartolo di messer Iacopo. Control over the bank and leadership in the *consorteria* tended to pass not to the direct descendants of previous heads, but to their brothers and cousins—older men with experience and skill.

Even without a recognized senior line, these great houses developed a strong sense of collective identity. Their numerous branches tended to live in close proximity to one another, in the same neighborhood or even on the same street. In 1427, for example, of the 60 Bardi households, 45 lived in the quarter of Santo Spirito, *gonfalone* of Scala, most of them on the street which even today bears their name, the *Via dei Bardi*.

The sense of solidarity was heightened by awareness of a common descent and pride in the accomplishment of virtuous ancestors. At Lucca, scribes writing in the thirteenth century are able to identify the ancestors of prominent lines from as far back as 991.[40] The adoption of a family name and coat of arms, the maintenance of a church or chapel in which prayers could be offered for the benefit of *consortes* living and dead, the burial of deceased members in a family crypt, the association of the house with a particular saint or saints—all these practices helped to enhance the individual's sense of identity and pride. This consciousness of the past led Italian, and especially Florentine, notables and authors to consult the records of their ancestors assiduously. One merchant-writer, Buonaccorso di Neri Pitti, became involved in a bitter dispute with a third cousin and with his daughter, over the possession of documents relating to their common, early forebears.[41] Another Florentine, Giovanni Morelli, wrote his memoirs in order to provide his own descendants with "true example" and "sound instruction" which would profit them "through the help of God and their own good intellects."[42] At least since the late thirteenth century, nearly all the great families of Florence seem to have kept *ricordanze*, which typically contained genealogies of their families from as far back as they could be traced.

The great urban *consorterie* combined solidarity of spirit with policies of pronounced economic individualism. Emancipation of the family's sons took place at very young ages, on which occasion they invariably received a certain amount of capital.[43] The young men thus enjoyed the autonomy and money they needed to make their start in business. The fortunes of the great mercantile houses were critically dependent on the early identification and encouragement of their most talented, most energetic youth. Individualism is apparent too in the administration of the family companies and banks. Partners in the company formed only a small and restricted circle within the larger *casata*. Among the 120 Bardi who swore to make peace in 1342, the first-named and the titular head of the house was messer Ridolfo di Bartolo Bardi. He was at the same time head of the Bardi bank; he and his partners were, in the judgment of Giovanni Villani, "the greatest merchants in Italy."[44] Still, the members of the Bardi *consorteria* and the partners in the bank were very different groups. The number of partners in 1310 was only sixteen, and only ten of these were related to the Bardi in the male line. One of the most active partners was a Machiavelli.[45] The number of partners, and the proportion of Bardi among them, did not change substantially through the bank's frequent reorganizations during the first half of the fourteenth century. Some members of the house of Bardi were employed as agents or factors in the bank, but surprisingly few. Of the 315 factors listed by Armando Sapori in his study of the Bardi bank, only nine can certainly be identified as members of the family. Perhaps the Bardi preferred that their sons gain experience by working in the banks of other families. Numerous Bardi were certainly depositors, but otherwise the great majority of the *consorteria* took no active role in the management or operations of the enterprise which bore their name.

To function effectively, the great family companies needed to maintain clear lines of authority and responsibility over the vital capital that supported their activities. A father or brother could not accept unlimited responsibility for the actions of sons or younger siblings who might be hundreds of miles from Florence. When the mercantile family came to include two or more adult males—whether a father and sons, or the sons of a deceased father—these natural partners tended rather quickly to divide the common patrimony, whether through emancipations and endowments, or through partitions of the paternal inheritance. True, the father and his sons, or the sons alone, then frequently reintegrated the patrimony, in whole or in part, through the creation of a company. But the notarial contract which created it, unlike the play of inheritance, spelled out clearly who owned what shares in, who could expect what profits from, and who could exercise authority over the common enterprise. The Tuscan commercial company, even in the thirteenth century, was not a spontaneous, natural association of heirs; it was, like Burckhardt's vision of the Renaissance state, a work of art.

The Dynastic Lineage

The appearance of the dynastic lineage is intimately connected with the rise of feudal principalities and the implantation of feudal institutions—fiefs and offices—widely across Europe in the post-Carolingian age. Contemporaries were very conscious of the emerging new form of family organization. A charter from the chartulary of the church of Grenoble in central France, written between 1080 and 1132 under the inspiration of a reforming bishop and saint named Hughes, tells how one lineage of counts came into being:

> After the destruction of the pagans [presumably the Magyars], because he found few inhabitants in the said diocese, Bishop Isarnus [late tenth century] gathered nobles, people of middle rank, and the poor from distant lands, and the land of Grenoble was consoled by these people. The bishop gave to these men castles to inhabit and lands to work, and over their castles and lands the aforesaid bishop held ownership and services, as pleased both parties. The aforesaid bishop and his successor Humbert [991–1025] held the said diocese as a true bishop ought to hold his own land and castles, as an allod, as land which he had taken from the pagans. For of the line of those counts who now rule throughout the diocese of Grenoble, none was found in his days (that is the days of Isarnus) who was called a count. But the said

bishop without protest from counts possessed in peace the whole
diocese . . . After Humbert, Mallenus was bishop of the said church
of Grenoble; in his day, Guigo the Old, the father of Guigo the
Fat [*Crassus*] unjustly began to possess those things which the
counts have at Grenoble, whether in episcopal lands, or in services, or in many churches or fields, or in gardens, so that out
of the entire diocese of Grenoble the bishop does not have one
whole farm under his dominion.[46]

After Guigo the Fat followed Guigo III, called "count of Albion,"
and Guigo IV, called the Dauphin.[47] They formed a dynastic lineage,
born in the turmoil of the post-Carolingian age, and winning for
itself office and lands.

All the old legal traditions of Europe—Roman and Germanic—
assumed that a landed patrimony was partible among heirs. The
spread of feudal tenure introduced much more varied inheritance
rules, affecting real property and the organization of families living
from it. The history of feudal tenures and offices is of course highly
complex, and the surviving records show only scattered points in a
broad and sweeping evolution.[48] Here, we do no more than sum-
marize the direction of that evolution and its apparent effects upon
the aristocratic lineage.

The fief was in origin a conditional, temporary, and non-hereditary
form of land tenure; the tenant or vassal could hold it only as long
as he fulfilled the required services. It thus differed from the allod,
which conveyed an unconditional, permanent, and hereditary title
to land. It is possible to distinguish two great swings in the evolution
of feudal tenure from the Carolingian age into modern times. From
its first appearances to roughly 1300, the fief tends to become both
heritable and partible, at least among male heirs. The rules governing
the devolution of feudal tenures, in other words, are gradually as-
similated to those governing the devolution of allods.

Then, from about 1300 and continuing well into the modern age,
landed noble families adopt ever more commonly a different strategy
of heirship. They entail part or all of their landed estates, over a
stated number of generations, sometimes in perpetuity. An entailed
estate cannot be sold or otherwise alienated. And the owner establishing the entail states exactly the line of devolution along which
the estate should pass. Usually, though not necessarily, he applies
a rule of primogeniture, but must stipulate what happens should the
preferred line become extinguished. Postponed male and female descendants are given movables or non-entailed properties, but the act
of entailment quite clearly creates a senior (or preferred) and cadet
(or postponed) branches within the descent group. The evolution of
feudal tenure, from indivision to partibility back to indivision, seems

to have occurred all over Europe.[49] Even in Italy, ancestral lands become entailed with increasing frequency from the fourteenth to the seventeenth centuries.[50] In consequence, the *consorterie* more and more came to resemble the dynastic lineages.

To be sure, many other factors influenced the course of this evolution in the various parts of Europe. One was the nature of the tenure. The more important or exalted the fief or office, the less likely it would be subject to division. In England, strategic castles which could under no conditions be divided were said to be under "the law of the sword."[51] To divide large territorial units—counties, marches, or duchies, not to mention monarchies and empires—seemed, at least after the Carolingian age, to breed strategic weakness or to invite internecine strife. Then too, the overlord had an interest in imposing a rule of undivided inheritance on fiefs, to assure that they would support the services he expected. But he usually had the power to impose this rule only on his immediate vassals. Rear and petty vassals were therefore more likely than great barons to gain the right to partition their fiefs. The dynastic lineage is thus most at home among the high feudal nobility.

Some points in this evolution are worth noting. In the capitulary of Quierzy-sur-Oise, dated 877, emperor Charles the Bald, on the eve of departing to campaign in Italy, declared that if a count should die while his son was with the emperor in Italy, the son should then succeed to his father's office.[52] He wanted the same rule to apply to rear vassals. So also, if one of his men should retire to a monastery, his office or "honor" should pass to a son or other close relative able to perform the service. The language is far from precise, but it seems not to envision a partition of the fiefs or the offices. In 1037, while besieging Milan, emperor Conrad II promulgated a "constitution concerning fiefs."[53] He affirmed the heritability in the male line of all fiefs great and small.[54] The line of devolution is as follows: son, grandson born of male issue, and brother from the side of the father. This is one of the earliest documents we possess showing the new agnatic bias in appointing heirs. Again the language is vague, but the constitution seems to assume that the fiefs will be kept integral. In 1158, in another constitution concerning fiefs, Frederick I Barbarossa, holding a general court at Roncaglia in Italy, ruled that "duchies, marches, and counties are not henceforth to be divided."[55] But all other fiefs could be partitioned, if the coheirs wished, provided only that all heirs swore fealty to the overlord.

In the German empire, the great territorial princes continue to follow a rule of strict primogeniture.[56] The Golden Bull of 1356, which defined the lay electors of the emperor as exactly four, also determined that only the first-born male heir could inherit the right to vote, and his territory, the *Kurland*, could not be partitioned. The higher German nobles followed a similar rule. They gave their ancestral lands, the so-called *Stammgüter*, to the first-born male. Their remaining possessions were divided among younger sons or given to daughters in dowry. In German lands, the lesser nobles and the urban patricians admit all their male heirs to the inheritance; they follow the model of the consortial lineage found also in Italy.

In northern France, in Normandy and Anjou, by the twelfth century small fiefs were also becoming subject to partition. There appears a distinctive type of tenure known as "parage." The sense of the term is that younger brothers hold their lands from an "equal," that is, the eldest brother, who in turn is responsible for all payments and services owed by the now divided fief. It admits younger sons into the inheritance, but still recognizes a senior line. The thirteenth-century Norman *Summa de Legibus* explains this tenure: "Fiefs are held through *parage* when a brother or a relative receives a part of the inheritance of his ancestors, which he holds from an older relative. The older relative is in turn responsible for all the individual obligations which the portions of the fief require and which are due to its principal lords."[57]

Even these scattered references make apparent the agnatic character of the dynastic lineage and its frequent division into senior and cadet branches. Primogeniture becomes the most common, but not the only, rule for selecting one among the heirs in preference to the others. (For example, English borough tenure calls the youngest male heir to the inheritance.) To judge from the Norman *Summa*, the dynastic lineage including the senior and cadet branches could extend over six degrees of kinship, that is, up to and including second cousins.[58]

In regard to both feudal tenure and the concept of nobility, England with its strong monarchy shows interesting variations from continental norms. After the conquest of 1066, the Norman and Angevin kings successfully established the principle that all land must supply service to the king. The nobility was thus divided into two great parts: the tenants-in-chief, lords spiritual and temporal, holding their lands directly from the monarch, probably about 200 (to judge from the Domesday Book); and the rear vassals or knights, who numbered between five and six thousand. This small aristocracy ruled in a land which, in 1066, had probably more than one million inhabitants.

As the service system evolved, all tenants who acquired a certain amount of property, equivalent to a *feudum militis* or knight's fee, were duty bound to serve as knights. On the other hand, those knights too poor to serve lost their status. Enjoyment of the title and status of knight thus depended less on blood than on landed possessions.

To maintain levels of service, English practice, undoubtedly responding to royal wishes, favored impartibility and primogeniture for male heirs. In statutes promulgated in the late thirteenth century, Edward I clarified and set the laws of medieval England governing real properties.[59] The practice of primogeniture and entailment assured that the dynastic lineage would prevail among the great landowners, and that senior and cadet branches would be socially differentiated.

At the pinnacle of the English aristocracy, the 200-odd peers claimed their status not directly through possessions but through the special favor of the king. As the king's tenants-in-chief, these barons and earls were obligated to give him counsel and to attend the plenary sessions of his court, the *curia*, traditionally held three times a year. By the late thirteenth century, the king invited the earls and barons through individual writs of summons. It is thought, but it is by no means certain, that the privilege of receiving this individual summons first distinguished, indeed identified, the peer.

The peer is noble, but, strange to say, not his siblings nor, as long as he lives, his sons. The king's favor, and not blood, confers nobility. The children of the peer are all commoners, though at the father's death the first-born male will succeed to his office and nobility. England has no cadet branches of noble houses, and no caste of nobles. This type of family organization is at the opposite end of the spectrum of lineages from that of the Italian *consorterie*. French, German, and Spanish lineages fall somewhere in between.

One exceptional source helps to investigate the internal organization of the dynastic lineage: the *History of the Counts of Guines*, written by a priest named Lambert of Ardres between the years 1201 and 1206.[60] Georges Duby has subjected this document to minute scrutiny, and we take advantage of his guidance.[61]

Lambert tells the story of two lineages, the counts of Guines and the lords of Ardres, whose separate patrimonies eventually passed to a single heir, Arnoul I of Guines (IV of Ardres), Lambert's patron. Ardres is a small town near Bouvines in northeastern France, and the patrimony of the counts spread over the linguistic frontier separating the Flemish speakers from the French. Lambert writes the tract to regain the favor of count Arnold, whom somehow he has offended. His history is a celebration of Arnold's glorious family line, a *tante nobilitatis genealogia*. He uses an impressive variety of sources in constructing it, including even courtly epics.[62] While Lambert pretends to find a count and an ancestor named Walbert as far back as Merovingian times, the historic founder of the lineage is Lambert the Great, also appropriately called the Old, who lived from about 918 to 965. The title and office pass to a first cousin, Ardolf; from that point Lambert traces the genealogy with considerable detail down to his own times, over a period of 250 years.

Although the counts distributed lands to all their male heirs, they bequeath the title and the ancestral estates, what Lambert calls the *hereditas paterna apud Guisnes,* to their eldest son. And this path of dynastic descent claims Lambert's exclusive attention. He apologizes for his failure to follow collateral lines, but he wishes to avoid "boredom and effort." He manifests little interest in younger sons and all daughters, even though they were "sons not feeble in arms and daughters fair of face."

The genealogical importance of women is much diminished. Count Robert, called Manasses, who died in 1142, had no sons, and his three younger brothers also failed to produce male offspring. "He grew old . . . fearing lest the seed of his body should give out, and the land of Guines should go to the [offspring] of one of his sisters . . . almost as if he should have at some time to beg an heir from foreign seed."[63] Manasses had two sisters, Adelis and Ghisla, both of whom had produced male offspring. But clearly he did not view a nephew through a sister as an appropriate heir to his title and lands. The avunculate tie, perhaps the most distinctive bonding under the old *cognatio,* had given way completely to the agnatic bias. The lineage survived through male seed. But the preference given to males could not always be respected. Manasses had to look for the perpetuation of his line to his daughter Rose and granddaughter Beatrice, his sole surviving direct heirs.

The counts proclaimed the solidarity of the lineage in many ways. They bore a family name, based on their "paternal inheritance of Guines." The same proper names, notably Arnold and Balduin, are repeated frequently in the line of descent. They had a common place of burial. Doubtless they had a coat of arms. And Lambert gave them a proud genealogy, beginning in myth, eventually spanning a quarter of a millennium.

In Duby's reconstruction, lineages such as that of the counts of Guines consciously pruned back the number of collateral branches by discouraging the marriages of younger sons. They were sent to do battle in the Holy Land or to search for an heiress at home; or they joined the Church. The result was that "the great noble families seem not to have multiplied in the course of the twelfth century. On the contrary, over-cautious restriction appears to have thinned them out and concentrated fortunes in fewer hands."[64]

The dynastic lineage thus stands in contrast to the consortial lineage best seen in Italy, which could grow within a few generations to include hundreds of male members and scores of branches. But similarities are present too. These two types, and all the intermediate forms between them, favored male descendants over females. A marked deterioration of the status of women in relation to their families of origin is evident too in the changing terms of marriage.

MARRIAGE

Even as kindreds were taking on a new orientation and complexity, changes of comparable influence were affecting the terms of marriage, ages at first marriage, and the internal structure of the medieval household.

Terms of Marriage

Widely across Europe, the terms of marriage were shifting to place the chief "burdens of matrimony" once again on the bride and her family. The change is clearest in Italy. From the early decades of the twelfth century, the documents, apparently for the first time since antiquity, make reference to the *dos* in its classical meaning, the true dowry.[65] Sometime about 1140, in what seems to be the earliest surviving medieval tract devoted to the dowry, a jurist named Martin Gosia repeats Justinian's stipulation that in legitimate marriage the contributions of bride and groom, or their respective families, had to be equal.[66] Later decretists and decretalists—commentators on Gratian's *Decretum* and on subsequent papal letters, respectively—reiterate that the bride must contribute to the capital of the new household a dowry at least equal to the groom's *donatio*.[67]

The acts of notaries working in the Italian port city of Genoa, dating from 1155, give us an abundant run of marriage agreements, unique for their age in Western Europe. The marriage contracts of Giovanni Scriba, dated from 1155 to 1164, show that in most instances the nuptial gifts of bride and groom were in fact equal.[68]

But equality was not long maintained. From the middle twelfth century, the governments of the Italian urban communes moved to limit the claims of wives upon their husbands' properties. In 1143, the commune of Genoa abolished the *tertia*, the right of the wife to one-third the household property after the death of her spouse, according to the Frankish custom followed in the city. A sketch in the pages of the contemporary chronicler Caffaro shows two women of Genoa weeping over their lost advantage.[69] The city at the same time decreed that the reverse dowry could not exceed one-fourth the value of the true dowry, and should at all events never surpass one hundred pounds of Genoese money. Alexandria in 1179, Volterra in

1200, Florence in 1253, and other cities imposed similar limits, both relative and absolute, on the grooms' contribution in relation to the brides'.[70] The spirit behind this campaign gained colorful expression in a phrase used several times in a Milanese compilation of customary law, dated 1216.[71] The text alludes to the *odium quartae,* the hatred of citizens (males, to be sure) for the wife's traditional claim in Lombard law to one-quarter of her husband's property at his death.

Individual marriage agreements, preserved by the thousands in the Italian notarial chartularies, record in detail the decline of the husband's nuptial gifts to virtual insignificance into the late Middle Ages.[72] At Genoa, already in the years 1200 to 1211, according to the marriage agreements redacted by the notary Giovanni di Guiberto, the bride usually brought more wealth into the marriage than did her husband.[73] At Florence, the statutory limit of 100 pounds on the husband's gift to his wife, set in 1253, was maintained throughout the subsequent Middle Ages.[74] But the steady debasement of the Florentine currency rendered the sum nugatory, as the dowry itself was leaping up in value.

Poets and preachers protested the rising costs of marriage, which the bride and her family were forced to meet. In the early fourteenth century Dante remarked in the *Divine Comedy* that the size of dowries was exceeding all reasonable measure, and he hearkened back to better days, in the eleventh and twelfth centuries, when the birth of a daughter did not strike terror into her father's heart.[75] His younger contemporary, the chronicler Giovanni Villani, penned a similar condemnation.[76] Inflation in dowries obstructed marriages, and the city governments worried that this would adversely affect the size of populations. In 1425 the Florentine commune established a special fund, the *Monte delle doti,* designed to help families arrange the marriage of their children, especially their daughters.[77]

Finally, contributions to the dowries of young girls, allowing them to marry, emerge as a common act of Christian charity from the thirteenth century. This form of charity seems not to have been much cultivated in the earlier medieval centuries. St. Ambrogio Sansedoni of Siena, who died in 1286, had a particular concern for the maidens of his city who could not marry, surely because they had insufficient dowries to attract a mate. "He also prayed for the maidens who ought to be joined in marriage, that God would unite them well in holy matrimony, for the salvation of their souls . . . From this there grew the custom, that every year marriageable young girls would go to the church of the Dominicans, to the tomb of St. Ambrogio, offering a candle, that they might obtain favor from the Lord, that they would be worthily joined in holy matrimony."[78] St. An-

toninus of Florence, who had a particular concern for the poor nobility of his city, "was especially generous in giving in marriage the
daughters of impoverished persons."[79] Charitable bequests in wills
now commonly include donations to poor and nubile girls.

Outside of Italy, the profusion of local customs, their instability,
and the limited number of surviving marriage agreements make a
steady evolution difficult to follow, but there are many indications
that the treatment of women in marriage was deteriorating from the
late twelfth century. In their monumental history of English law,
Pollock and Maitland conclude that the rise of the feudal order,
which closely linked tenure with military service, inevitably cur-
tailed the rights and claims of widows and other women.[80] In the
thirteenth century the English woman lost all capacity to own chat-
tels or movables, which at her marriage passed completely under
the ownership of her husband.[81] Analogous changes can be found
elsewhere in Europe. In some regions the dower, the portion of the
husband's property assigned to his wife at marriage, at one time, at
the husband's death, passed to his widow in full ownership, but later
she acquired only a right of lifetime usufruct. In 1205, at the request
of his French vassals, King John of England declared that widows
could no longer claim one-half the acquisitions made by their households while their marriages endured, but were to be content with
their dowers.[82] The goal of all these complex and frequently obscure
changes seems to have been to limit acquisitions of property by
women through marriage gifts or any other means.

The Spanish kingdoms held on longest to the older practices.[83]
Grooms continued to convey the *donatio* to the brides through the
thirteenth century.[84] But even there the true dowry triumphs in
the late Middle Ages. In Iberia only the timing, not the direction,
of the evolution differed from that of other European regions.

How are we to explain these striking shifts in the terms of Western
marriage? Several factors contributed. Women were valued members
of the household in early medieval society. Within the aristocracy,
they fulfilled many important administrative functions, from managing estates to making yearly gifts to the knights at court. On lower
social levels, they played an indispensable role in many processes
of production; they dominated the manufacture of cloth, including
such skilled operations as dyeing. In the central and late Middle
Ages women lost some of these functions. The growth of bureau-
cratic offices limited, though it never fully extinguished, their importance as administrators. Christine de Pisan, writing in the early
fifteenth century, still advises that the daughters of barons be taught
how to read, as later in life, when married, they would have to read
the estate accounts for their frequently absent husbands.[85] Never-

theless, women were not so indispensable in high administration as they once were.

Their role in economic production also diminished, especially in cities.[86] Guilds dominate cloth production within towns, and only under special circumstances could women become guild members. Males now take over nearly all phases of cloth manufacture, including dyeing. The contribution of women is limited to such relatively unskilled work as spinning and washing. Late in the Middle Ages, the rise of an important silk industry enhanced the role of women, who were apparently more dexterous than men and better able to work the fine threads. But this is a late development.

The contributions women made through service or skill to their families thus diminished, especially in the middle ranges of society and especially in cities. Families were no longer eager to retain the services of daughters. In the fifteenth century, a Florentine matron, Alessandra Macinghi-Strozzi, complains that nothing can be accomplished in a household, as long as marriageable daughters are present.[87] She clearly regarded daughters as a burden and not an asset.

A second, perhaps even more important reason for the deteriorating status of the nubile girl was the changing marriage market. To be sure, religious beliefs, values, customs, and the like played a role of major importance in the making of marriages, as they defined who was eligible for marriage, who was desirable as a partner, and how courtship should be conducted. Governments also influenced the negotiations, setting, for example, minimum or maximum limits to the size of the marriage gifts. But at all times both custom and law left considerable scope for a system of bidding and response, for market interactions, in sum. In medieval times, to be sure, the true agents operating on this market were usually not individual men and women, but families and lineages, with sons and daughters to place in marriage. Within the limits set by religion, custom, and law, these families bargained, looking for the best terms for themselves and their offspring.

What determined the negotiating strength of a family seeking to gain a spouse for a son or daughter? The physical attraction, the health, and the social connections of the young man or woman are the most obvious considerations. But one other, less immediately evident factor was the relative number of men and women actively seeking a mate. If, for example, more men are seeking brides than there are brides to be had, the men will have to bid competitively for the scarce women and offer attractive terms in order to win a bride. The terms of marriage will therefore come to favor women; and some men will not succeed in the competition and will not be able to marry at all.

Although the numbers of male and female babies are approximately the same, this biological fact does not guarantee that there will be equal numbers of brides seeking grooms and grooms seeking brides when the children reach maturity. One or the other of the sexes may endure higher mortalities during childhood, reflecting different standards of nourishment or treatment in the household. Differing functional responsibilities, as, for example, military services demanded from young men, may also affect rates of relative survival. Families may also promote the marriages of sons but not of daughters, or the reverse.

Evidence of imbalance on the marriage market abounds for the period of the central and late Middle Ages, at least among the nobility and the townspeople. According to Georges Duby, the great lineages of northern France in the twelfth century strove to place in marriage all their daughters but only the first-born of their sons.[88] To marry, the younger sons had to win a prize at war or on crusade, or successfully woo an heiress; many were not even given this chance, but had to accept an ecclesiastical career.

Their professional preoccupation with war also eroded the ranks of young noblemen. An English survey dated 1185, entitled *Rotuli de dominabus*, shows the distribution of sexes within a segment of the Anglo-Norman nobility.[89] The document lists the possessions and children of widows over whom the king, Henry II, exercises rights of wardship. The ages of the widows range from 18 to 70, and of course many of their offspring are already mature. Among the offspring females outnumber males by 155 to 138. The reason for this seems apparent. In a social group made up of professional fighters, young men faced greater risk of death than young women, who were excused from warfare under the code of chivalry. If this group practiced endogamy, some of these women would never find a husband, and all of them would have to compete under unfavorable terms.

Medieval society in the central Middle Ages was acquiring a marked plurality of women over men. In the early twelfth century, according to the contemporary life of St. Hugh of Grenoble, religious houses for women were too few to receive all those who wished to enter.[90] In the towns of Flanders and the Rhineland, from the late twelfth century, unattached, unmarriageable women reached extraordinary numbers, raising what historians traditionally call the *Frauenfrage*, the "woman question."[91] Many of these women became beghines, religious who followed no recognized rule and lived either at home or in communes known as beguinages. A report dated 1328, "On the motives of founding beghinages," gives a good insight into the social origins of their plight. Two sisters, Johanna and Margherita of Constantinople, who were in succession countesses of Flanders and Hainaut, saw that their territories "greatly abounded in women, for whom suitable marriages according to their condition . . . were not possible, because of their number and the poverty of their parents." In consequence, "honest and noble young women, impoverished, had to go about begging or to lead a life injurious to both themselves and their relatives." The two countesses therefore "founded in various parts of Flanders certain spacious places, which are called Beghine courts, in which the aforesaid women, daughters or maidens might be received."[92]

Several saints tried to serve these hapless women. We have already mentioned St. Ambrogio Sansedoni of Siena.[93] The fourteenth-century German mystic Heinrich Suso was also aware that "in many places [of Germany] there were many women, both religious and lay, who because of the fragility and mobility of soul fell greatly into vices. The miserable persons had no one, to whom they dared confess."[94] In Spain, in the early sixteenth century, St. John of God also had a special concern for "women of slender means," unable to marry, who lived by begging in the city. He distributed meat, fish, coal, and wood among them, and supplied them with "silk, wool, and linen, which they made into fabric and thus earned an income."[95]

The "decision theory" of the economists predicts that the bad terms which women faced when contemplating marriage should have prompted them to seek a mate at younger ages, while favorable terms enjoyed by males should have encouraged them to marry late.[96] The data on marital ages seem to confirm this prediction.

AGES AT FIRST MARRIAGE

Evidence on ages at first marriage is most abundant and clearest from Mediterranean lands, but there are indications that a comparable pattern was common also in the European north.

Ages of Women

St. Adalheid, later the wife of emperor Otto I, was first married in the middle tenth century at age 16, but the marital practices of the high aristocracy may not have been typical of society as a whole.[97]

When the references to marriage ages multiply from the thirteenth century, they consistently show that Italian girls were very young when given to their husbands. St. Umiliana dei Cerchi of Florence, born in 1219, was married at the age of 16.[98] St. Humility, born in 1226 of rich, presumably noble parents in the Romagna, was married in 1241 at age 15, and was already widowed by age 24.[99] According to the life by Raymond of Capua, when Catherine of Siena reached marriage age, "that is, 12 years," she was kept at home and made to wash her face and neck, to make her pleasing to men.[100] St. Clare of Pisa, daughter of the despot Pietro Gambacorta, born in 1362, was betrothed at age 7, married at 12, and widowed at 15.[101] St. Francesca de' Ponziani, patroness of Rome (1384–1440), was also only 12 when she was married.[102] According to the life of St. Catherine Palantina, who was reared in Milan and died in 1478, the brothers of a friend, Dominica Ruffini, forced their sister into marriage at age 15.[103] The father of another friend, Giuliana, tried unsuccessfully to make his daughter marry at age 17.[104]

The Statutes of the commune of Pistoia, dated 1296, forbid the marriage of girls before their twelfth year.[105] By comparison, the Edict of Liutprand, dated 731, forbade the marriage of boys younger than 13. The status of the sexes had been reversed, between the early and late Middle Ages.

For 30 Florentine women, whose birth dates and wedding dates between 1251 and 1475 are given in published family memoirs, the average age at first marriage is 17.2 years.[106]

Extant population surveys allow us on occasion to measure marriage ages across entire communities. At Prato in 1372, estimated age at first marriage for city girls was 16.3 years; at Florence in 1427, it was 17.6 years.[107] Girls in the Florentine countryside were somewhat older at first marriage in 1427; their average age was 18. The average ages rise a little as the fifteenth century progresses. At Florence in 1480, it was 20.8 years for women, and 21.1 at Prato in 1470.

Contemporaries were well aware of the young ages of brides, and many disapproved. We have already cited Dante, who thought that the "tempo," the age, at which girls were marrying was unreasonable.[108] The Florentine domestic chronicler Giovanni Morelli, writing in the first decade of the fifteenth century, hearkened back to olden times, presumably the twelfth century, when girls were married at 24 or 25.[109] In his own days, he asserts, fathers were reluctant to wait until age 15, before giving their daughters in marriage.

The evidence for marriage ages from outside Italy is less abundant and less varied, but still indicative. The father of St. Flor, who lived in Provence in the early fourteenth century, wished to have her married at age 14.[110] A study based on marriage contracts from Toulouse, in southern France, in the fourteenth and fifteenth centuries, concludes that brides were typically age 16.[111] St. Hildeburgis, from the region of Chartres in northern France, was given in marriage just as her childhood had ended and she was entering adolescence.[112] According to traditional calculations of the ages of life, she was probably about 14.

Guibert of Nogent, who wrote a lively autobiography in 1155, tells of a woman of the town of Angers who married, in his phrase, "as a little girl."[113] Her limbs continued to grow after marriage, and she could not later remove the wedding ring given her as a child bride. According to the life of St. Roger the Abbot, who was born in England but passed his career chiefly in France, "a certain woman was married as a young girl by her parents . . . As she passed the years of youth, her finger grew larger, and the ring sorely squeezed it."[114] The ring had to be miraculously removed. The late medieval French satire, "The Fifteen Joys of Marriage," describes a similar predicament.[115] The wife asks her old and miserly husband for a new gown; her wedding dress has become too short for her, as she has continued to grow since her marriage.

In the middle thirteenth century, Philippe de Navarre advised that boys not be allowed to marry before completing their twentieth year, but girls could be "willingly" placed with a husband after their fourteenth.[116] St. Marie of Maillac, born in 1331 near Tours, was given in marriage "after twelve years."[117] St. Françoise d'Ambroise was born in 1427 and was married in 1442, at the age of 14, to the duke of Brittany.[118] "It isn't rare," writes Erasmus, "to see, especially among the French, a girl hardly ten years old married, and a mother at 11."[119]

In England in the middle twelfth century, the parents of St. Christina of Markyate forced her into marriage, when, in the opinion of the editor of her life, she was 18 or 19 years old.[120] The *Rotuli de dominabus* of 1185 gives the ages of the widows listed and those of their dependent children.[121] Subtracting the age of the oldest child from the age of the mother tells us how old these women were at the birth of their oldest surviving child. (We exclude women over 30, as many of their adult children were doubtless already dead.) For 14 widows younger than age 30 in the survey, the average age at which they gave birth to their first surviving child was 18.4 years. They must have been age 17 or younger at first marriage. For example, the lady Alda must have been younger than 14 when she married, as her eldest child in the survey was 16 and she only 30. The lady Emma has a daughter already married at age 18 and another unmarried at 16, suggesting that the common age of first marriage fell between these two ages.

The widows mentioned in the *Rotuli* belong, to be sure, to the high English aristocracy, and their behavior may not have been typical of all English society. The many studies of manors and villages yield disappointingly little data on marriage ages.[122] But in a canonical marriage case dated 1332–33, which clearly involved commoners, the bride at the time of marriage was "almost fourteen years," and in another case, "twelve or more."[123] And ought we to dismiss the testimony offered by England's greatest poet of the Middle Ages, Geoffrey Chaucer? His wife of Bath tells the reader that she took the first of her five husbands when she was only in her twelfth year.[124] The wife of Thomas More was 16 or 17 when she married Thomas in 1504 or 1505; she died in 1511, at age 23.[125] Thomas was 26 or 27, from a middle-class London family, and his wife a "country girl." He would have preferred the hand of her still younger sister, but the father wanted his daughters to be married in order of age. Erasmus must have thought that these ages were appropriate, since he models his own conceptions of the ideal marriage on the More household.

In Flanders, St. Godelive de Ghistelles seems to have been born in 1052, married in 1067 at about age 15, and murdered by her husband in 1070.[126] St. Mary of Oignies, born about 1177, was forced into marriage about 1191; her contemporary biographer, Jacques de Vitry, gives her age as only 14.[127] About the same time, the parents of St. Yvette from the town of Huy in modern Belgium (d. 1228) similarly forced their daughter to accept a husband. Yvette was only 13; she bore three children in rapid succession, and then was widowed, at the age of 18.[128] St. Ida of Louvain (d. 1300) reached the "Pythagorean forks" at age 18, that is, she had then to choose between marriage or the religious life.[129] In the fourteenth century, the father of St. Lidwina of Schiedam sought to have her married when she was 12.[130] Lidwina was beautiful and attracted many eager suitors, but her mother, protesting that the girl was too young, resisted her husband's efforts. A disease, which struck her at age 15 and made her an invalid for life, settled the dispute. In Erasmus' *Colloquies*, a maiden who resists marriage (the *virgo misogamos*) is described as 17; and a new mother is "scarcely past 16."[131]

In the Rhineland, St. Christina of Stommeln, a village near Cologne (d. 1312), allegedly fled from her family home when her parents tried to force a husband upon her; she was then age 12.[132] St. Hedwige of Bavaria (d. 1243) was married at age 12 to Henry, duke of Silesia and of Poland.[133]

Some years ago, Richard Koebner examined marriages in the late Middle Ages, for both the German nobility and the town patriciates.[134] Noble girls were especially young at first marriage. In the noble family of Wittelsbach, from 1300 to 1520, four brides were between 12 and 13 years; eight about 14; and two about 15. Among the Hohenzollern, five brides were between 12 and 13; five about 14; and five about 15. And among the Nassau, one was 12; two were 14; and three were 15. Among the patricians of the town of Frankfurt, the average age of 43 brides was 18.8 years. The mother of the artist Albrecht Dürer was married at age 15.

Still farther east, St. Dorothea of Montau in Prussia was born in 1347, and was married at the age of 17 to an artisan of Gdansk named Adalbert.[135] She is rare among the saints in that her parents were peasants and her husband a workingman. At the opposite end of the social scale was St. Bridget of Sweden (d. 1373), from the high aristocracy, who was married at age 13, although she and her husband did not consummate the marriage for another year.[136] Her daughter Karin or Catherine must have been married well before her eighteenth year; at that age she left her husband in Sweden to reside with her mother in Rome.[137]

The data on marriage ages for women are very scattered and of varying reliability. Women of the nobility and of the towns dominate the listings. It is likely that peasant girls were older at first marriage than their urban or noble counterparts. The Tuscan surveys suggest as much.[138] The father of one peasant girl mentioned in an Italian life wants her to marry at age 17, but she is able to resist his demands for another 10 years.[139] But if the evidence is scattered and uneven, it is nonetheless remarkably consistent. Girls in the central and late Middle Ages were usually very young when they first married. This seems not to have been exclusively a Mediterranean pattern, but marked the careers of medieval women wherever we can trace them.

Ages of Men

The men's ages at first marriage are even more difficult to determine than the women's. Widowers remarried more commonly and more quickly than widows, and most descriptions of marriages do not mention whether the groom has been married before. The ages of marriage for males seem also to have been more subject to change than those of females, and were more sensitive to conditions favoring or obstructing the formation of new households. Thus, at Prato in 1371, the population was rebounding from an epidemic that had struck only eight years before; men married at an average age of 24—exceptionally young for an Italian population.[140] In 1427, under stabilized demographic conditions, that age had risen by three years, to 27. The age of females at first marriage responded to the same conditions by increasing only a single year, from 16 to 17.

It is therefore difficult to discover a single, consistent pattern of masculine marriage ages for all places and periods during the central and late Middle Ages. It may be, for example, that those ages dipped low during the time of most vigorous demographic expansion, in the eleventh and twelfth centuries. Guibert of Nogent says that his own father was a "mere youth," and "young and dull-witted," when he married about the middle eleventh century.[141] The Englishman Burthred, who tried unsuccessfully to claim Christina of Markyate as his bride, is described as *iuvenis* and even *adolescens* by Christina's biographer.[142] The *Rotuli de dominabus* records a certain Reginald, living with a wife at age 24; a Hamo son of Hamo, who "took a wife" at age 20; and a William, who was married at age 17.[143]

But the picture sharpens after the middle and late twelfth century, so that from about 1200 it is clear that many men were postponing marriage, or refusing it altogether. Philippe of Navarre does not want men to marry before they are 21 years old, but he does not state his preferred age.[144] In contemporary terminology, *iuvenis* and its romance equivalents were virtually synonymous with "bachelor" or "celibate."[145] Philippe's own decision to extend the age of *jovens* to the fortieth year suggests that he viewed a society in which many men, up to that age, were still unmarried. Georges Duby has noted that in the twelfth century the soldier of fortune Guillaume le Marechal married at age 45, and that one of the counts of Guines, Arnold, took a bride 13 years after he was dubbed a knight, which would have made him age 30 or probably older at his marriage.[146]

In courtly literature, male figures often convey the impression of mature years at their marriages, and often betray extreme reluctance to marry at all. King Mark of Cornwall, in the romance of *Tristan and Iseult*, agreed to marry only after his barons threatened to make war against him, if he persisted in celibacy.[147] The bride he chose, Iseult, must have been a generation younger than himself, if she was (as seems appropriate) the same age as her lover Tristan, Mark's nephew. The Carolingian hero Aymeri delayed marriage until well after the emperor had given him the rich city of Narbonne; even after he had made his fortune, he yielded with misgivings to the entreaties of his vassals to marry.[148] In the late thirteenth-century poem *Hervis de Mez*, the king of Spain, suitor of the young and fair Beatris, is variously represented as 60 or 80 years old; for 20 years his barons have been urging him to find a bride, which means that he was 40 at the youngest, before he thought about, or was reminded of, marriage.[149] Beatris declares that she would much prefer a young, brave, and strong knight, even if, she adds significantly, he has no property. The two nubile heroines in *Tirant lo Blanc*, Stephanie and Carmesina, are both 14; and their suitors, Diaphebus and Tirant, clearly much older, as they had experienced many adventures before meeting the girls.[150]

In the fourteenth century in England, the wife of Bath, who first married at age 12, describes the first three of her five husbands as "goode men, and riche, and old."[151] Her fourth husband was presumably close to her in age, and the fifth is explicitly described as younger. But few women married five times, so her first three marriages must represent the usual pattern. As mentioned, Thomas

More was 26 or 27 years old at his marriage, and his bride was ten years younger.[152]

In the late Middle Ages, writers again nourished the view that men in former times were older at marriage than their own contemporaries. An Italian chronicler, who in 1354 praised the *mores* of men in the early thirteenth century, affirmed that males then refrained from marriage until age 30.[153] The Florentine Giovanni Morelli offers still more precise comments. The usual age of marriage for men in the twelfth and thirteenth centuries was, in his estimation, 40 years, and he tells his readers not to be surprised, as this was the custom.[154]

Of 56 Florentine males, whose birth dates and wedding dates between 1251 and 1475 can be found in published family memoirs, the average age at first marriage is 28.87 years.[155] In the city of Florence in 1427, men were nearly 30 at first marriage, and they selected as brides girls more than 12 years younger than themselves. The Florentine case is doubtless an extreme example. At Verona, in 1425, the average age difference between husband and wife was 7 years.[156] Still, men were remarkably mature at first marriage.

Adalbert was much older than his young and pretty wife, Dorothea of Montau. Once, when they were traveling, she was asked: "Beloved sister, where do propose to take this Joseph? Are you trying to lead him to the restorative fountain of youth?"[157] To be sure, it is possible to give examples of men who were quite young at first marriage, particularly in the high aristocracy. The husband of St. Bridget of Sweden was 18 at his marriage—five years older than his bride.[158] Koebner's study of the marriage ages of German nobles and city patricians concludes that some men in both classes married young, though most were past age 20.[159] Out of 17 male Hohenzollern, one was age 16 at marriage; five were between 18 and 19; and 11 were over 20. Among the Wittelsbach, two were between 14 and 15, one 16; three 18; eight, between 19 and 20; and 24 still older. The patricians seem even older than the nobles at first marriage. Of ten members of the Walther family of Augsburg, one was married at age 19, but all the others were age 24 or older. A Nicholas Muffels of Nuremberg married at 21, but he remarks that he was exceedingly young. Dürer married at age 24. A moralizing poem of the epoch advises the male not to marry "until he becomes 30 years old."[160] Taken together, the marriage pattern among the German nobles and patricians studied by Koebner suggests that males married in their early and middle twenties to girls well below twenty, with a difference between them of from six to eight years. This is not so great a difference as is found in Florence, but it is still not what would be regarded as a modern marriage pattern.

The great differences in ages between bride and groom made intergenerational marriages common. Guibert of Nogent gives a striking example of one, with complications. The wife of Enguerrand of Coucy spurns her husband because of his age and obesity.[161] She takes as her lover a handsome youth, presumably of her own age; to cover their scandalous liaison, she marries him to her daughter, and establishes them in her castle. In this strange ménage, the bonds of marriage linked two older males to two younger females across three generations; but the bonds of marriage were not those of emotional and sexual attachment.

Exactly the same arrangement appears in the life of the Premonstratensian abbot St. Frederick of Hallom, who died in 1175. A young man becomes engaged to a girl not yet of marriage age. While waiting for his fiancee to grow up, he and her mother begin a love affair, and the two eventually murder her betrayed husband.[162] Had the marriage ever occurred, the groom would likely have been a generation older than his bride.

The reluctance of some men to marry young indicates that some men would not marry at all. From the late twelfth century, the figure of the confirmed bachelor becomes common in the sources. A cousin of Guibert of Nogent "refused to be bound by a layman's laws. The marriage net could not hold him; he never allowed himself to be entangled in its folds."[163] According to Guibert, no married woman was safe in his company. Bachelors crowded the towns as well as the courts. The son of St. Yvette of Hui caused great pain to his widowed mother, as he sowed his wild oats for years within the city, together with lascivious companions, presumably also unmarried.[164] For a long time and despite his mother's frequent entreaties, he gave no thought to his soul's salvation, or to marriage.

The males' reluctance to marry was prevalent enough to serve as a major theme in that bizarre, twelfth-century Latin poem, *The Complaint of Nature*, by Alain of Lille. In the poetic allegory, Nature herself worries that males were failing to replenish the race through marriage; they either ignored love altogether or exercised other sexual options, characteristically barren. "Of such of these men as profess the grammar of love," Nature remarks, "some embrace only the masculine gender, some the feminine, others the common or indiscriminate."[165] Hymen, husband of Venus and patron of marriage, also appears, in garments once decorated "with ideal pictures . . . of the events of marriage" but now in tatters.[166] The neglect of males has reduced him to this ragged state.

This then seems to be the common marriage pattern within medieval society from about the year 1200. It is most visible, and was probably most pronounced, in Mediterranean lands, but is frequently encountered also in the north. Sparse as the information is for this area of Europe, it seems consistently to point in the same direction. In this common medieval pattern, the male delays marriage until his middle or late twenties, but the female marries before her twentieth year. And the bride's family must now assume the larger share of the costs involved in establishing the new household. The crowded Europe of the thirteenth century thus returns to a pattern of marriage which, in its basic form, closely resembles that of the classical Roman empire.

5 | DOMESTIC ROLES AND FAMILY SENTIMENTS IN THE LATER MIDDLE AGES

In Normannorum regionis confinibus quidam vicus vo-
catus est Ramis: ubi vir manebat juxta saecularis vitae
statum prae omnibus vicinis suis prosapia clarus, honoris
non minus et divitiarum ubertate circumfluus. Ad pros-
peritatis etiam suae cumulum, matrimonii copula hones-
tatus dignissima, filiorum procreatione pollebat: quorum
curam supra omnia gerens in illis enutriendis non minimum laborem impendebat, quia in hoc quoque omnium
naturalis intentio hominum quasi maximam suae beati-
tudinis partem consistere putat.

Within the boundaries of Normandy there is a village
called Ramis. There a man lived who by the standards of
secular life surpassed all his neighbors in the dignity of
his lineage, and he abounded in honor and no less in wealth.
To crown his prosperity, he was distinguished by a most
worthy marriage and was fertile in producing children. He
expended no little effort in rearing them, taking care of
them above all things. For it is the natural bent of all
human beings, to believe that in this lies the largest part
of their happiness.

—Bernard of Anjou, *Miracles of Ste. Foi*, 994

THE CORNER of the medieval household that historians
have found most difficult to penetrate has been its cultural and emotional life—the roles assigned to father,
mother, and children; the rewards in love which followed on good performance; and the bonds which knitted the members. Statistical records yield almost nothing on the emotional life
of families, and it remains hard to judge how well the hortatory and
didactic writings reflect the real world. Limited information has
allowed the field of household history to become overgrown with
many dubious assertions concerning the Middle Ages. The medieval
family has become the negative stereotype against which later families are compared, in order to show the alleged benefits of modern-
ization.

Thus, if we are to believe Philippe Ariès, medieval parents did
not recognize their children to be children, and did not respond
emotionally to their special qualities.[1] Distinguished historians affirm that the affective family, comprised of loving spouses, loving
parents and children, is a modern, even recent creation.[2] Were medieval people really cold and indifferent toward their closest relatives, with whom they shared the most personal and penetrating

experiences of life? The judgment seems dubious indeed, and is at all events more truly based on silence than on documented evidence.

SOURCES, SECULAR AND SACRED

The records of the Middle Ages are poor in depicting the sentiments commonly present in households, but probably no poorer than those that illuminate, or conceal, domestic emotions in other periods of Western history. A full tradition of prescriptive literature, on religious or secular grounds, instructs family members, fathers in particular, how they should manage their households.[3] Although this genre is useful, it is always impossible to determine from such works alone whether the good counsel was ever followed. The medieval sources do have a special sort of biographic writing, often passionate in tone, about passionate persons. These are the lives of saints, and they are very many. The *Acta Sanctorum*, the great collection of saints' lives which the Bollandist society has been publishing since the seventeenth century, makes reference by my count to 3,276 individual saints who died before 1500.[4] Of these named saints, 2,754 are men and 522 women, for a sex ratio of 528 men per 100 women. The numbers of saints are not distributed evenly across the Middle Ages; rather, the ranks of the blessed grow threadbare as the epoch wanes. Only 87, barely 3 percent, flourished in the period after 1348. The declining number of saints primarily reflects the much more stringent controls which the papacy was imposing on local cults from about the year 1200.

Three changes in the thinning ranks of late medieval saints are worth mentioning. The first is the "feminization" of sainthood. The French scholar, André Vauchez, uses this term in his recent, massive study of sanctity in the medieval centuries.[5] Women, to be sure, are always in the minority among the blessed; the court of heaven did not admit men and women saints (or at least, famous saints) in anything approaching equal numbers.[6] Still, the sex ratio of saints after the middle of the fourteenth century—264 men to every 100 women—favors them more than in the earlier medieval period. A second characteristic of sainthood from the thirteenth century is that now most saints—even those originally from rural areas—are town dwellers. One reason for this is that the Dominicans and Franciscans were the great promoters of sainthood in the late Middle Ages, and these mendicant orders pursued their apostolate primarily in cities. But perhaps the prominence of mendicant orders and mendicant saints is itself a reflection of the growing importance of cities in the cultural life of the central and late Middle Ages. The urbanization of sainthood in the late medieval world lends a special prominence to saints from the more heavily citified regions of Europe: northern Italy, the Rhineland, and Flanders. This band of cities cuts across the European heartland, south to north, like a sash. But other European regions—such as England and Sweden—also contribute some notable figures.

A third characteristic of late medieval sanctity is its strongly mystical orientation. Unlike the saints of early Ireland, and of the early Middle Ages generally, holy people in the later epoch are not primarily wonderworkers, channeling divine power into human affairs. Catherine of Siena confesses her inability to raise the dead, during a plague outburst in the city.[7] The saint of her time is typically a mystic and a visionary, bringing divine illumination to human consciousness. Late medieval saints are frequently given to acts of heroic asceticism, but primarily their lives emphasize interior experiences—powerful visions, rapturous conversations with God and His saints. Perhaps we can speak of an internalization of sanctity in the late Middle Ages. This intense cultivation of the sentimental life, a badge of late medieval sanctity, has produced unique materials for what is perhaps the most difficult of all branches of history—the history of emotion.

The lives of these preeminently urban saints depict numerous domestic scenes, usually associated with the birth, childhood, adolescence, and sometimes marriage, of their holy subjects. With only rare exceptions, they describe family events and relationships with scant sympathy. The Church's attitude toward the natural family remained throughout the Middle Ages reserved, even suspicious. The claims of kin competed with the claims of God. Jesus himself had warned: "He who loves father and mother more than me is not worthy of me" (Matt. 11.37). Many great medieval saints—Francis of Assisi and Thomas Aquinas among them—entered the religious life over the staunch opposition of their families.[8] Catherine of Siena warned her followers, women in particular, against excessive attachment to their husbands and children.[9] Conjugal love, maternal love, could disguise forms of worldly entanglements. The medieval Church saw no absolute value in close and emotional family attachments.

In the accounts of saints' lives, close relatives often appear in villainous roles. "It is a dictum of secular wisdom," the eleventh-century hagiographer Drogo of Bergues affirms, "that all mothers-in-law hate their daughters-in-law."[10] Margaret of Cortona, widowed young, seeks to return to her father's home.[11] But her father, now remarried, throws her out at the instigation of his new wife; for a while she must earn her living as a prostitute. Angela of Foligno in Italy, and Yvette of Huys in Flanders, are mistreated by their husbands; they thank God and rejoice when death takes both husband and children from them.[12] Adalbert, the husband of Dorothea of Montau, beats her; once, he struck her so cruelly that her teeth nearly cut through her upper lip.[13]

Besides describing the harsh realities of the secular world, the lives make use of family images in an even more interesting way—as metaphorical descriptions of the saints' mystical experiences. These abound in allusions to brides and bridegrooms; to motherhood, childhood, paternity. In their struggle to achieve sanctity, the saints break free from family entanglements, but not at all from familial sentiments. It is almost as if these single, widowed, often abandoned persons found compensation for domestic satisfactions in and through mystical experiences. They reconstituted, as it were, in a religious context, the emotional rewards that families ideally held out to their members. My point is that the evocations of motherhood, childhood, and fatherhood contained in the lives must bear some correspondence with the ways in which mothers, children, and fathers were viewed in the real world. These images were designed to evoke an emotional response on the part of readers or listeners; the sentiments expressed in a devotional context must have had parallels in feelings that prevailed in the natural family, for which we have no records. The religious biographer and the devotional writer or preacher play upon sentiments already familiar to their audiences. On occasion too, they try to shape the sentimental ties of family members by pointing out examples in the lives of saints. Family imagery, family models, in religious devotion and in daily experience: each echoed and reinforced the other.

The life of Catherine of Siena offers a fine example of this easy transfer of sentiment between the religious and domestic spheres. As a child growing up in a large family, Catherine would pretend that her father was Christ, her mother our Blessed Lady, and her brethren the apostles.[14] Catherine lived within two families, and she didn't much bother to separate her emotional worlds, one from the other.

MARRIAGE

The Learned Tradition

Medieval attitudes toward marriage and women (the two themes are inextricably intertwined) were profoundly ambivalent. The civilization sustained a well-embedded tradition of misogynistic literature—one of its less attractive inheritances from the ancient world.[15] It comes to a climax in the long allegorical poem of the thirteenth century, *The Romance of the Rose*.[16] The poem itself becomes an object of controversy in the learned world of the late Middle Ages, separating the defenders of women (and indirectly, of marriage) from those who would denigrate them.[17]

Alongside this misogynistic current there existed another one praising women, especially the good wife. Already in the late eleventh century, a poet named Marbode, bishop of Rennes, a figure of some importance in the period's renaissance of Latin letters, wrote a series of poems on women; he condemns prostitutes, but bestows lavish praise on the *mulier bona*, the good wife.[18]

> Of all the things that God has provided
> For human benefit, we think that there is nothing lovelier,
> Nothing better, than a good wife, who is part of our
> Body, as we are part of hers . . .
> There is nothing that we do not do together;
> We are similar in all things, saving the difference in sex . . .
> These [the wife's services to the household] are so useful to
>   us, so convenient
> That if they were lacking, the good order of life would be
>   diminished.[19]

Not only does the good wife bring children into the world, assuring the survival of society, but she performs many other services as well. She cares for the sick. "For who would assume the care of a nurse, if not a woman? Without her no one born could prolong his life." She cooks and keeps house, spins wool and flax, and weaves cloth. She is crucial in maintaining the *honestas vitae*, the good order of domestic life. Of course, Marbode's poem can be regarded as a school exercise; he was, after all, a bishop, and did not himself benefit from the feminine services he praised so highly. Nonetheless, it is remarkable that a man of the eleventh century wrote this poem in praise of the married woman. Not all the clerical scholars of the age were misogynists.

The surge of humanism in the fourteenth and fifteenth centuries greatly enriched writings supportive of marriage and the family. About 1400, the "civic humanists" of Florence—notably Coluccio Salutati and Leonardo Bruni—maintained that the active life was superior to the *vita contemplativa*.[20] The ideal human type was the married man, the *paterfamilias* who took an active interest in the affairs of his household and community. Leonardo Bruni, for example, chides Boccaccio for his condemnation of the marriage of Dante. His eloquent words are worth quoting: "Man is a social animal, as all philosophers agree; the fundamental union, which by its multiplication creates the city, is that of husband and wife. Nothing can be accomplished where this union does not exist. And this love alone is natural, legitimate, and allowed."[21]

St. Bernardino of Siena, who is considered to be on the margin of the humanist movement, in his own praises of the good wife seems to echo Marbode: "the most beautiful and useful thing in a house [is] to have a beautiful, tall wife, who is wise, virtuous, temperate, and such as to bear children."[22]

Fifteenth-century Italian humanists energetically culled from classical literature stories and aphorisms favorable to married life. Plutarch's *Moralia* proved to be an especially rich mine of example and citation. About 1415 or 1416, in celebration of the marriage of a Florentine friend, a young Venetian scholar named Francesco Barbaro wrote a tract on marriage and domestic life. He made liberal use of Plutarch, but his parade of erudition does not conceal an authentic enthusiasm for marriage: "What greater pleasure, than to decide together all things, even while spared the concerns of the household? Than to have a modest wife, a companion in good days and bad, a spouse and a friend? To whom you can confide your most private thoughts regarding your affairs? Whose sweetness and company sooth all your cares and woes? Whom you love so much that you think that a part of your own life depends on her well-being?"[23]

In the north of Europe, in the late fifteenth and early sixteenth century, Erasmus of Rotterdam, "prince of scholars," echoes and further embellishes these sentiments. His praise of marriage was in part a critique of the monastic life, as in the story out of the *Colloquies*, the *Virgo Misogamos*.[24] In it a young girl of seventeen rejects marriage in favor of the convent, only to regret her decision. But in numerous works, perhaps most eloquently in his *Encomium Matrimonii*, he affirms that marriage is the very foundation of the social order.[25] "And to what conclusion do these things point? To this surely: that we should recognize that all things both stand and are maintained by the married couple, and without it all things would break apart, perish, and slip away."[26]

Why was marriage rehabilitated in the fifteenth century, preeminently by the Italian and northern humanists? Certainly the influence of classical authors such as Plutarch played a role. But the writers were also living in the context of depopulated Europe. The radical loss of population seemed to put in jeopardy the continued survival of the human race.[27] Could they have been insensitive to their social surroundings? Did they not recognize that marriage and procreation needed to be promoted, if the community was to survive this shocking fall in numbers?

But the views on marriage of eleventh century poets and even of the later humanists confine us to the educated elite of the medieval world. Although written in Latin, the saints' lives reflect popular attitudes better than does the literature of the learned. They must, of course, be used with circumspection. We must try to filter out those elements directly governed by dogmatic assumptions from those that are not. Obviously, it is the latter that attract our principal interest.

Marital Metaphors

Saints' lives typically express abhorrence at sexual relations, and seem never to depict a happy, holy marriage, with normally frequent sexual intercourse. In the marriages of saints, either the couple agree early to remain continent, or the sainted partner, most frequently the wife, endures dreadful sufferings in the fulfillment of her marital duties. Sexual intercourse causes St. Francesca of Rome (d. 1440) to vomit, to the point of throwing up blood.[28] In their negative treatment of sex, the lives reflect an ancient, ecclesiastical prejudice.

But despite the horror of sexual relations, the lives indicate that marriage, the most intimate of human attachments, did engage the emotions of the partners. One example (already cited) was the ninth-century life of St. Severus of Ravenna, the poor wool worker who became in later life bishop of his city; he asked to be buried with his wife and daughter. This family, which lived a common life on earth, wished to stay together even in the grave.

Many of the marriages encountered in the lives are mystical. Usually they unite Christ and a female saint. However, the Dominican mystic Heinrich Suso courts and is married to Holy Wisdom.[29] Clearly the implication is that marriage brought about the closest possible spiritual and emotional union.[30] The imagery sometimes goes beyond the spiritual into the physical, even the erotic. The union of Angela of Foligno (d. 1309) with Christ is especially passionate. "And thus prepare yourself to receive him," Angela is told, "who has betrothed you with the ring of his love; and the marriage is already made; and therefore in a new way he [meaning Christ] wishes union and copulation [*copulam*]."[31] The life of St. Ida of Louvain (d. 1330) explicitly compares the saint's union with her spouse, Christ, with the embrace of lovers. She gains "joyous experience" by "strongly joining herself to her husband Christ the Lord."[32] God instructs the English mystic Margery Kempe how she should express her devotion: "There I must needs be homely with thee, and lie in bed with thee. Daughter . . . when thou art in thy bed, take Me to thee as thy wedded husband . . . Boldly take Me in the arms of thy soul and kiss My mouth, My head, and My feet, as sweetly as thou wilt."[33] The sexual imagery measures the emotonal intensity of many such lives.

One of the most interesting of these spiritual marriages unites a male saint with the Virgin Mary. This was St. Hermann of Steinfeld (died between 1230 and 1241), who became a member of the Premonstratensian order. As a boy growing up in Cologne, he develops a particular attachment to the Virgin. At age seven, he makes her (or her statue in a church) the gift of an apple, and he plays with the little boy Jesus. Once he cuts his foot on a nail, and goes to Mary's statue to be comforted. She scolds him for traipsing about the city streets without shoes, and tells him where to find the money to purchase a pair. Mothers look after their children.

As an adult, living in a monastic house, he is given the Virgin herself in marriage, in recognition of his life-long devotion to her. She is no longer the caring mother, but the radiant bride. One evening, while praying in the monastery church,

> he saw in the middle of the choir a young girl of ineffable beauty, marked by royal bearing, and next to her two beautiful young men standing on her left and on her right, whom he knew to be angels, ready to do service to so great a lady. The happy Brother, soon to be happier, stood there, admiring the newness and sweetness of the vision. He heard one of the angels speaking thus to the other: "To whom do we marry this virgin?" The other replied: "To whom shall we marry her, if not to the Brother here present? . . ." "It is fitting," he said [to Hermann], "that this glorious girl be married to you . . ." The Angel took his right hand and joined it to the hand of the most sacred virgin, and performed the marriage with these words: "Behold," he said, "I give this virgin to you as a wife, even as she was married to Joseph; and you shall take the name [of Joseph] together with the wife."[34]

The life makes no allusion to physical union, as the model for this marriage is clearly Mary's relationship with the original Joseph. Still, it is an exemplary picture of the affectionate, supportive relations of a man and a woman, of husband and wife. The author, Hermann's contemporary and doubtless a member of his order, even condemns fellow churchmen who demean and denigrate women.[35] Mary is Hermann's *carissima amica*, his sweetheart, his counselor and consoler.

> We [his fellow canons report] heard that it often happened to him . . . that, as he was occupied with prayers and meditations in a corner of the monastery, he would hear the voice of his Lady and dearest friend, standing across from him. He would go to her and, in some secret place, sitting together, he would answer Blessed Mary, as she asked him about all the details of his daily doings; and he in turn would ask of her, whatever he wanted. In such conversations, he passed in peace the nighttime

hours. With such a supporter, he bore all sorts of adverse happenings. By the breasts of such an consoling mother he was warmed. By such a teacher, by her instructions, he learned of many doubtful and uncertain matters.[36]

This deeply affectionate marriage is of course imaginary, but in his portrayal the author projects into the mystical realm a contemporary social ideal.

MOTHERHOOD

Nursing

According to Plutarch, nature had placed the breasts of the human female high upon her body, so that she would embrace her baby as she nursed him, and so develop affection for him.[37] This quaint teleology of breast location appears again in humanistic writings.[38]

Even the saints' lives express a similar sentiment. "For so it is arranged by nature," reads the life of St. Brigid of Ireland, "that nurses always bestow the affection of their spirit on those to whom they provide the milk of their flesh."[39]

Many women saints are granted the privilege of nursing the baby Jesus; they thereby not only provide nourishment to the sacred child, but they also enlarge their own affection for him. In one of her visions, St. Lidwina of Schiedam in Holland (d. 1433) observes that the breasts (including her own) of the entire heavenly chorus of virgins swell with milk on Christmas day, as they think of nursing the baby Jesus.[40] St. Gertrude of Oosten similarly gains indescribable joy in meditating on the infancy of Christ; the breasts of this virgin overflow with milk from the feast of Christmas until that of the Purification.[41] Once, when Margaret of Cortona (d. 1297) was feeling depressed, "he . . . who turns the sadness of the elect into joy, suddenly appeared, blond and little and whiter than snow, lying back in the cradle; and then rising to the mother's breast he sat in the virgin's lap."[42] It would be hard to miss the emotional flavor of these and many other passages which could be cited.

Intercession

Nurse to babies, the mother is also protector and intercessor of her growing and grown sons. The difference in age between the husband and wife, the consequent unequal measures of time separating fathers from children and mothers from children, made the father an older, distant, but powerful figure. The father could do favors for his sons, but his very presence, once his sons had reached maturity, could block them from attaining and enjoying marriage and property.

Conflicts between the male generations seem particularly acute in the twelfth and thirteenth centuries, when the old clung tenaciously to life, property, and power. Within noble society, as Duby reminds us, conflicts, even rebellions, of sons against their fathers, the *jeunes* against the old, were commonplace.[43] To cite familiar examples, emperor Henry IV at the start of the twelfth century, and Henry II of England at its close, faced successive revolts from their dissatisfied sons. In imaginative literature, in *Hervis de Mez*, the young hero repeatedly collides with his bourgeois father, who will not give him the support he needs, and who in turn objects to his son's prodigal ways.[44]

It was fundamentally over the use of property that the young Francis of Assisi disputed with his parsimonious father, who objected to his charities. In a memorable scene before the bishop of Assisi, Francis strips and returns all the clothes his father had given him.[45] Naked he had been received into his father's care, and naked he departs. The saint thus had personal reasons for affirming that questions of property were the source of all disputes in the world.

The mother, on the other hand, was ideally placed to serve as intermediary between the often conflicting male generations. She remained much nearer in years to her children, was easier to approach, and emotionally more committed to their welfare. She frequently assumes the role of intermediary in the literature of feudal society. In the epic *Les Narbonnais*, Aymeri of Narbonne sends his six oldest sons from his court, to make their fortunes in the world virtually without their father's aid. His wife, Hermengarde, their mother, protests against the harshness of this decision, to the point of suffering blows from her unyielding husband.[46] Aelis, mother of Hervis of Metz, urges her husband to apologize for striking their son.[47] A historian writes about the place of the mother in the French epics: "In extreme need, the heroes betake themselves to their mother, with whom they always find love, counsel and help. She takes them under her protection, even against their father."[48] The mother of Francis of Assisi similarly sought to reconcile father and son, and took the risk of removing the chains with which his father had bound him in the dungeon of their home.[49]

In sum, the medieval marriage pattern isolated the wife and mother in the family and shortened the generational distance between her and the children. The mother was well placed to listen and to speak, to convey pleas and proposals in both directions. The mother's unique position within the natural family could not fail to affect cultural attitudes toward motherhood itself and its functions. Medieval religious culture witnesses from the twelfth century on an extraordinary growth in veneration of the Virgin Mary. Mary, in traditional

Catholic teaching, is not only the mother of Jesus but also, in a spiritual sense, of the entire Christian family. Used to seeking the help and intercession of their natural mothers, medieval people seem to have sought comparable services from their spiritual mother in heaven. Their secular hopes and gratitude find their counterpart in Marian devotions.

The saints' lives of the late Middle Ages overflow with depictions of Mary as intercessor, and other women saints assume that function too.[50] But the lives also attribute to these holy women another function, less recognized but perhaps equally indicative of the role of the mother in the medieval home.

Spiritual Families, Holy Instruction

Female saints of the late Middle Ages attract bands of followers, who form a kind of spiritual family. The saint calls them her children, and they call her their mother. The best known of these spiritual families is doubtlessly the "joyous brigade" which followed Catherine of Siena. She is to them, in a name brimming with affection, their "little mother."[51] One of her followers, the notary ser Barduccio di Piero Canigiani, describes himself at her death as "a feeble infant, orphaned by the death of so great a mother."[52] Catherine, he affirms, was the "mother of a thousand souls."[53] But Catherine is far from alone in recruiting a spiritual family. A century earlier, Margaret of Cortona similarly attracted a large following of both sexes. "Who can count," her biographer (also her confessor) asks, "how many were the Spaniards, Apulians, Romans and others coming to her, that they might be instructed?"[54] This instruction and exhortation earned her the title of *mater peccatorum*, the "mother of sinners."[55] Her younger contemporary, Angela of Foligno, also becomes the center of a spiritual fellowship of men as well as women.[56] The Flemish widow, Yvette of Huy, attracts disciples from overseas.[57] St. Marie of Maillac, who lived in Tours in the late fourteenth century, "by her words fervently directed along the way of salvation both sexes and all ages."[58] These groups are in no sense organized religious communities. They are, as they claim to be, the spiritual family of a saintly mother.

The mother prays and intercedes for her children. But perhaps the most remarkable of her services is religious instruction. These holy women are teachers and preachers. St. Juliane of Liège (d. 1258), orphaned at five, is sent to a convent to be educated. She reads Augustine and Bernard of Clairvaux, and memorizes the latter's lengthy commentary on the Song of Songs, "for she ardently loved the amatory canticles." Many important people come to seek her counsel, "although in her entire life she bore badly the visits of high personages."[59] The virgin St. Rose preaches publicly against the heretical rulers of her native Perugia, and she and her followers are exiled from the city.[60] The blind St. Sibillina of Pavia (d. 1367) receives numerous visitors, both lay and religious, and is "very involved in the conversion of sinners."[61] Her biographer expresses amazement "that a lay woman could speak so profusely and easily about divine things, and discourse at times about mysteries with such suitable vocabulary. A certain religious once said that she could not have been more eloquent in the expression of theological words, had she attentively read the meditations of St. Bernard or the soliloquies of St. Augustine."[62] Often these spiritual mothers include in their following men in holy orders; the priests frequently serve as their confessors and biographers. But it is the women, and not their ordained disciples, who are the voices of holy wisdom. Catherine's meditation and exhortations to her spiritual family are today classics in the religious literature of the late Middle Ages; they have gained for her the official honor and title of doctor of the Church.

Not Catherine's equal in sublime theology, but still important in this context, are the English mystics, the rather conventional nun, Julian of Norwich, and the quite unconventional wife, Margery Kempe. The latter's *Book* (1436) in particular further illustrates the role of women as religious preachers to a predominantly lay audience.[63] We do not have works of comparable size and power from the other spiritual mothers. It is, however, interesting to note that the life of Angela of Foligno is recorded in the first person.[64] She spoke to her family, and she speaks to us, directly.

The mother, fount of sacred wisdom: it is a surprising juxtaposition. The medieval Church was traditionally suspicious of lay preaching, and above all wary of women pretending to offer religious instruction. Yet despite this ancient prejudice, women assume that function commonly in the late medieval towns.

This fact suggests that historians perhaps have not sufficiently recognized the importance of women, of mothers, as receptacles and transmitters of sacred values. In other words, the spiritual families led by holy women, who were sources of divine knowledge and exhorters to religious perfection, imitated the natural family, where presumably mothers assumed a comparable if less visible role in the religious training of children. We have long had hints that this was so. Not much after 1400, the Florentine Dominican, Giovanni Dominici, writes a tract on "family care," in which he includes much advice on the religious training of children.[65] The tract is addressed to a woman, and the assumption is that she has the chief responsibility for implementing the counsels. The followers of Catherine, Angela, Sibillina, and many other holy women were likely continuing a religious education begun by their mothers.

The structure of late medieval urban families aided women in this function. Since urban girls were young at first marriage, and grooms mature, mothers were therefore destined for longer, closer contact with their children than the aging fathers. Death would call many fathers early in their children's lives; affairs of society and state would take many others out of the home. The mother was the steadier tie to the older generation and its values. Preeminently mothers instructed and exhorted the little children. But structural peculiarities of the late medieval family are surely not the total explanation for the mother's role as cultural, and here religious, repositories of wisdom. We must concede importance also to the spontaneous effort of women to socialize their children in appropriate ways.

As anthropologists remind us, possession of knowledge, and perhaps sacred knowledge above all, is a principal avenue to status and power in any community. Catherine of Siena exerts power in fourteenth-century Europe through the revelations granted her. She also enjoys the honor, respect, and ultimately the veneration of her followers and the wider world. Urban mothers too may have basked in the unrecorded prestige of their own private circle.

The image of the wife and mother in the didactic literature is singularly passive.[66] She follows without complaint or initiative the instructions of her patronizing husband. The saints' lives at least suggest that this is a biased picture; the mother played a far more active role, and enjoyed higher prestige and status, than we have hitherto appreciated.

Obstruction

The youth of women at first marriage and the relatively advanced age for men had at least one other important social effect. Despite the risks of childbirth, wives had a good chance of surviving their husbands. Still young as widows, they were in a position to block the transmission of the family patrimony, in whole or in part, to the younger generation. In traditional India under seemingly comparable conditions, the devoted widow or suttee was expected to immolate herself upon her husband's pyre—a personal sacrifice which also conveniently freed the family property for the next generation.[67] In medieval Europe governments and families could only limit the widow's claims upon the property of her husband and restrict her capacity to acquire or to manage other possessions. In the middle of the twelfth century the Statutes of Pisa already complain that "mothers, in demanding [return of] the dowry and the reverse dowry from their sons, more often than not show not maternal affection but a step-mother's lack of familial feeling."[68] "The female sex," reads a commonplace of the legal literature, "is most avaricious and most tenacious and more eager to receive than to give."[69] In the late sixteenth century, the commune of Correggio in Italy tried to restrict acquisitions by women "for the public good and for the conservation of families and of male lines, which are often ruined by the excessive bequests and donations which daily are made to women, without having regard to the conservation of the male line."[70]

The medieval mother can be at various times a gracious inter-cessor and an avaricious parent, who blocks by her longevity the devolution of property to her needy children. Small wonder that medieval society sustained contrary impressions of women.

CHILDHOOD

Few today support Ariès' thesis that medieval parents ignored their children. On the contrary, as civilization grew more complex, more critically based on learned skill, medieval society had to invest heavily in the training of the young. And where treasure is, so also is the heart.

The lives give many examples of a passionate involvement with childhood and children. The devil himself uses the attraction of children as a trap to waylay saints. The devil knows, for example, that Gertrude van Oosten, though unmarried, dearly loves babies and children. "For this reason," her life relates, "the devil often transformed himself not into an angel of light, but into the form of a crying and hurting child, so that he might preoccupy the soul of the virgin, and distract her from God and things divine."[71] The devil conjures up a similar vision before the eyes of Christina of Stommeln, who passed most of her life in Cologne. She sees in a vision a husband, wife, and baby. The woman, playing sweetly with the child, declares to Christina: "There is no delight greater than this delight, by which a husband is joined to his wife; there is no delight like to this delight, which a mother has in her child."[72] For six weeks this serene (if diabolical) domestic group appears before Christina, subtly tempting the lonely, abandoned girl to jealousy and despair. The medieval family was not a cold community founded upon indifference; the devil has keener insight than many modern historians.

Even more than the bait of family feeling to tempt the saints, the cult of baby Jesus was the chief arena for the expression of sentiments concerning childhood, sacred and profane. The cult of the holy infant was widespread. The English Cistercian Aelred of Rievaulx writes in the twelfth century a passionate meditation on twelve-year-old Jesus; in his writings some have detected homosexual tendencies.[73] Francis of Assisi is credited in his legend with the erection of the first Christmas crèche.[74] Anthony of Padua or of Lisbon, in the early thirteenth century, was seen hugging a boy in his chamber, the child Jesus; his embrace of the holy boy later becomes a permanent part of his iconography.[75] Heinrich Suso similarly is favored with a vision of Jesus as a charming schoolboy, the ideal pupil for teachers everywhere.[76] Women were not alone in admiring the baby Christ.

And yet, in this cult, women seem especially prominent and passionate. Many examples could be given of these outpourings of maternal affection. Angela of Foligno one day sees in the consecrated host Jesus as "a big boy." "And I had great delight in watching him . . . he was of such beauty and so well dressed, that it cannot be described. And he seemed about twelve years old."[77]

Another time, on the feast of the Purification, the Blessed Mother comes to visit her, carrying the infant Jesus. Mary collapses into a chair "as if tired from a journey." She hands Angela the child: "O loved one of my son, take him."[78] The baby's eyes are closed, and he is all bundled in swaddling clothes.

> While I stood there suddenly he stayed in my arms all naked, and he opened and lifted his eyes and looked at me . . . and immediately in the look of those eyes I felt and had so much love, that I was completely overwhelmed. For so much splendor came from those eyes, and fire of love and joy, that it cannot be described. And then suddenly there appeared an immense, ineffable majesty, and he said to me: who does not see me little, will not see me great . . . And he added: I come to you, and I offer myself to you, that you will offer yourself to me. And then my soul in wonderful and indescribable fashion offered itself to him; finally I gave my whole self to him, and all my children.[79]

The children she mentions were her spiritual, not her natural family. For them, for her, union with God was the embrace of a naked baby.

It is fair to assume that the cult of the infant Jesus exploited real attitudes toward babies. "How sweet in the womb, sweet in the lap, sweet burden in the arms, light weight to the shoulders, is the child to the mother, Christ to Mary."[80] This last passage comes from the life of Yvette of Huy.

St. Ida of Louvain was often favored with visits by the infant Jesus, from which she drew "immense joy." She even worshiped him with the wise men. Once, a fellow nun had slandered her. The holy child comes at night while the culprit is sleeping, pounces upon her in her bed, and beats and kicks her with his little fists and legs. He throws this childish tantrum because she has offended his beloved Ida.[81]

Another day, Ida gives the infant Jesus a bath, with the help of St. Elizabeth, mother of the Baptist. They fill the tub with tepid water, and gently place the holy child in it. "As he sat there, this the most chosen of all babies, like playing babies, clapped with both hands under the water and in the manner of infants swirled and splashed the water, and got everything around him wet and himself all wet, before they could wash him . . . When the bath was over, she lifted the baby from the water, and put him in her lap wrapped in towels, playing intimately with him like a mother does. She wonderfully exulted in her saving God, more than can be said or imagined."[82] Whoever wrote this life had observed babies taking baths and enjoyed the sight. Ida does not want to return the holy child, and a "most pleasant dispute and argument pleasing beyond measure" breaks out among the women.[83]

FATHERHOOD

The final example of familial imagery in a devotional context is perhaps the most central to our subject, and also the most difficult to interpret. This is the cult of St. Joseph, patron and protector of the Holy Family.

Joseph is all but invisible in early medieval writings. The *Patrologia Latina* of J. P. Migne, consisting of more than 200 volumes of doctrinal writings before the year 1216, does not, in its index of cited saints, provide a single reference to Joseph. About 1200, St. Hermann of Steinfeld is given by an angel the name of Joseph, but the real Joseph does not otherwise play a role in his legend.[84] Indeed, he loses his name and dignity as Mary's consort to another man, without complaint. Late medieval saints' lives are surfeited with visions, but not of Joseph. When he appears, which is rarely, he is called *senex*, "old man"; he is honored, but he does not appear as a powerful intercessor.[85] The fifteenth-century preacher Bernardino da Feltre complains that painters represent him as a *vechiarello*, a powerless old man.[86]

But in the fourteenth century, several prominent churchmen undertake a vigorous campaign to promote devotion to Joseph. Chief among them was Jean Gerson, the chancellor of the University of Paris around 1400. In tract, sermon, and poem, he celebrates the Josephine image and proposes that the Church establish for him a major feastday.[87] In promoting Joseph, Gerson also changes his traditional shadowy, weak image. Joseph must no longer be regarded as the feeble old man, as writers and artists have wrongly depicted him. He must have been only about 36 when he married Mary, as this is the age which Aristotle identifies as the prime of life.[88] Who else but a vigorous man could have guarded the Holy Family during seven years of exile in Egypt? Subtly, even if reverently, Gerson must also downplay the image of Mary. She was only 13 or 14 years at marriage, a mere *pucelle*. She was scarcely capable of guiding the family through its parlous adventures. Mary was young, poor, simple, accustomed to home, ignorant of foreign lands.[89] Joseph, still in Gerson's embroidery of the Biblical tale, takes complete command of the harassed family. He convinces the pharaoh to let them live in Egypt, pursues his trade as carpenter, earns money for the family, and protects his wife and baby against the many threats mounted against them. "He wasn't at all," Gerson concludes, "old, ugly, ineffectual, feeble, and, so to speak, incapable of work."[90]

Joseph is the *sedulus administrator*, but he also bound to his wife and child, and they to him, by bonds of deep affection. And he is demonstrative in showing that love. "Joseph bears him," reads a poem, "Joseph leads him, Joseph soothes him with kisses"—meaning of course the child Jesus.[91] "What fragrance," exclaims Bernardino da Feltre, "when he holds in his arms the king of Paradise!" And then in rapture from his meditations: "Oymi, I can't bear this any longer!"[92] So great are the bonds of mutual affection that, in the opinion of the doctors, Joseph, like Mary herself and Jesus, must have been taken bodily into heaven. There they constitute a loving family, the ideal for all families. As Bernardino da Feltre explains, "in Paradise, the order of love (*charitas*) and of relationship (*propinquitas*) is preserved, since grace does not destroy nature."[93]

This effective manager and loving father deserves many honors. The French theologian Pierre d'Ailly counts twelve *honores* that Joseph enjoys.[94] Bernardino da Feltre asserts that the rulership of the whole world by right belongs to Joseph.[95] It is because Mary, the Mother of God, and God himself in human form, were subject to his authority and remain in loving subjugation even in heaven.[96] Grace does not destroy the natural order, but perfects it.

It is not hard to see why the cult of Joseph would have had appeal during the late Middle Ages. The raging plagues, tenacious famines, and recurrent wars menaced many households; then if ever the times required that heads of families be attentive, efficient, caring, loving, comforting. The world, in Gerson's view, was Egypt.[97] Bernardino tells of a rich townsman whose home was attacked during the course of a political upheaval. The townsman prays before a statue of Joseph that he keeps in his house. The saint intervenes to save his person, his family and his fortune.[98]

Yet some puzzling aspects of the late medieval cult of Joseph remain. Did it spontaneously appear among the faithful, or was it disseminated by great churchmen and saints such as Pierre d'Ailly, Jean Gerson, Bernardino da Siena, Bernardino da Feltre? For other purposes, I have collected the names of 30,000 Florentine males of the office-holding class, from the late fourteenth century until 1530.[99] Not until the sixteenth century is any one of them called Giuseppe, Joseph, today a common Italian name. And in the early sixteenth century still only one citizen is called after the head of the Holy Family.

Why were prominent leaders of the late medieval Church so zealous in promoting devotions to Joseph? Was it a reaction against the feminization of sainthood and sanctity? Perhaps they believed that in their tumultuous times, fathers needed stronger spiritual patrons and models than the ranks of recent saints were supplying. The late medieval cult of Joseph may not have grown spontaneously. But at least it shows what some doctors thought was appropriate status, behavior, and honors for fathers.

Saints' live and other sources show beyond question that the medieval family was not an emotional desert. But the structure of the household and the experiences of the epoch reinforced distinctive roles for husbands and wives, parents and children. The poems of Marbode of Rennes and the life of St. Hermann-Joseph indicate that the misogynist tradition, which was antimarriage as well as anti-women, at no time ruled all of medieval society. To some at least, the wife was helpmate and companion; upon her the *honestas* of the household was totally dependent. The demographic disasters of the late Middle Ages, the menace of a radically falling population, helped strengthen this positive assessment of marriage and its contributions to society.

The large age difference between husband and wife, which had increased since probably the twelfth century, placed the mother midway between the generations of fathers and children. She was thus ideally placed to serve as mediator in generational conflicts. Perhaps still more remarkable was the role of mothers as repositories of sacred wisdom, as channels through which a significant part of the cultural inheritance passed from the old to the young. This lent to the mother prestige and influence within the household, perhaps more than we have recognized. The experiences of the closing Middle Ages seem particularly to have affected the role of father. Again, the dreadful epidemics threatened the survival of families and lineages. To counter the dangers, the father had to be the attentive,

assiduous; a hard-working manager, supporting his family and leading it to safety. St. Joseph, in a new interpretation, became the perfect
model of paternal solicitude.

The ravages of the times emphasized the fragility of human relations; people paid more attention to children and showed a greater
willingness to invest in their welfare.[100] But we ought not to assume
that medieval people were ever indifferent to their offspring. Bernard
of Anjou, writing about the year 1000, surely was correct in affirming
that most human beings, and his contemporaries among them, find
in rearing their children the largest part of their happiness.

6 | THE HOUSEHOLD SYSTEM
IN THE LATE MIDDLE AGES

E certo in questo separare l'assidua conversazione insieme
e familiarità, loderò chi imiterà el buon padre di famiglia
aggravato dalle spese, el quale non in un dì rende la famiglia e le spese minori, per non dare di se ammirazione
alla moltitudine, ma ne' dì passati ne mandò el maestro
de' cavagli e serbossi una sola cavalcatura, oggi licenza
quelli senza cui opera la famiglia ben si può governare, e
di tempo in tempo ne manderà persin de' suoi a quello
essercizio e a quell' altro altrove.

In breaking off close social contacts along with coresidency, I recommend as an example the good father of family who is burdened with expenses. He does not in a single
day reduce both the household and the expenses, so as not
to provoke public astonishment. Rather, days ago he dis-
missed the master of the horses and retained only one
indispensable mount. Today he lets go those servants
without whose work the household can still function. And
from time to time he will send away even his own kin, to
one or another employment elsewhere.

—Leon Battista Alberti, *Della famiglia*

T HE RADICAL loss of population during the late Middle
Ages did one service for historians. The governments of
the epoch almost continuously engaged in exhausting
wars and desperately searched for the resources to wage
them. To meet their pressing fiscal needs, they took precise counts
of their subjects and made exact assessments of their wealth. Communities were minutely scrutinized, even as violence flared and
numbers dwindled. The age of political arithmetic, if not yet mature,
was in its infancy. Notable among these late medieval harbingers
of a closely watched society are the English poll tax surveys of 1377–
1381, and the Florentine Catasto of 1427–1430.[1]

Better statistical records promise at least partial answers to such
fundamental questions as, what factors determined the size and
structure of medieval households? And how, if at all, did the medieval coresidential group differ from those of the modern or indus-
trial world? For the first time, we can roughly sketch what
anthropologists would call the household formation system, if not
of the entire medieval society, then at least of some communities
within it.

IDEALS

The household is a coresidential community with parents and children—the primary biological descent group—at its core. The household members are simultaneously caught up in dynamic processes, and this is what renders the analysis of household systems so complex. As stable associations, households reflect largely static cultural ideals, indicating who should appropriately live together, how long, and under what terms. Rules too, which are also slow to change, govern marriage, inheritance, fostering, adoption, employment of servants, and other events which, directly or indirectly, add or subtract members to and from the household. Under these overarching ideals and rules, some members engage in productive enterprise, while all members are subject to the inexorable processes of aging. Here, we shall first examine these static sets of values and prescriptions, and then we shall consider the playing out of the processes they were intended to direct.

Religious Ideals

The medieval Church espoused a forceful though far from comprehensive ideal of domestic life. Two crucial texts from the Old Testament underlay its teachings. According to Genesis 2.24, when Adam took to wife the newly created Eve, he pronounced: "Wherefore a man shall leave father and mother, and shall cleave to his wife, and they shall be two in one flesh." The obligations of husband to wife take precedence over duty to his parents: there are limits, in sum, to patriarchal power.

Children were nonetheless obligated to respect and, when needed, to support their parents. The fourth commandment in the Vulgate version of the Bible enjoins them: "Honor thy father and mother, as the Lord thy God hath commanded thee, that thou mayest live a long time" (Deut. 5.16).

St. Paul cited both these texts in elaborating his own, highly influential statement concerning domestic morality. The state of marriage he regarded as inferior to that of virginity and even widowhood, but it is nonetheless holy. The husband holds authority over the body of his wife, and she over his (1 Cor. 7.4). Either can claim the marital debt, even when the other is unwilling. Divorce is forbidden, except from an infidel spouse. And in words which medieval Christians heard many times in the course of their lives, Paul instructed the faithful:

> Let wives be subject to their husbands as to the Lord, because
> a husband is head of the wife, just as Christ is head of the

Church . . . Husbands, love your wives, just as Christ also loved the Church . . . Even thus ought husbands also to love their wives as their own bodies. He who loves his own wife, loves himself. For no one ever hated his own flesh; on the contrary he nourishes and cherishes it, as Christ also does the Church.   (Eph. 5.21–29)

So also, according to Paul, children should obey their parents, but fathers must not nag their children, lest they become discouraged. The family, in Pauline doctrine, is not a patriarchal despotism but a moral economy in which all members are bound to service.

Another crucial scriptural text in shaping the familial values of the Middle Ages was the parable of the prodigal son. The younger son claims from his father his share in the inheritance, takes the wealth to a foreign land, and squanders it in riotous living. Destitute and deserted, he returns to ask forgiveness and to beg for scraps of food from his father's table. His father welcomes him and arranges a great feast to celebrate his return. The faithful older brother refuses in anger to attend the celebration, the like of which was never offered him. The father explains: "Son, thou art always with me, and all that is mine is thine; but we were bound to make merry and rejoice, for this thy brother was dead, and has come to life; he was lost, and is found" (Luke 16.31–32). Love for family members, the text insists, transcends and transforms personal weakness and failure.

The scriptures offered counsels as well as commands, in regard to property as well as persons. One text, favored by medieval preachers, cautioned the father against distributing his property before his death: "Give not to son or wife, brother or friend, power over thee while thou livest; and give not thy estate to another, lest thou repent, and thou entreat for the same . . . For it is better that thy children should ask of thee than that thou look towards the hands of thy children . . . In the time when thou shalt end the days of thy life, and in the time of thy decease, distribute thy inheritance" (Eccles. 33).[2]

The family ideal implied in these teachings is familiar. Marriage is monogamous and permanent; the family itself, stable and cohesive. Parents must be honored and obeyed, and their children must aid and support them in old age and illness (Eccles. 3.14). The wise father will retain control over the patrimony until his death, but his patriarchal power is not absolute. A son or daughter may leave father and mother and cleave to a spouse. The moral claims of the old family are subordinate to those of the new.

These values saturated the religious culture of the Middle Ages. In imposing the same sexual morality on all social classes, the teachings helped in the early Middle Ages to make households similar and commensurable, as we have argued. In giving precedence to family of marriage over family or origin, they blocked the development of a full-blown patriarchal system in Europe. And they recommended that mutual goodwill and love, not paternal authority or even self-interest, join together family members.

Secular Ideals

Alongside these religious values, secular ideals also defined goals and recommended appropriate strategies for achieving them. The patrilineage, which dominated the elite circles of late medieval society, was founded on the principle that the claims of offspring to shares in the patrimony be limited. Its spirit seems well reflected in the quip of the fifteenth-century humanist, Leon Battista Alberti, that three sons, like three villas, were too many.[3]

Classical antiquity had developed a rich literature concerned with "economics" or the laws of household management, but the tradition did not survive the debacle of the western empire. From the ninth century it makes a partial reappearance in the "mirrors of princes," which advise the ruler not only on public affairs but also on the management of the palace and the education of children.[4] Apparently the first medieval author to write on "economics" in the classical sense is the thirteenth-century Dominican Vincent of Beauvais, who included a treatise on household management in the *Speculum morale*, one of the four divisions of his monumental encyclopedia.[5] Important too in this burgeoning tradition is the *De regimine principum* of Egidius Colonna (Giles of Rome), which offers much advice on the general problems of household administration and the training of children; it forms a bridge between the early-medieval "mirrors" and the late-medieval tracts offering guidance to prominent but not princely lay families.[6]

The disasters of the late Middle Ages powerfully stimulated interest in effective household management. There was no assurance that the radical decline in human numbers, between the early fourteenth and the early fifteenth centuries, would ever be reversed. The conscientious household head was eager to find counsel and wisdom, to assure the continuity and prosperity of his lineage. And improving command of the classical heritage enhanced accessibility to the large body of comment and counsel that ancient authors had devoted to households.

The best known example of the new literature is *Four Books on the Family*, which Alberti wrote in the middle 1430s.[7] Alberti's ideal household is large, stable, and supportive. In an oft-quoted passage, the old and experienced Giannozzo Alberti urges the Alberti sons to live together as long as possible: "To make of one family two requires double expenses . . . I have never been pleased with the division of families, with [brothers] going out and coming in through more than one door; and my spirit would never have allowed me to let Antonio my brother live without me under another roof."[8]

Giannozzo elsewhere declares: "I would have all my relatives live under one and the same roof, warm themselves at one and the same fire, and sit down at one and the same table." He also wants them to live "under the shadow of a single will"; the father should rule his wife, married and unmarried sons, daughters and daughters-in-law, and all household members, and control the family patrimony until his death.[9]

In spite of Giannozzo's enthusiastic support of the large and undivided family, comparatively few households were able to achieve this level of solidarity.[10] Even in Alberti's own lifetime, in 1427, the average size of Florentine households was only 3.8 persons, and 4.4 in all of Tuscany.[11] The number of truly big households of the kind Alberti envisions is exiguous; those in the city containing more than 10 persons constitute only 3.6 percent of the total of 10,000. The ideal of the large and extended family, eloquently propounded by Alberti and others, was seldom realized.

RULES

Monogamy and Exogamy

The rules of monogamy and exogamy imposed by the medieval Church were remarkably strict, and remained so even after the Fourth Lateran Council reduced the number of degrees within which marriages could not occur from seven to four. The point of the prohibition, we have argued, was initially to prevent rich and powerful males from collecting or retaining more than their share of women. For example, if a household contained one married and several unmarried brothers and the married brother died, his widow could not marry any of his siblings. Unless she was content to remain a widow, she would have to leave the household if she wished to remarry. The departure of widows was a common occurrence, and often highly aggravating to the male affines she left behind.[12] Similarly, a male could not marry sisters, neither simultaneously (like the Merovingian king Clothar) nor sequentially. And a son could not marry his widowed stepmother (and thereby assure her continued presence in the household). In forcing widowed women to look outside their present household membership to find a new mate, the rule of exogamy reduced the possibilities that two or more married couples would be continuously found in the same residence. The rules also improved the chances that even poor males would find a mate. This too may have helped sustain a situation in which one married couple, but usually only one, would be present in most households.

Inheritance

In the common medieval view, the rules of inheritance were closely tied to those of exogamy. For example, in his eleventh-century treatise "On the Degrees of Kinship," the Italian reformer and saint Peter Damian explained that the right to inherit from a person and the right to marry that person were mutually exclusive.[13] A man is not allowed to marry a woman from whom he might also inherit; the same applies to women. Rich households, in consequence, could not easily conserve their patrimonies by arranging marriages among their own heirs. The woman must marry out, and she inevitably takes some property with her. The circulation of women thus also produced a circulation of capital. Both sets of rules—respectively governing incest and inheritance—worked against disproportionate accumulations whether of women or of wealth in a few powerful households.

In his famous thesis, the French sociologist and social reformer Frédéric Le Play (1806–82) argued that a direct and strong connection existed between the practice of partible or impartible inheritance and family organization.[14] Le Play as a social reformer deplored the equal division of inheritances among heirs prescribed by the Napoleonic Code. The practice, he believed, produced small and impoverished farmsteads, and encouraged growth in population beyond the limit of what the resources could comfortably support. The traditional (and preferable) form of family organization was, in his own coinage, the *famille souche,* or "stem family." It resembles, on a more humble social level, the dynastic lineage considered in Chapter 4.

The stem family was organized to preserve the integrity and productivity of the ancestral farm upon which and from which it lived. The farm was passed on intact from the family chief to a single heir, usually the oldest but sometimes the youngest or the one whom the father designated. Only the inheriting son was allowed to marry while remaining on the farm, and he often took a wife even before the death or retirement of his parents. His siblings, if they wished to remain in the parental house, had to stay celibate. Typically, therefore, the stem family was vertically extended over three generations. It included the old parents; a single married son and his unmarried siblings; and the children of the young married couple.

The system, Le Play fervently believed, assured good care of the land, protecting it from ruinous divisions; and good care of the people supported by it. The discipline it imposed prevented excessive population growth. Finally, the stem family offered all its members material and psychological help, even while denying to most of them the chance to marry.

Impartible inheritance and the stem family thus seemed to Le Play inextricably joined. In contrast, in those areas of Europe where partible inheritance prevailed, different forms of household organization took root. The several brothers, all of whom had claim to a share of the inheritance, might keep their common patrimony undivided, even after one or more had married. The result was the joint-family household, also often called by its French name, *frèrèche*.[15] The *frèrèche* was laterally extended. Sooner or later, the inheriting brothers would likely divide their home and patrimony. Partible inheritance thus led to a proliferation of small farms. It did not maintain the same fine balance between population and resources that the system of the stem family achieved.

In his pioneering investigation of thirteenth-century English peasants, George C. Homans accepted Le Play's thesis as valid for England too.[16] In the champion areas of the English midlands, where impartible inheritance was the rule, he concluded that the peasants organized their households according to the model of the stem family. One son received the family holding, and his siblings who remained on the farm did not marry. Conversely, areas of partible inheritance, such as Kent in the southeast or the western borderlands, and also Wales and Ireland, contained many joint family households or the small menages resulting from the division of properties.

Homans, however, did not have the use of statistical data, and in the light of recent research his conclusions seem impressionistic and arguable. Zvi Razi, for example, in his study of the manor of Halesowen near Birmingham, brings forth much statistical information, which shows little or no relationship between inheritance customs and family organization.[17] The prevailing custom at Halesowen was impartible inheritance, and all the land presumably passed to the eldest son. But parents often bestowed some holdings on younger siblings, while reserving the major portion for the principal heir. These sons and daughters began families of their own, even though they received only small portions of their parents' property. Presumably they supplemented their meager harvests through work as hired hands. Even the inheriting son often helped his younger brothers or sisters acquire land, sometimes assigning them parts of his own patrimony. Finally, landless males in the countryside might hope to acquire land through advantageous marriages with propertied widows or heiresses.

People, in sum, found ways around the customary rules. And doubtless too, in regions of partible inheritance, parents might favor one offspring over the others. At all events, at Halesowen and surely elsewhere too, younger sons were not forced to remain celibate. The community was not divided into propertied household heads and their landless and celibate younger siblings. The requirement that younger siblings remain celibate, which the system of the stem family demanded, was simply too harsh to command full compliance.

Finally, in areas of Europe where short-term, non-inheritable leaseholds were common, inheritance customs might affect the behavior of great landholding families, but not that of the peasants who worked the land. The terms of land tenure, in other words, might be just as important as inheritance customs in influencing family organization. One region of Europe where the relations of land tenure and family structure can be observed in great detail is Tuscany in 1427.

Tenures

As recorded in the Catasto, peasant homesteaders settled on the Florentine domains in 1427 fell into three principal categories. (A homesteader for our purposes is a peasant who owns or leases, and works through his own efforts, a complete farm or productive unit, including the house in which he and his family reside.) Peasants owning their own farm, the *podere,* accounted for 6,979 households, or 18.19 percent of the total of 38,368 households in the entire countryside.[18] In other words, the inheritance custom of the region (which prescribed partibility) would have directly affected only about one of five rural families.

Just about as many as the freeholders were peasants who held their *poderi* under the famous sharecropping contract known as the *mezzadria.* This was a precarious tenancy, renewable after short terms (usually one, three, or five years). Under its terms, the landlord (*oste*) supplied his tenant (*lavoratore*) not only with a complete farm, but also with a large part of what he needed to work it—animals, seed, fertilizer, and loans.[19] The owner received in turn one-half the harvest. Sharecropping households numbered 7,263, or 18.2 percent of the total. Farms given out for fixed rents were 1,640 (4.24 percent); artisans and merchants headed 2,193 (5.7 percent) of the rural households; and those who give no indication of their occupation are 20,293 (52.84 percent).

From the whole Tuscan data we shall isolate the rural quarter of Santo Spirito, which stretched south of the city into the Chianti hills. It was a relatively homogeneous zone in the highly variegated Tuscan countryside; both the "poderization" of tenures and the use of the *mezzadria* were well advanced. The following analysis will include only households with a male head. We look first at the households without taxable lands.

In 1427 households without landed property in rural Santo Spirito were quite numerous—1,652, or 21.94 percent of the total of 7,530. Inheritance customs could have had no influence upon this rural proletariat. Yet Table 6.1 shows that the households of the landless still show considerable variations, when tested by such simple measures as average size or percentage of family heads appearing with living wives. (The group of leaseholders or *affictuarii* is very small and perhaps not fully representative.) Sharecroppers on the one hand, and artisans and men without known occupation on the other, lived in quite different domestic surroundings. In spite of their apparent destitution, sharecropping households contain on the average over 5 members; those of the artisans, only 3.64; and those without stated occupation, 4.20. Nine out of ten sharecroppers have wives, but only three out of four in the equally destitute group of artisans and men of unknown employment. These considerable differences require an explanation.

The farm held under the *mezzadria* was in effect an impartible tenure. It was designed to be a complete productive unit, and the *oste* who owned it was not likely to undermine its productivity by assigning its different fields to different heirs. The peasant-owned farm was, on the other hand, subject to the rule of partibility. Did the practical partibility or impartibility of the lands affect the organization of these peasant families?

As Table 6.2 illustrates, the difference among the households headed by a peasant proprietor, a leaseholder, or a sharecropper are minimal.

Table 6.1. Male household heads without taxable land, rural quarter of Santo Spirito, Tuscany, 1427.

Occupation	Households	Members	Average Size	Percent married
Not stated	517	2176	4.20	77.17
Leaseholders	59	266	4.50	88.13
Sharecroppers	894	4492	5.02	90.38
Artisans	197	718	3.64	73.60

Source: Florentine Catasto of 1427–30.

Table 6.2. Male household heads with and without taxable land, rural quarter of Santo Spirito, Tuscany, 1427.

Occupation	Households	Members	Average size	Percent Married
Not stated	3219	13240	4.11	83.22
Peasant owners	630	3727	5.91	90.56
Leaseholders	370	2212	5.97	91.82
Sharecroppers	2533	14818	5.84	90.77
Artisans	663	3022	4.55	83.07
Merchants[a]	115	664	5.77	81.57

Source: Florentine Catasto of 1427–30.

a. Men whose stated profession would make them members of a major guild if they lived in the city.

The three groups have both large households (an average of 5.91, 5.97 and 5.84 persons respectively) and high proportions of married household heads. Upon a closer inspection of the data, the wives of sharecroppers turn out to be somewhat more fertile. One out of nine wives in this category appears without children, as opposed to one out of five among the peasant proprietors.[20] Sharecroppers may have felt less restraint in adding another child and heir to the family, as they held little or no property in their own name. And the system of proportionate rent shifted some of the costs of supporting the additional mouth onto the landlord. For the countryside as a whole, the population of sharecroppers is noticeably younger than that of any other occupatonal group.[21]

The tables do, however, isolate one factor that powerfully affected the rural households of Santo Spirito, dividing them into two principal groups. This was access, whether by lease or inheritance, to a full farm or productive unit. All peasant homesteaders—proprietors, leaseholders, and sharecroppers—live in households very different in composition from those of rural artisans and people of unknown occupation. These inhabitants of the countryside must have earned their living by cultivating scattered parcels of land and by working as hired hands. Not in possession of a family farm, they hired out their services to the homesteaders.

This Tuscan evidence demonstrates that the rules of inheritance and the terms of tenancy exerted only a weak influence on family organization. The decisive factor was responsibility for a complete farm or *podere*. This in turn made the household system in rural Tuscany effectively two-tiered. Those who enjoyed the use of a farm lived in large domestic communities, which were usually headed by a married couple. Those who did not lived in much smaller households, which frequently lacked a married chief.

Although the data are not as clear, the peasant households of medieval England may have been organized in a similar fashion. For example, Edward Britton studied 128 families of Broughton, Huntingdonshire, in the period 1288 to 1340, on the basis of manorial court rolls.[22] He divides them into four categories, which he labels A, B, C, and D. The classification reflects the number of times the male head of the family served in some official capacity at the manorial court, with Category A including the most prominent residents, and D the least. He argues persuasively that the men who appear most frequently at court also head the richest families.

The differences in household organization across the four categories are quite pronounced. Category A includes 36 percent of the households, but more than one-half the population. Category C contains a little more than half the village households and only a little more than one-third the population. Category B is small in size (12 percent of the households) and intermediate in its characteristics; it may not constitute a coherent group. And Category D consists of persons who appear sporadically at court—outsiders to the village, drifters, and the like. Almost nothing can be ascertained about the domestic life (if they had one) of the floating population.

The real contrast shows up in the two large categories, A and C. The households in Category A are large, those in C quite small. It is harder to compare marital arrangements, as Britton notes that "in the discussion of internal family structure . . . the bulk of information relates to A families." But even this suggests that many of the small C households lacked a married couple. And the richer households have proportionately more women and children (or at least yield more data about children). They dominate certain economic activities, such as ale brewing.

It is quite clear that the households within the village of Broughton were not cut from a single mold; sharp differences separate the most prominent one-third of the families from those beneath them on the social scale. The rich families seem to have been the true centers of production within the village, and this implies that they recruited workers from the less resourceful homes. The peasants of Broughton do not look very different from the Tuscan peasants of a later period.

It remains to inquire whether, when, and why individuals may have passed back and forth between the two tiers. This in turn requires that we examine the dynamic aspects of the household system, the processes underlying the largely static ideals and goals, rules and circumstances, we have so far considered.

PROCESSES

The two chief functions classically associated with households are reproduction and production: the procreation and rearing of children, and the material support of household members.

As far as we can judge, at no moment in its long history did the medieval population multiply without restraint, or even at high biological rates. The chief external check upon the increase in numbers was death rates, which soared to fabulous levels during the great epidemics of the closing Middle Ages. But apparently too, alongside this "positive check" (to resort to Malthusian terminology), "preventive checks" were also functioning, to reduce levels of nuptiality and perhaps even of marital fertility.

Marriage and Property

As far as surveys allow us to discern, at all times medieval society contained large numbers of adult men and women living without a spouse and who were sexually inactive, even outside the religious life. The medieval family more often than not has few children. In the great ninth-century survey of St. Germain-des-Prés, the paucity of children attributed to the households makes it hard to see how the community was even maintaining its numbers. Social changes after the twelfth century obstructed marriage particularly for women, and the large numbers of unmarriageable girls, especially in the towns, posed the much-discussed *Frauenfrage*, the "woman question," of the period. As mentioned, the donation of dowries to poor girls, allowing them to marry, became in this late medieval world a principal expression of Christian charity.

From earliest medieval times, the institutions of dowry and reverse dowry required that either or both bride and groom own some property, at least within some segments of society. From the central Middle Ages, it had also become essential that the groom engage in an occupation or profession. In the countryside, the young man would usually have to own or lease his own farm. In the city he had to be well embarked and successful in his trade before contemplating marriage. Marriage (and a license to procreate) was thus closely linked with the ownership, or at least the productive use, of property.

There were, to be sure, differences between urban and rural marriages, which also help explain the "demographic deficit" of towns, their failure to match the countryside in rates of reproduction. Usually, the young peasant had first to marry before he undertook the cultivation of a farm; he needed the help of a wife and eventually children. In the city, the merchant or artisan had first to achieve success in his trade before taking a wife and assuming the burdens of a family. In a rural setting, marriage was prerequisite to productive performance; among urban dwellers, it was its recognition and reward. But in both environments, marriage was closely linked with property or a job, and the enjoyment of income.

The control of marriages thus seems to have been the most important preventive check regulating the numbers of the medieval community. This means in turn that the long-term demographic trend affected nuptiality, and with it the number, size, and composition of medieval households. In periods of demographic expansion, as in the late thirteenth century or again after 1460, the heightened competition for farms or jobs made it difficult for young men to leave their households of origin. They lingered on, swelling the size and adding to the complexity of the domestic units. Conversely, in periods of demographic decline, as in the late fourteenth century, powerful incentives were called into play, encouraging early marriages and early departures of young persons from their parents' homes. Landlords feared that as the population shrank, tenures would be abandoned; city employers faced difficulties in recruiting workers; and the governments were threatened with diminished revenues. The common reacton to falling population was to reduce rents, offer higher wages, and lower taxes—all of which were designed to attract younger people to the farms and the jobs, and into marriage.

It is interesting that younger marriages did not mean larger households; quite the contrary. A community in the early stages of growth is likely to contain many young families, still with few children and a simple structure. The big and complex households, once thought typical of traditional society, are typical only of certain periods of high population densities. They more truly reflect efforts to limit marriages and expansion, rather than vigorous growth.

Economic trends also affected the number, size, and character of households. The number of households in a community depended on the number of farms in the countryside or of "basic" jobs (that is, those remunerative enough to support a family) in the city. Expansion in the area of settlement (which occurred in the central Middle Ages) or the introduction of new industries should have given a powerful thrust to population expansion. Indeed, roughly from the year 1000 to 1250 these movements were occurring simultaneously, although we do not have precise statistics to illustrate their relationship.

Molded by powerful demographic and economic forces, the medieval household was not characterized by a timeless uniformity or stability. For example, at the small town of Prato in Tuscany, average household size was 4.1 persons in 1298–1305, 3.5 persons in 1372, and 3.7 persons in 1427. In the city of Florence the average figure was 3.8 persons in 1427, 4.89 in 1469, 5.20 in 1480, and 5.66 in 1552.[23]

The sensitivity of household size and structure to long-term demographic and economic trends argues strongly that population dynamics in medieval society was already at least partially functioning as a self-regulating or homeostatic system. Population growth unaccompanied by economic expansion pushed up the age (or reduced the possibilities) of marriage, especially for males.[24] Although the age of marriage for women is usually considered the chief determinant of marital fertility, if a mature male marries a young bride, his wife is likely to be widowed when still relatively young. Many of these medieval widows did not remarry; they were effectively freed from the risk of pregnancy, while still biologically capable of bearing children.

How effective was this "preventive check" in protecting the medieval world from crises of overpopulation? The question raises one of the great, still unresolved problems of medieval demographic history. Around 1300, the population in many European areas had attained extraordinary size. For example, the region of Tuscany in Italy may have had 2 million people by then, and would not contain comparable numbers until after 1850.[25] Many other examples of similarly crowded regions could be cited.[26] Without the aid of a developed technology or efficient transport, how could such numbers have been supported? Many historians agree that they could not in fact have been supported. For them, the great demographic catastrophe of the middle and late fourteenth century ill conceals a true Malthusian reckoning.

There is an apparent discrepancy in our evidence: the medieval population system shows some characteristics of a self-regulating mechanism, but it does not seem to have been powerful enough to ward off a Malthusian crisis in the fourteenth century. The explanation is admittedly speculative. The need to preserve property and manage it efficiently did work to regulate marraiges, but the regulations became effective only above a certain threshold of wealth. The poor, without access to land or capital, were not under pressure to practice restraint in their marriages.

The marital behavior of Florentines in 1427 suggests such a threshold. We can divide the approximately 10,000 households of the city into quartiles based on ascending wealth (see Table 6.3), and then calculate the distribution of presumably fertile married couples across them (the wife not older than 47). The poorest 25 percent of Florentine households contains 25.20 percent of the married couples—a nearly perfect match. But the second quartile in

Table 6.3. Married women without recent babies (0–2 years old), by age, Florence and the rural quarter of Santo Spirito, 1427.

Ages	Florence			Santo Spirito		
	Married women	No babies	%	Married women	No babies	%
13–17	236	174	73.72	229	185	80.78
18–22	1236	406	32.84	1225	462	37.71
23–27	1092	295	27.01	1120	289	25.80
28–32	1173	434	36.99	1227	354	28.85
33–37	702	317	45.15	852	275	32.27
38–42	711	479	67.36	993	552	55.58
43–47	490	450	91.83	639	521	81.53

Source: Florentine Catasto of 1427–30.

ascending wealth contains only 21.10 percent of the married, the third 22.41, and the richest 30.30. In other words, the influence of wealth upon marriage seems to have no effect on the poorest quarter of the urban households.

In the decades before the Black Death, when rents were high and wages low, the poor formed a particularly large segment of the population. They were presumably not subject in their demographic behavior to the kind of discipline that the ownership or care of important resources imposed. Perhaps it was this large and unrestrained social group that provoked the Malthusian crisis of the middle fourteenth century.

But the great mortalities conferred certain benefits on those who survived them. Rents fell, wages grew, and terms of tenancy improved for the cultivators. Income was now more fairly distributed across society. A large proportion of the people came to enjoy the ownership of, or at least access to, significant land and capital. A larger segment of society was thus brought into the demographic system of controlled growth already in existence. If fourteenth-century Europe did indeed suffer an authentic Malthusian crisis, it was destined to be the last in its experience.

In their splendid reconstruction of the population of England in early modern times, Wrigley and Scofield conclude that already in the middle sixteenth century, the preventive check (specifically the limitation of marriages) weighed more than the positive check (disease and starvation) in controlling the numbers of English people.[27] Was it perhaps out of the readjustments of the late Middle Ages that England, and with her Europe, first developed effective means of avoiding the terrible crises of excessive numbers?

Fertility

In the communities of the Middle Ages, nuptiality was undoubtedly the chief lever used to push forward or hold back the rates of growth or decline. But was there also control of fertility within marriage? Did the effort to balance population and resources promote primitive practices of contraception?

Condemnations of contraception—of the use, for example, of *venena sterilitatis* or "poisons of sterility"—are found scattered through the moral literature since the days of the Church fathers.[28] Even in Merovingian times, the mother of St. Germain, the future bishop of Paris, tried to abort him with a potion. Noble women in twelfth-century France may have practiced some form of birth control.[29] In the fifteenth century, the great preacher Bernardine of Siena was particularly outspoken in his censures:

> And so I advise you [women of Siena] that you bring your daughters tomorrow, and I promise you that never shall you hear a more beneficial sermon. I don't say that your married daughters should come, I say both the married and those to be married . . . I have grave forebodings about you, as I believe that very few of those in the married state will be saved. Out of 1000 marriages, 999, I believe, are of the devil.[30]

And he elsewhere exclaims: "Oh, in how many unspeakable and unbelievable ways do husbands abuse their wives! Who could ever state them with decency?"[31] Are these charges grossly exaggerated, or do they suggest that the practice of contraception really was widespread within Tuscan towns of the fifteenth century?

The question leads us to look again at one of the best illuminated of all medieval communities, the city of Florence in the fourteenth and fifteenth centuries. But even here the data are still not entirely satisfactory. For example, the numerous family memoirs (*ricordi*) yield many direct references to births, and these suggest that Florentine wives were about as fertile as biology allowed.[32] Yet the *ricordi* represent the behavior of a particular, privileged class, the elite of Florentine merchants. It cannot be assumed that their actions were typical too of their less advantaged neighbors.

The surveys, and particularly the great Catasto of 1427, illuminate all social groups, but they do not record vital events, at least not comprehensively.[33] They present a still picture of Tuscan society at a particular moment in time. We can isolate particular groups—babies and women of child-bearing years, for example—and examine their associations. But almost always alternate hypotheses can be proposed to explain the relationships. Still, the surveys at least can show patterns of association within the Florentine or Tuscan population, and specify the problems that have to be explained. One such problem is that rural wives and rich wives in the city appear with many more babies than do the urban poor and middle-class married women.

In looking for evidence of contraception in Tuscan marriages, close attention should focus on married women, young enough to bear children, who nonetheless appear in the survey without a recent baby. A recent baby is here taken to be an infant registered in the Catasto as age 2 or younger. We exclude, however, babies added after the first redaction of the survey, because wealthy households were more likely than the poor to keep the tax office informed of additional births.[34]

Table 6.3 shows, for categories of ascending ages, the percentage of married women appearing without a baby age 2 or younger, in the city of Florence and in the rural quarter of Santo Spirito. To minimize the influence of favored ages, the categories center on numbers evenly divisible by 10 and 5.

Up to approximately age 22, apparently barren married women are actually more numerous in the countryside than in the city, but this doubtless reflects generally later first marriages for women in rural areas. Married but childless women are fewest in the city in the age category 23–27, indicating that these were the years of maximum fertility in the urban marriages. Thereafter their numbers grow substantially, and this implies an early decline in the fertility of urban wives. So also, after the middle 20s, the differences in the apparent fertility of urban and rural wives grow progressively more marked. At approximately age 35, nearly one-half the urban wives appear barren, as opposed to less than one-third in the countryside. Possible differences in the death rates of babies between city and countryside do not offer an adequate explanation for this early decline in urban fertility. Presumably a baby born to a woman age 25 would not be subject to substantially greater risks of dying than one born to a mother age 30. Yet many more urban wives age 30 appear without a recent baby, than do those of age 25.

The decline of fertility among married women at an earlier age in Florence than in the countryside is *prima facie* evidence of some control of fertility within the urban marriage. But we cannot assume that all urban wives were equally fertile—or infertile. To identify the fertile and infertile groups, we again divide the 10,000 households of the city into four quartiles, by ascending order of wealth, and count the numbers of married women who appear with a baby age 2 or under (additions of babies are excluded).

The contrast in apparent fertility among the four quartiles is very marked, and the richest women appear with substantially larger numbers of babies. The richest 25 percent of the households contain 30.30 percent of the married women and 37.07 percent of babies age 2 or younger. The third quartile contains 22.41 percent of the married women and only 21.88 percent of the babies. While the poorest urban households may well have suffered higher infant mortalities than the richest, it is not likely that middle-class mothers in this third quartile lost many more babies than did the richest matrons. In other words, if some urban wives were controlling their fertility, they must be sought primarily among the poor and middle-class households, and less so among the rich.

In Table 6.4, we contrast the third and fourth quartiles, which together comprise the richest half of the Florentine population.

All the women of the city, even the richest, reach their peak fertility in their middle 20s, but the wealthiest quartile of Florentine wives surpass in their apparent fertility not merely the destitute, but also women in the quartile immediately below their own, who make up with them the richest half of the Florentine population. The difference at approximate age 25 is particularly striking, amounting to 10 points. How can we explain this sharp contrast, not between the destitute and the propertied, but between the Florentine middle-class and the rich? It seems reasonable to conclude that families with limited resources wanted limited numbers of babies, and somehow achieved that goal. Even the fertility of the richest wives falls off at a notably early age, in comparison with married women of the countryside. Were they too limiting their fertility late in their marriages?

The evidence is admittedly indirect, but it does imply that married

Table 6.4. Married women without recent babies, by age, in the third and fourth quartiles of Florentine households, by ascending wealth, 1427.

Ages	Third quartile (233–817 florins)			Fourth quartile (over 817 florins)		
	Married women	No babies	%	Married women	No babies	%
13–17	49	37	75.51	91	76	83.51
18–22	276	100	36.23	446	112	25.11
23–27	198	61	30.80	426	87	20.42
28–32	239	88	36.82	388	137	35.30
33–37	158	67	42.40	187	84	44.91
38–42	148	102	68.91	171	111	64.91
43–47	112	102	91.07	107	95	88.78

Source: Florentine Catasto of 1427–30.

couples of the low and middle classes within the city were particularly prone to the practices that Bernardine condemned. Great wealth conveys many advantages, and wealthy couples apparently found it easier to respect the Church's hard prohibition of contraception within marriage.

Entrances and Exits

Birth was the chief way of entering the household, and death the chief exit. But the medieval household gained and lost members in other ways over the entire course of its developmental cycle. The Catasto of the city of Florence offers a unique opportunity to observe these entrances and exits, in fact the transfer of members at different ages from one household to another. Table 6.5 shows the distribution by sex and by age across the usual four quartiles of urban households, arranged in ascending order of wealth.

It helps to clarify Table 6.5 to note that the survey respondents had strong preferences for certain ages (especially those ending in 0 or 5), and that certain segments of the population were more prone than others to report their ages in those rounded numbers. The poor were particularly given to this error, and women also showed a stronger propensity than men to report their years at these preferred ages.[35] To offset this tendency, we center our intervals at preferred ages (ending in 0 and 5), but even this strategy cannot entirely offset the influence of age heaping. This practice helps explain otherwise puzzling shifts in numbers, particularly at the higher age levels.

According to the "law of the Catasto," the survey did not count servants or apprentices with the households of their masters, but with their families of origin. This obscures one of the chief conduits by which persons transferred from one household to another. Nor does the census track babies sent forth from the home to be nursed, as they too would be counted with their families of origin.

We might expect that 25 percent of the households would contain roughly 25 percent of the population, both of women and of men, but the table shows that this is clearly not the case. The richest fourth of the households consistently contains more than one-quarter of the population. Differential death rates, especially between rich and poor, may have affected these distributions. The poor may have higher mortality than the rich, especially among children; this may have been a factor in the tendency of the richest households to gather in ever larger proportions of growing children. On the other hand, the real contrast in the table is not between the rich and the destitute, but between the richer quarter and the remaining three-quarters of the households. It is not likely that members in households with capital between 217 and 817 florins had a different ex-

Table 6.5. Distribution of household members by age, sex, and wealth quartiles (in florins), Florence, 1427.

	Wealth quartile				
	First (0–33)	Second (34–216)	Third (217–817)	Fourth (over 817)	Totals
Households	2518	2523	2482	2511	10034
Percent	25.09	25.14	24.73	25.02	99.99
Married women	1264	1107	1124	1520	5015
Percent	25.20	22.07	22.41	30.30	99.98
Ages 0 to 2					
Women	332	337	371	557	1597
Percent	20.78	21.10	23.23	34.87	99.98
Men	386	355	378	715	1834
Percent	21.04	19.35	20.61	38.98	99.97
Sex ratio	116	105	102	128	115
Ages 3 to 7					
Women	459	463	522	935	2379
Percent	19.29	19.46	21.94	39.30	99.98
Men	566	490	580	1094	2730
Percent	20.73	17.94	21.24	40.07	99.98
Sex ratio	121	106	111	117	115
Ages 8 to 12					
Women	356	352	433	792	1933
Percent	18.41	18.21	22.40	40.97	99.99
Men	431	362	517	979	2289
Percent	18.82	15.81	22.58	42.76	99.97
Sex ratio	121	103	119	124	118
Ages 13 to 17					
Women	285	227	326	580	1418
Percent	20.09	16.00	22.99	40.90	99.98
Men	286	299	412	783	1780
Percent	16.06	16.79	23.14	43.98	99.98
Sex ratio	100	132	126	135	126
Ages 18 to 22					
Women	273	256	321	409	1259
Percent	21.68	20.33	25.49	32.48	99.98
Men	323	273	358	529	1483
Percent	21.78	18.40	24.14	35.67	99.99
Sex ratio	118	107	112	129	118

Table 6.5 (*continued*)

	Wealth quartile				
	First (0–33)	Second (34–216)	Third (217–817)	Fourth (over 817)	Totals
Ages 23 to 27					
Women	209	225	208	350	992
Percent	21.06	22.68	20.96	35.28	99.98
Men	292	297	372	520	1481
Percent	19.71	20.05	25.11	35.11	99.98
Sex ratio	140	132	179	149	149
Ages 28 to 32					
Women	263	249	253	385	1150
Percent	2.86	21.65	22.00	33.47	99.98
Men	296	333	391	534	1534
Percent	19.29	20.40	25.48	34.81	99.98
Sex ratio	113	134	155	139	133
Ages 33 to 37					
Women	216	160	173	225	774
Percent	27.90	20.67	22.35	29.06	99.98
Men	243	227	316	394	1180
Percent	20.59	19.23	26.77	33.38	99.98
Sex ratio	113	142	183	175	152
Ages 38 to 42					
Women	241	213	199	241	894
Percent	26.95	23.82	22.25	26.95	99.97
Men	233	272	296	362	1163
Percent	20.03	23.38	25.45	31.12	99.98
Sex ratio	97	128	149	150	130
Ages 43 to 47					
Women	194	174	179	182	729
Percent	26.61	23.86	24.55	24.96	99.99
Men	209	162	181	299	851
Percent	24.55	19.03	21.26	35.13	98.98
Sex ratio	108	93	101	164	117

Source: Florentine Catasto of 1427–30.

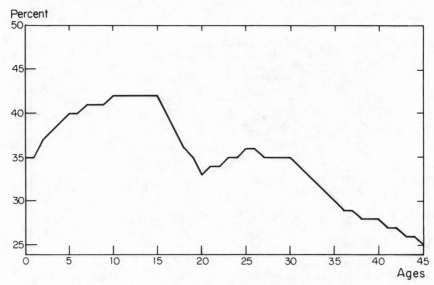

Figure 6.1. Males in the richest quartile of Florentine households, 1427.

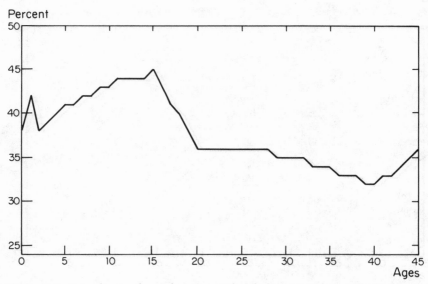

Figure 6.2. Females in the richest quartile of Florentine households, 1427.

perience of mortality than those in the quartile households assessed at more than 817 florins. And if differential death rates partly explain declining proportions of children in poor households, they do not explain the opposite phenomenon: the apparent drift of young adults from richer to poorer homes. We would argue, in sum, that the shifting proportions of men and women across the four quartiles primarily reflect actual transfers of persons in and out of households, and across wealth categories.

Table 6.5 again indicates that the household system was two-tiered. A set of wealthy and large households formed up to a quarter of the total, and a contrasting set of poorer and smaller households made up the remaining three-fourths. Members were continuously transferring back and forth between the two sets.

The overall pattern in the circulation of members between the sets was similar for men and for women, but there are also some significant differences in the movements of the two sexes. The richest households tend to gather in both boys and girls as they age, from birth up to their middle teens. At exact age 15, the 25 percent of wealthy households contain 45 percent of the boys and 43.5 percent of the girls (as opposed to 39 percent and 35 percent respectively of the cohort of babies, age 0–2).

This drift of children primarily means that wealthy households were taking in orphaned relatives. The incoming children probably also included many young relatives who had lost their fathers, and whose mothers had remarried and deserted them.[36] The mother joined the household of her new husband, but usually did not take her children with her. The kindred of her late husband had to look to their care. Some of the children were the illegitimate offspring of the family head who received them. Then too, some households took in children and supported them solely "for the love of God."[37]

If we had data on servants and apprentices, we would undoubtedly observe an even more massive drift of young persons into and out of the homes of the wealthy. We know from other sources that "life-cycle" servants were numerous at Florence, as widely in traditional society. These young people, girls especially, spent their years of late childhood in service; they thereby earned their keep and accumulated from their earnings the dowry they needed for marriage.[38] While the young servants had no claim on the household resources, nonetheless they shared many of its advantages, such as a better diet, assured shelter and clothing, and the like.

The remarkable conclusion is that the set of wealthy households was carrying, as it were, disproportionate numbers of the community's children through the dangerous years of early life. This top quartile was rearing nearly one-half the children. Because servants are excluded, we can assume that the true proportion is in fact much higher. Conversely, the poorer households were consigning many of their children into the care of the wealthy.

After their middle teens, both boys and girls begin to slip down the categories of wealth. The fall is sharpest between the interval ages 13–17 and 18–22. The proportion of men found in the richest quartile then slips from 44 to 35.6 percent, a fall of over 8 points. The proportion of girls also slides from 41 to 32.5 percent, again by almost 8 points. At these ages many young men were leaving the households where they had been reared, and striking out on their own. For girls, this was the period of marriage (the average age of first marriage for girls at Florence was 17.6 years).

Girls usually married downward, for several reasons. Their husbands, at approximate age 30, were not likely to be as wealthy as their fathers, who would be about 50. Then too, the age difference between men and women at first marriage was very great (approximately 13 years). Men married late, and many, especially younger sons, were not allowed or did not wish to marry at all. The young women seeking grooms were likely to be more numerous than the young men in search of brides. The marriage market was thus unfavorable for women. If they wished to marry at all, some girls would have to accept mates from social levels less exalted than their own.[39]

The social status of males stabilizes through their late 40s. The proportion of males found in the richest quarter hovers around 35 percent. A favorable marriage, at approximately age 30, helped shore up their social position. But the slippage of women continues after their early 20s. The richest households no longer contain many women in their 40s; the figure hovers around 25 percent. And the sex ratio of the wealthy soars to 150 and more, showing three men for every two women in middle age.

Why are aging women leaving the wealthiest households? We must again look to the operations of the marriage market. The large age difference between husband and wife meant that many wives would be widowed at comparatively young ages. At the dissolution of the marriage, the widow received her dowry, but Florentine law did not recognize community property. In other words, she received no share of the acquisitions which her household had made during her years of marriage—a crucial disability.

The woman now faced an obvious choice: either to remarry, or live in widowhood. But if women entered first marriage under unfavorable terms, the terms became even worse in any subsequent unions. The Catasto shows that as the age of the husband advances, so also does the difference in years separating him from his wife; the widower who remarried usually chose a wife younger than the spouse he had lost. Aging widowers preferred fresh young maidens, and this either reduced the chances of a widow to remarry, or worsened her terms for taking another spouse.

If she chose widowhood, the likelihood of social slippage was even greater. Widows were a numerous but not a particularly wealthy group at Florence. In the poorest quartile of households, women actually outnumber men in the age bracket 38 to 42, and are nearly as many between 43 and 47 (the attraction of age 40 for women has an influence here). The social immiseration of older women, often deplored in our own society, had a medieval precedent.

In sum, vertical social mobility for Florentine women was not unknown, but in the aggregate was limited to childhood. After her middle teens, when the woman married she took a downturn, and would slip still further if she had to remarry or live as a widow. Boys also slipped downward as they entered adult life and moved out from their households of origin. But mastery of a trade or profession, and the favorable terms with which they entered marriage, shored up their social position. Women were dependent on marriage alone to define their status, and the Florentine marriage pattern did not treat them well.

The Household System

The two-tiered system of households was not limited to Florence alone. All our evidence, from all periods and places of the medieval world, indicates that rich households were bigger, and presumably more complex, than the poor. Britton's study of the families of Broughton shows that the richest third of the households contained more than one-half the population.[40] Although the data do not permit precise tracking of movement in and out of these households, it is likely that such movement was related to age. On a more general level, the group of rural historians associated with J. Ambrose Raftis at Toronto has been able to show considerable variation in the peasant households of medieval England. The conclusion seems safe that several types of households (at the very least two) existed simultaneously in medieval society. And the study of the linkages and flows among them ought now to be a principal goal of future research.

In a recent, stimulating study, the English demographer J. Hajnal identifies two kinds of the "pre-industrial household formation system," the one characteristic of northwest Europe in the early modern period, and the second of India and China.[41] One of the rules governing household formation in northwest Europe is: "Young people before marriage often circulate between households as servants."

The medieval household system reconstructed on the basis of the Florentine data resembles Hajnal's model in that the flow of young persons in and out of households in relation to their ages is crucial to it. It differs, however, in two important ways. The flow of young people among households is not, at Florence, limited to servants. And the movement is across wealth categories, up or down the social scale. Hajnal seems to assume that the transfers are predominantly horizontal, that is, between households of comparable wealth and social status. He does not explore the possibilities that the giving and receivng households differed in the resources they commanded, and that the transfers were in different directions at different ages. These issues merit further examination.

At Florence, the system treated badly certain members of the community, most notably older women. Impoverished widows filled the ranks of the Florentine *miserabiles*. But the system also performed some notable services for the community. The most resourceful households reared a disproportionate number of children; they passed their parlous early years in a privileged environment. And it gave a large proportion of the population—more than could otherwise be expected—some exposure to elite society and its way of life. Perhaps too, it lessened class antagonisms and produced a more integrated community. In young adulthood, many of these persons transferred back into smaller, poorer households. But surely they retained throughout their lives some social and cultural benefits from their childhood experiences.

CONCLUSION

THE STUDY of medieval households requires the use of scattered, diverse, and usually difficult sources, but even out of them a coherent picture emerges. The end of slavery and the insistence of the Church on both monogamy and exogamy reduced the range of variation that had marked households in ancient societies. No longer could a rich senator call hundreds of slaves into his personal service; nor could a barbarian chief gather in numerous wives and concubines, to the deprivation of less privileged males. This is not to suggest that Roman and barbarian households were similar. The importance of large kindreds among the barbarians, the *Sippe*, obscured the division among households, and the *Sippe* themselves differed greatly in numbers, wealth, and prestige. The classical Mediterranean world did not know, or had long since lost, such kindreds. But neither Romans nor barbarians possessed a symmetrical household system—symmetrical in the simple sense that the rich lived with their wives and children in a manner comparable to the poor. A great social achievement of the early Middle Ages was the imposition of the same rules of sexual and domestic conduct on both rich and poor. The king in his palace, the peasant in his hovel: neither one was exempt. Cheating might have been easier for the mighty, but they could not claim women or slaves as a right. Poor men's chances of gaining a wife and producing progeny were enhanced. It is very likely that the fairer distribution of women across society helped reduce abductions and rapes and levels of violence generally, in the early Middle Ages.

The marriage pattern was a powerful factor in molding the internal life of families. Late ages at first marriage for both men and women—a custom which Tacitus recognized already among the barbarian Germans—seem to have been the norm in medieval society through to the eleventh and twelfth centuries. In the later Middle Ages, the age of first marriage for girls drops, most notably among the nobility and in the cities, while that for males remains high or moves even higher. This change is linked with a shift in the terms of marriage. Under the barbarian model of the early Middle Ages, the groom, or his family, assumed the chief costs in the establishment of the new household, but in the later medieval period, the bride, or those providing for her, had to assume the larger share of the "burdens of matrimony." The classical dowry, which had all but disappeared in the West in the early medieval centuries, makes a triumphant return.

The peculiar structure of the household in the central Middle Ages helped shape domestic roles and emotions. It was difficult for partners widely separated in age to become true companions and helpmates, but that ideal is still encountered in the literature, alongside a continuing misogynism inherited from the ancient world. The huge loss of population in the later medieval centuries helped inspire much more positive attitudes toward marriage, given eloquent expression by Leonardo Bruni in Italy, Erasmus in the north, and other humanist scholars. Set between the generations of fathers and children, mothers frequently assumed the functions of intermediaries, and they also passed on cultural values down the generations. Deeply involved in socializing the young, mothers were instrumental in preserving and enriching the cultural tradition. Amid the tumult of the late Middle Ages, several great churchmen vigorously promote devotions to St. Joseph; the veneration he attracts seems thinly to disguise a cult of paternal care. In conditions that contemporaries likened to Joseph's Egypt, the cult lent encouragement to fathers. The crisis of family life in the late Middle Ages drew more attention to children. But had they ever been really forgotten? Parents delighted in them for about as far back as there are records. The medieval family was never dead to sentiment; it is only poor in sources.

I have said that from approximately the year 700 medieval households were commensurate—a quality evident in their utilization in many surveys and censuses. But if the differences among households were reduced, they were not entirely erased. Rich households were at all times larger and more complex than those of the poor. By the end of the Middle Ages, in certain favored areas such as Tuscany, we can see how the rich and poor units were combined under an integrated system. The system shows two salient features. The rich households were deeply involved in production or some other form of social service. In rural areas, for example, many would be associated with large and productive farms; in the city, with important commercial or administrative functions. The top tier recruited workers, usually young in age, from families with fewer resources. These transfers of persons across levels of wealth meant that a significant proportion of the population passed their young years amid favored surroundings. This process blocked the encrustation of social classes and may have helped produce a more integrated society.

These observations on medieval households yield a general conclusion regarding the study of households in history. Not all medieval households were centers of production or even of reproduction, if we include in the latter category the rearing of children without interruption through to adulthood. Indeed, from two-thirds to three-quarters of households—to make a rough judgment from English and Italian data—were not. This means that the study of households everywhere cannot be limited to individual domestic units, taken in isolation. Rather, the system joining them must be reconstructed and examined. The system, together with the separate households, helped assure that reproduction and production would be carried on somewhere in society, and that this civilization would survive.

REFERENCES

The following list of references is divided into sources and studies, as is conventional in historical works. All references in the notes cite the author's last name (or occasionally title or abbreviated title, when the work is a series) and the date of publication; the date ascribed to ancient and medieval authors represents the date of publication of the edition used here. Also included below are full citations for abbreviations, such as *ASS* or *MGH*. which are conventionally used in medieval studies.

SOURCES

Adam of Bremen. 1917. *Gesta hammaburgensis ecclesiae pontificum. MGH* in usum scholarum. Hanover and Leipzig.
—— 1959. *History of the Archbishops of Hamburg-Bremen,* trans. F. J. Tschan. Columbia University Records of Civilization. New York.
Aelred of Rievaulx. 1971. *The Works of Aelred of Rievaulx, 1: Treatises, The Pastoral Prayer.* Cistercian Fathers Series, 2. Spencer. Mass.
Alain de Lille. 1908. *The Complaint of Nature,* trans. Douglas M. Moffat. Yale Studies in English, 36. New York.
Alberti, Leon Battista. 1960. I libri della famiglia, *Opere volgari,* ed. Cecil Grayson. I:1–341. Scrittori d'Italia, 218. Bari.
Amalfi. 1917, 1951. *Codice diplomatico Amalfitano,* ed. R. Filangieri. 2 vols. Naples and Trani.
Ancient Roman Statutes. 1961. *Ancient Roman Statutes: A Translation with Introduction, Commentary, Glossary and index,* ed. Allan Chester Johnson, Paul Robinson Coleman-Norton, and Frank Card Bourne. Austin.
Aquinas, Thomas. 1882–1948. *Sancti Thomae Aquinatis Opera omnia iussu impensaque Leonis XIII.* 16 vols. Rome.
Aristotle. 1921–28. *The Works of Aristotle,* ed. W. D. Ross. 12 vols. Oxford.
—— 1946. *The Politics of Aristotle,* trans. with an Introduction, Notes, and Appendices by Ernest Barker. Oxford.
ASF. Archivio di Stato di Firenze.
ASS. 1643– *Acta sanctorum quotquot toto orbe coluntur.* Antwerp.
Augustine. 1837. *Opera omnia.* Paris.

—— 1894. *De genesi ad litteram libri xii*, ed. J. Zycha. Corpus scriptorum ecclesiasticorum latinorum, 28, 1. Prague and Vienna.

—— 1952. *The City of God*, trans. G. Walsh and Grace Monahan. The Fathers of the Church: A New Translation. New York.

—— 1955. *Treatises on Marriage and Other Subjects*, trans. Charles T. Wilcox and others. The Fathers of the Church: A New Translation. New York.

—— 1963. *Confessions*, trans. Rex Warner, with an Introduction by Vernon J. Bourke. New York and Toronto.

Ausonius. 1967–68. *Ausonius*, with an English trans. by Hugh G. Evelyn White. 2 vols. Loeb Classical Library. Cambridge, Mass. and London.

Aymeri de Narbonne. 1887. *Aymeri de Narbonne. Chanson de Geste*, ed. Louis Demaison. Société des anciens textes français, 25. Paris.

Barbaros, Francesco. 1915. "De re uxoria liber," ed. A. Gnesotto, *Atti e memorie della R. Accademia lucchese di scienze, lettere ed arti di Padova*. 32: 7–105.

—— 1978. "On Marriage," trans. Benjamin Kohl, in *The Earthly Republic: Italian Humanists on Government and Society*, pp. 177–228. Philadelphia.

Battaglia da Rimini, Marcha di Marco. 1913. *Breviarum italicae historicae*, ed. Aldo Francesco Massera. Rerum Italicarum Scriptores, n.s. 16, pt. 3. Città di Castello.

Bede. 1971. *Baedae opera historica*, with an English Trans. by J. E. King. Loeb Classical Library. Cambridge, Mass., and London.

Bernard of Anjou. 1899. Miracula s. Fidis matyris aginnensis auctore Bernardo scholastico, in *AB* 8: 54–85.

Bernardino da Feltre. 1964. *Sermoni del beato Bernardino Tomitano da Feltre*, ed. P. Carlo Varische da Milano, O.F.M. Cap. 3 vols. Milan.

Bernardino da Siena. 1888. *Le prediche volgari di San Bernadino da Siena dette nella Piazza del Campo l'anno mccccxxvii*, ed. L. Banchi. 3 vols. Siena.

—— 1950–65. *Opera Omnia*, ed. PP. Collegii S. Bonaventurae. 9 vols. Florence.

Bethada. 1922. *Bethada Náem nÉrenn. Lives of Irish Saints*, ed. and trans. Charles Plummer. 2 vols. Oxford.

Bobbio. 1905. *Codice diplomatico del monastero di S. Columbano di Bobbio fino all'anno mccviii*, ed. Carlo Cipolla. 3 vols. Fonti per la storia d'Italia. 52–54. Rome.

Bologna Stat. 1937. *Statuti di Bologna dell'anno 1288*, ed. Gina Fasoli and Pietro Sella. Studi e Testi, 73. Città di Vaticano.

Bongi, S., ed. 1886. "Statuto inedito della casa de' Corbolini," *Atti della R. Accademia lucchese di scienze, lettere ed arti* 24: 471–87.

Bracton. 1968–77. *On the Laws and Customs of England*, ed. George E. Woodbine and trans. Samuel E. Thorne. 4 vols. Cambridge, Mass.

Bruni, Leonardo Aretino. 1847. "De Florentinorum Republica," trans. from the Greek by B. Moneta, in *Philippi Villani Liber de civitatis Florentiae famosis civibus . . . et de Florentinorum litteratura principes fere synchroni scriptores*, ed. G. C. Galletti. Florence.

Caffaro. 1890–1929. *Annali genovesi di Caffaro e de' suoi continuatori dal MXCIX al MCCXCIII*, ed. Luigi Belgrano. Fonti per la storia d'Italia. 11–14bis. Genoa.

Cáin Adamnáin. 1905. *Cáin Adamnáin: An Old-Irish Treatise on the Law of Adamnan*, ed. and trans. Kuno Meyer, in *Analecta Oxoniensia*, Medieval and Modern Series, 12. Oxford.

Canones Theodori. 1929. *Die Canones Theodori cantuariensis und ihre Uberlieferungsformen*, ed. Paul Finsterwalder. Vienna.

Caterina da Siena. 1913. *Le Lettere di S. Caterina da Siena ridotte a migliori lezioni*, ed. P. Misciatelli. 2nd ed. Siena.

———— 1943. *The Dialogue of the Seraphic Virgin Catherine of Siena*, trans. Algar Thorold. Westminster.

Chaucer. 1933. *The Poetical Works of Chaucer*, ed. F. N. Robinson. Cambridge.

Christine de Pizane. 1982. *The Book of the City of Ladies*, trans. Earl Jeffrey Richards. New York.

Civil Law. 1932. *The Civil Law, Including the Twelve Tables, the Institutes of Gaius, the Rules of Ulpian, the Opinions of Paulus, the Enactments of Justinian, and the Constitutions of Leo*, trans. S. P. Scott. 17 vols. Cincinnati.

CI. 1954. *Corpus Iuris Civilis*, ed. P. Krueger, T. Mommsen, R. Schoell and G. Kroll. 3 vols. Berlin.

Codice Diplomatico Longobardo. 1929–33. *Codice diplomatico longobardo*, ed. Luigi Schiaparelli. 3 vols. Fonti per la storia d'Italia. 62–64. Rome.

Colonna, Egidio. 1858. *Del reggimento de' principi . . . transcritto nel 1228*, ed. Francesco Corazzini. Florence.

Consuetudini di Milano. 1866. *Liber consuetudinum Mediolani anni 1216*, ed. Francesco Berlan. Milan.

Corpus Documentorum Inquisitionis. 1889–1906. *Corpus Documentorum Inquisitionis Haereticae Pravitatis Neerlandicae*, ed. Paul Fredericq. 5 vols. Ghent.

Corpus Iuris Canonici. 1879. *Corpus Iuris Canonici*. Editio secunda Lipsiensis of E. Richter, ed. E. Friedberg. 2 vols. Leipzig.

Corvey. 1843. *Traditiones corbeienses*, ed. Paul Wigand. Leipzig.

Coûtumiers. 1896. *Coûtumiers de Normandie*, ed. E. J. Tardif. Rouen and Paris.

CS. 1966. *Vitae sanctorum Hiberniae ex codice olim salmanticensi nunc brusellensi*, ed. W. W. Heist. Subsidia Hagiographica, 28. Brussels.

Damian, Peter. 1853. "De parentelae gradibus, ad Johannem episcopum caesenatensem," *PL* 145: 191–208.

Dante. 1960. *Le opere di Dante. Testo critico della Società dantesca italiana*, 2nd ed. Florence.

Dhuoda. 1975. *Manuel pour mon fils. Introduction, texte critique, notes*, par Pierre Riché, trad. par Bernard de Vregille et Claude Mondesert, S.J. Sources chrétiennes, no. 225. Paris.

Dio. 1960. *Dio's Roman History*, trans. Earnest Cary. Loeb Classical Library. 9 vols. Cambridge, Mass., and London.

Dominici, Giovanni. 1860. *Regola del governo di cura familiare*, ed. D. Salvi. Florence.

—— 1927. *On the Education of Children*, trans. A. B. Coté, Washington, D.C.

Echternach, 1929–30. *Geschichte der Grundherrschaft Echternach im Frühmittelalter*, by Cornelius Wampach. Luxembourg.

Erasmus. 1703. *Opera omnia*. 10 vols. in 11. Leiden.

Farfa. 1879–88. *Il regesto di Farfa compilato da Gregorio da Catino*, ed. I. Giorgi and U. Balzani. 5 vols. Rome.

Florence. Stat. 1910–21. *Statuti della Repubblica fiorentina*, ed. R. Caggese. 2 vols. Florence.

Freising. 1905. *Die Traditionen des Hochstifts Freising, I: (744–962)*, ed. Theodor Bitterauf. Quellen und Eröterung zur bayerischen und deutschen Geschichte, neue Folge, 4. Munich.

Fulda. 1850. *Codex diplomaticus fuldensis*, ed. Ernst Friedrich Dronke. Cassel.

—— 1913. *Urkundbuch des Klosters Fulda*, ed. E. Z. Stengel. Marburg.

Gerson, Jean. 1960–1973. *Oeuvres complètes. Introduction, texte, et notes*, par Mgr. Glorieux. 10 vols. Paris.

Giovanni di Guiberto. 1939–40. *Notai liguri del sec. XII, 5: Giovanni di Guiberto (1200–1211)*, ed. M. W. Hall-Cole, H. C. Krueger, R. G. Reinert, and R. L. Reynolds. 2 vols. Documenti e studi per la storia del commercio e del diritto commerciale italiano, 17–18. Turin.

Giovanni Scriba. 1905. *Il cartolare di Giovanni Scriba*, ed. Mario Chiaudano and Mattia Moresco. 2 vols. Regesta chartarum Italiae, 19–20. Rome.

Gregory of Tours. 1884–1969. *Gregorii Turonensis Opera*, ed. W. Arndt and Br. Krusch. 2 vols. *MGH* Ss rerum merovingicarum. Hanover.

—— 1927. *The History of the Franks*, trans. O. M. Dalton. 2 vols. Oxford.

—— 1951. *Historiarum libri X*, ed. B. Krusch and W. Levison. *MGH* Ss rerum merovingicarum. Hanover.

Grenoble. 1869. *Cartulaires de l'église cathédrale de Grenoble dits cartulaire de Saint-Hughes*, ed. E. Jules Marion. Collection de documents inédits sur l'histoire de France. Paris.

Guibert of Nogent. 1970. *Self and Society in Medieval France: The Memoirs of Abbot Guibert of Nogent*, ed. John F. Benton. New York and Evanston.

Herodotus. 1963. *Herodotus*, with an English trans. by A. D. Godley. Loeb Classical Library. Cambridge, Mass., and London.

Hervis von Metz. 1903. *Hervis von Metz: Vorgedicht der Lothringer Geste*, ed. E. Stengel. Gesellschaft für romanische Literatur, 1. Dresden.

Hesiod. 1967. *The Homeric Hymns and Homerica*, ed. and trans. Hugh G. Evelyn White. Loeb Classical Library. Cambridge, Mass., and London.

ILCV. 1961. *Inscriptiones latinae christianae veteres*, ed. Ernestus Diehl. 4 vols. Berlin.

Irish Penitentials. 1963. *The Irish Penitentials*, ed. Ludwig Bieler, with an Appendix by D. A. Binchy. Scriptores Latini Hiberniae, 5. Dublin.

Isidore. 1911. *Isidori Hisspalensis episcopi etymologiarum sive originum libri XX*, ed. W. M. Lindsay, Oxford.

Juvenal. 1965. *Juvenal and Perseus*, trans. G. G. Ramsey. Loeb Classical Library. Cambridge, Mass., and London.

Kempe, Margery. 1944. *The Book of Margery Kempe, A.D. 1436*, ed. W. Butler Bowdon. London.

Lambertus. 1879. Lamberti Ardensis Historia comitum Ghisnensium, ed. J. Heller, in *MGH Ss*, 24, pp. 550–642. Hanover.

Laws of Alamans and Bavarians. 1979. *Laws of Alamans and Bavarians*, trans. Theodore John Rivers. Philadelphia.

Leges Alamannorum. 1966. *Leges Alamannorum*, ed. K. Lehmann. Editio altera, ed. K. A. Eckhardt. *MGH Legum Sectio I*, vol. 5, part 1. Hanover.

Leges Burgundionum. 1892. *Leges Burgundionum*, ed. L. R. de Salis. *MGH Legum Sectio I*, vol. 2, part 1. Hanover.

Leges Langobardorum. 1962. *Leges Langobardorum: Die Gesetze der Langobarden*, ed. Franz Beyerle. 2nd ed. 2 vols. Witzenhausen.

Leges Visigothorum. 1894. *Leges Visigothorum*, ed. Karolus Zeumer. *MGH Legum Sectio I*, vol 1. Hanover.

Leo Marsicanus. 1846. *Chronica*. ed. G. Pertz. *MGH Ss* 7. Hanover.

Les Narbonnais. 1898. *Les Narbonnais: Chanson de Geste*, ed. Herman Suchier. Société des anciens textes français, 42. Paris.

Lex Salica, 1949. *Lex Salica*. ed. Karl August Eckhardt. *MGH Legum Sectio I*, vol. 4, part 2. Hanover.

Liber magistri Salmonis. 1906. *Liber magistri Salmonis* (1222–26), ed. A. Ferretto, in Atti della Società Ligure di Storia Patria, 36.

Life of Christina. 1959. *The Life of Christina of Markyate, A Twelfth-Century Recluse*, ed. and trans. C. H. Talbot. Oxford.

Livy. 1967. *Livy in Fourteen Volumes*, with an English trans. by B. O. Foster. Loeb Classical Library. Cambridge, Mass., and London.

Lorsch. 1768–70. *Codex principis olim Laureshamensis abbatiae, diplomaticus*. Mannheim.

⸻ 1966–72. *Codex Laureshamensis. Lorscher Codex. Urkundenbuch der ehemahligen Fürstabtei Lorsch . . . ins Deutsche übertragen von Karl Josef Minst*. Lorsch.

Lucca Mem. e Doc. 1818–37. *Memorie e documenti per servire all'istoria del ducato di Lucca*, IV, pts. 1 and 2, and V, pts. 2 and 3. Lucca.

Lucca Reg. 1910–19. *Regesto del Capitolo di Lucca*, ed. P. Guidi and O. Parenti. Regesta chartarum Italiae, 6, 9, 18. Rome.

Lucretius. 1965. *On the Nature of the Universe* (De rerum natura), trans. James H. Mantinband. New York.

Macinghi negli Strozzi, Alessandra. 1877. *Lettere di una gentildonna fiorentina del secolo XIV ai figli esuli*, ed. Cesari Guasti. Florence.

Marbode of Rennes. 1984. *Liber decem capitulorum. Introduzione, testo critico e commento*, ed. Rosario Leotta. Rome.

Marius Aventicensis. 1894, 1961. Marii episcopi aventicensis chronica, A. CCCCLV–DLXXXI, ed. Theodor Mommsen, in *MGH, Auctores antiquissimi*, 11: 225–39. Hanover.

Martorelli, Joanot, and de Galba, Marti Joan. 1984. *Tirant lo Blanc*, trans. David H. Rosenthal. New York.

MGH. 1826– *Monumenta Germaniae Historica*. Leipzig and Hanover.

MGH Capit. 1893–97. *Capitularia regum Francorum,* ed. A. Boretius and V. Krause. 2 vols. *MGH Legum Sectio II,* 1. Hanover.

MGH Conc. 1906, 1979. *Concilia, II: Concilia aevi karolinorum,* ed. Albertus Werminghoff. *MGH Legum Sectio III.* Hanover and Leipzig.

MGH Const. 1893– *Constitutiones et acta publica imperatorum et regum. MGH Legum Sectio IV.* Hanover.

MGH Dipl. 1879– *Diplomata regum et imperatorum Germaniae.* Hanover.

MGH Ep. 1887– *MGH. Epistulae Karolini Aevi.* Berlin.

Milan. Consuet. 1872. *Le due edizioni milanese e torinese delle Consuetudini di Milano dell'anno 1215, cenni ed appunti.* ed. Francesco Berlan. Venice.

Morelli, Giovanni di Paolo. 1969. *Ricordi,* ed. V. Branca. 2nd ed. Florence.

Muratori. L. A., ed. 1739–42. *Novus thesaurus veterum inscriptionum.* 4 vols. Milan.

Novalesa. 1898. *Monumenta novalensia vetustiora raccolta degli atti e delle cronache riguardanti l'abbazia della Novalesa,* ed. Carlo Cipolla. Fonti per la storia d'Italia, 31 and 32. Rome.

Ovid. 1962. *The Art of Love and Other Poems,* trans. J. H. Mozley. Loeb Classical Library. Cambridge, Mass., and London.

Pactus legis salicae. 1962. *Pactus legis salicae,* ed. K. A. Eckhardt. *MGH Legum Sectio I,* vol 4, part 1. Hanover.

Pardessus. 1943–49. *Diplomata, chartae, epistolae, leges aliaque instrumenta ad res Gallofrancicas* spectantia prius collecta a De Brequigny et La Porte du Theil, nunc nova ratione ordinata plurimumque aucta edidit J. M. Pardessus. 2 vols. Paris.

Passio Perpetuae et Felicitatis. 1972. Passio Perpetuae et Felicitatis, in *The Acts of the Christian Martyrs,* ed. Herbert Musurillo, pp. 106–31. Oxford.

Passiones vitaeque sanctorum. 1913–29. *Passiones vitaeque sanctorum aevi Merovingici,* ed. B. Krusch and W. Levison. 2 vols. *MGH Ss rerum merovinicarum,* 6–7. Hanover and Leipzig.

Paul the Deacon. 1878. *Historia Langobardorum,* ed. Waitz. *MGH Ss in usum scholarum,* 48. Hanover.

PG. 1857–66. *Patrologiae cursus completus,* Series graeca, ed. J. P. Migne. Paris.

Philippe de Novarre. 1889. *Les quatre âges de l'homme,* ed Marcel de Fréville. Société des anciens textes français, 27. Paris.

Pisa Stat. 1870. *Statuti inediti della città di Pisa del XII al XIV secolo,* ed. Francesco Bonaini. Florence.

Pistoia Stat. pot. 1888. *Statutum potestatis communis Pistorii anni MCCLXXXXVI,* ed. L. Zdekauer. Milan.

Pitti, Buonaccorso. 1905. *Cronaca, con annotazioni,* ed. A. Bacchi della Lega. Bologna.

PL. 1841–64. *Patrologiae cursus completus,* Series latina, ed. J. P. Migne. Paris.

Plautus. 1916. *Plautus,* trans. Paul Nixon. 4 vols. Loeb Classical Library. Cambridge, Mass., and London.

Plutarch. 1920. On Affection for Offspring. *Plutarch's Moralia in Sixteen*

Volumes, trans. W. C. Helmbold. Loeb Classical Library. VI: 330–57. Cambridge, Mass., and London.

——— 1965. *Makers of Rome: Nine Lives of Plutarch*, trans. Ian Scott-Kilvert. Harmondsworth.

Polybius. 1960. *Polybius: The Histories*, trans. W. R. Paton. 6 vols. Loeb Classical Library. Cambridge, Mass., and London.

Romance of the Rose. 1971. *The Romance of the Rose by Guillaume de Lorris and Jean de Meun*, trans. Charles Dahlberg. Princeton.

Rotuli de dominabus. 1913. *Rotuli de dominabus et pueris et puellis de XII comitatibus* [1185], ed. John Horace Round. Publications of the Pipe Roll Society, 35. London.

Ss. Scriptores rerum Germanicarum.

St. Gallen. 1863– *Urkundenbuch der Abtei St. Gallen*, ed. Hermann Wartmann. Zurich.

St. Germain. 1844, 1886–95. *Polyptych de l'abbé Irminon*, ed. B. Guérard; reprinted with some revisions as *Polyptych de l'abbaye de Saint Germain-des-Prés*, ed. A. Longnon. Paris.

St. Victor. 1857. *Cartulaire de Saint Victor de Marseille*, ed. B. Guérard. 2 vols. Paris.

Scriptores Historiae Augustae. 1960. *Scriptores Historiae Augustae*, with an English trans. by David Magie. Loeb Classical Library. Cambridge, Mass., and London.

Seneca. 1971. *Naturales Quaestiones*, ed. Thomas H. Corcoran. Loeb Classical Library. Cambridge, Mass., and London.

Stubbs, William, ed. 1951. *Select Charters and Other Illustrations of English Constitutional History . . . to the Reign of Edward the First*, 9th ed. rev. by H. W. C. Davis. Oxford.

Syntagma. 1880. *Institutionum et regularum iuris romani syntagma*, ed. Rudolfus Gneist. Leipzig.

Tablettes Albertini. 1952. *Tablettes Albertini: Actes privés de l'époque vandale*, ed. C. Courtois, L. Leschi, C. Perrat and C. Saumagne. Paris.

Tacitus. 1911. *De Germania*, ed. C. Halm. Leipzig.

Tertullian. 1954. *Opera*, II: *Opera monastica*. Corpus Christianorum, Series latina, 2. Turnholt.

Theodosian Code, 1955. *The Theodosian Code and Novels and the Sirmondian Constitutions*, trans. and ed. with Commentary, Glossary, and Bibliography by C. Pharr, with T. S. Davidson and M. B. Pharr. Introduction by C. D. Williams. Princeton.

Thomas of Celano. 1904. *Life of St. Francis of Assisi*, ed. H. G. Rosedale. London.

Tirant lo Blanc. See Martorell, Joanot.

Tristan and Iseult. 1945. *The Romance of Tristan and Iseult*, as retold by Joseph Bédier, trans. Hilaire Belloc. New York.

Valerius Maximus. 1888. *Valerius Maximus factorum et dictorum memorabilium libri novem*, ed. C. Kemp. Leipzig.

Varro. 1974. *Satires ménippées*, traduction et commentaire par J.-P. Cèbe. Collection de l'école française de Rome. Rome.

Villani, Giovanni. 1823. *Cronica di Giovanni Villani a miglior edizione ridotta.* Florence.

Vincent of Beauvais. 1624. *Bibliotheca mundi,* III: *Speculum Doctrinale,* II, Liber sextus, De arte economice. Douai.

Vita Caterine. 1866. *Vita Caterine auctore Fr. Raimundo Capuano,* in *ASS,* Aprilis III: 853–959.

Vita Hedwegis. 1884. Vita sanctae Hedwegis, in *Monumenta Poloniae Historica* 4: 501–661. Lvov.

Vita Liutbirgae. 1939. *Vita Liutbirgae virginis: Das Leben der Liutbirg,* ed. O. Menzel. *MGH, Deutsches Mittelalter,* 3. Leipzig.

Vita Mathildis. 1841. *Vita Mathildis Reginae. MGH, Ss,* 4. Hanover.

Vita Melaniae. 1889. "Vita sanctae Melaniae junioris auctore coaevo et sanctae familiari," in *Analecta Bolandiana* 8: 16–63.

Vitae patrum. 1878. *Vitae patrum, PL,* vols. 73–74. Paris.

Vitae sanctorum. 1910. *Vitae sanctorum Hiberniae,* ed. C. Plummer. Oxford.

Volterra Stat. 1951. *Statuti di Volterra,* ed. Enrico Fiumi. Florence.

Xenophon. 1970. Leo Strauss, *Xenophon's Socratic Discourse: An Interpretation of the Oeconomicus,* with a literal trans. by Carnes Lord. Ithaca and London.

STUDIES

AB. Analecta Bollandiana

AESC. Annales-Economies-Sociétés-Civilisations

Anné, Lucien. 1941. *Les rites des fiançailles et la donation pour cause de mariage dans le Bas-Empire.* Dissertationes ad gradum magistri in Facultate Canonici Iuris consequendum, ser. 2 t. 33. Louvain.

Ariès, Philippe. 1965. *Centuries of Childhood.* New York.

—— 1973. *L'enfant et la vie sous l'Ancien régime.* 2nd. ed. Paris.

Arnold, Klaus. 1980. *Kind und Gesellschaft im Mittelalter und Renaissance.* Paderborn and Munich.

Astolfi, Riccardo. 1970. *Lex Julia et Papia.* Padua.

Balon, Joseph. 1963– *Ius Medii Aevi. Traité de droit salique. Etude d'exégèse et de sociologie juridiques.* Namur.

Bec, Christian. 1967. *Les marchands écrivains. Affairs et humanisme à Florence, 1375–1434.* Paris.

Bellomo, Manlio. 1961. *Richerche sui rapporti patrimoniali tra coniugi. Contributo alla storia della famiglia medievale.* Milan.

—— 1966. *Profili della famiglia italiana nell'età dei comuni.* Catania.

BHL. 1892–1913. *Bibliotheca Hagiographica Latina antiquae et mediae aetatis,* ed. Socii Bolandiani. 2 vols. Subsidia Hagiographica, 6. Supplementi. Subsidia Hagiographica, 12. Brussels.

Benson, Robert L., and Constable, Giles, eds. 1982. *Renaissance and Renewal in the Twelfth Century.* Cambridge, Mass.

Berges, W. 1938. *Die Fürstenspiegel des hohen und späten Mittelalters.* Schriften der *MGH.* Leipzig.

Biller, P. P. A. 1982. "Birth Control in the West in the Thirteenth and Fourteenth Centuries," *Past and Present*, 94: 3–26.

Boesch, Hans. 1900, 1979. *Kinderleben in der deutschen Vergangenheit. Mit Abbildungen nach den Originalen aus 15.–18. Jahrhundert.* Monographien zur deutschen Kulturgeschichte, 5. Leipzig and Cologne.

Boswell, John. 1981. *Christianity, Social Tolerance and Homosexuality in Western Europe from the Beginning of the Christian Era to the Fourteenth Century.* Chicago.

Bouchard, Constance R. 1981a. "Consanguinity and Noble Marriages in the Tenth and Eleventh Centuries," *Speculum* 56: 268–87.

——— 1981b. "The Origins of the French Nobility: A Reassessment," *American Historical Review* 86: 501–32.

Bourgeois, Emile. 1974. *Le capitulaire de Kiersy-sur-Oise, 1877. Etude sur l'Etat et le régime politique de la société carolingienne.* Geneva.

Brenner, Robert. 1976. "Agrarian Class Structure and Economic Development in Pre-Industrial Europe," *Past and Present* 70–73: 30–75.

Brissaud, Y. B. 1972. "L'infanticide à la fin du moyen âge," *RHDFE* 50: 229–56.

Britton, Edward. 1977. *The Community of the Vill. A Study in the History of the Family and Village Life in Fourteenth-Century England.* Toronto.

Brunt, P. A. 1971. *Italian Manpower, 225 B.C.-A.D. 14.* Oxford.

Buckland, W. W. 1966. *A Manual of Roman Private Law.* 3rd ed. rev. by P. Stein. Cambridge.

Bullough, Donald. 1969. "Early Medieval Social Groupings: The Terminology of Kinship," *Past and Present* 45: 3–18.

Byrne, Francis. 1971. "Tribes and Tribalism in Early Ireland," *Erin* 22: 128–65.

Carcopino, Jerome. 1940. *Daily Life in Ancient Rome*, ed. Henry T. Rowell, trans. E. O. Lorimer. New Haven.

Catherine of Siena. 1943. *The Dialogue of the Seraphic Virgin Catherine of Siena*, trans. Algar Thorold. Westminster.

CEH. 1941– *Cambridge Economic History.* Cambridge.

Chadwick, Norah. 1970. *The Celts.* London.

Champeaux, E. 1933. "*Jus sanguinis.* Trois façons de calculer la parenté au Moyen Age," *RHDFE* 4th ser. 12: 241–90.

Charles-Edwards, T. M. 1972. "Kinship, Status and the Origins of the Hide," *Past and Present* 56: 3–33.

Coleman, Emily R. 1974. "L'infanticide dans le haut Moyen Age," *AESC* 29: 315–35.

Conrad, Hermann. 1956–62. *Deutsche Rechtsgeschichte; ein Lehrbuch.* 2nd ed. 2 vols. Karlsruhe.

Corbett, Percy Ellwood. 1930. *The Roman Law of Marriage.* Oxford.

Csillag, P. 1976. *The Augustan Laws on Family Relations.* Budapest.

Dauvillier, Jean. 1933. *Le mariage dans le droit classique de l'église depuis le décret de Gratian jusqu'à la mort de Clément V (1314).* Paris.

Del Treppo, Mario, and Leone, Alfonso. 1977. *Amalfi medioevale.* Biblioteca di studi meridionali, 5. Naples.

Dennys, Rodney. 1982. *Heraldry and the Heralds.* London.

Devroey, J.-P. 1981. "Les méthodes d'analyse démographique des polyptyques du Haut Moyen Age." In *Histoire et Méthode,* ed. M.-A. Arnould et al. Acta Historica Bruxellensia, 4: 71–88.

Dewindt, Edwin Brezette. 1972. *Land and People in Holywell-cum-Needingworth.* Toronto.

Doherty, Charles. 1982. "Some Aspects of Hagiography as a Source of Irish Economic History," *Peritia* 1: 300–28.

Donahue, Charles, Jr. 1983. "The Canon Law in the Formation of Marriage and Social Practice in the Later Middle Ages," *Journal of Family History* 8: 144–58.

Duby, Georges. 1964, 1968. "Au xiie siècle: les 'jeunes' dans la société aristocratique," *AESC* 19: 835–46. Trans. in *Lordship and Community in Medieval Europe,* ed. Fredric L. Cheyette. New York.

——— 1973. "Structures et parenté et noblesse dans la France du nord aux 11e et 12e siècles," in *Hommes et structures du Moyen Age,* pp. 267–85. Paris.

——— 1978. *Medieval Marriage. Two Models from Twelfth-Century France,* trans. Elborg Forster. Baltimore and London.

——— 1983. *The Knight, the Lady and the Priest. The Making of Modern Marriage in Medieval France,* trans. Barbara Bray, with an introduction by Natalie Zemon Davis. New York.

Duncan-Jones, Richard. 1982. "Population and Demographic Policy," in *The Economy of the Roman Empire. Quantitative Studies.* 2nd ed., pp. 259–319. Cambridge.

Ercole, Franco. 1908. "Vicende storiche della dote romana nella pratica medievale dell'Italia superiore," *Archivio giuridico* 80: 393–490, and 81: 34–148.

Erickson, Carolly, and Casey, Kathleen. 1978. "Women in the Middle Ages. A Working Bibliography," *Medieval Studies* 37: 340–59.

Esmein, Adhémar. 1929–35. *Le mariage en droit canonique,* ed. R. Génestal. Paris.

Falletti, Louis. 1966–67. "De la condition de la femme pendant le haut moyen-âge," *Annali di storia del diritto: Rassegna internazionale* 10–11: 91–115.

Famille et parenté. 1977. *Famille et parenté dans l'occident médiéval.* Rome.

Fossier, Robert. 1968. *La terre et les hommes en Picardie jusqu'à la fin du XIIIe siècle.* Paris.

——— 1980. "Les structures de la famille en occident au Moyen-Age," in *XVe Congrès International des Sciences Historiques. Rapports* 2: 115–32. Bucharest.

Friedlaender, Ludwig. 1968. *Roman Life and Manners under the Early Empire,* trans. Leonard A. Magnus. 4 vols. New York.

Fustel de Coulanges, Numa Denis. 1885. "De la constitution de la famille," in *Recherches sur quelques problèmes d'histoire,* pp. 219–52. Paris.

Galy, Charles. 1901. *La famille à l'époque mérovingienne. Etude faite principalement d'après les récits de Grégoire de Tours.* Paris.

Gaudemet, J. 1952. "Les transformations de la vie familiale au Bas Empire et l'influence du Christianisme," *Romanitas: Revista de Cultura Romana* 5: 58–85.

Gies, Frances and Joseph. 1978. *Women in the Middle Ages.* New York.

Goffart, Walter. 1974. *"Caput" and Colonate: Towards a History of Late Roman Taxation.* Toronto.

—— 1980. *Barbarians and Romans, A.D. 481–584. The Techniques of Accommodation.* Princeton.

Goldthwaite, Richard A. 1968. *Private Wealth in Renaissance Florence. A Study of Four Families.* Princeton.

—— 1980. *The Building of Renaissance Florence. An Economic and Social History.* Baltimore and London.

Goody, Jack. 1983. *The Development of the Family and Marriage in Europe.* Cambridge and New York.

Goody, Jack, and Tambiah, S. J. 1973. *Bridewealth and Dowry.* Cambridge.

Goody, Jack, Thirsk, J., and Thompson, E. P., eds. 1976. *Family and Inheritance: Rural Society in Western Europe, 1200–1800.* New York.

Grabmann, Martin. 1926. "Die deutsche Frauenmystik des Mittelalters," *Mittelalterliches Geistesleben. Abhandlungen zur Geschichte der Scholastik und Mystik,* I: 469–88. Munich.

Guilhiermoz, Paul. 1902, 1960. *Essai sur l'origine de la noblesse en France au Moyen Age.* Paris and New York.

Hajnal, J. 1953. "Age at Marriage and Proportions Marrying," *Population Studies* 7: 111–36.

—— 1965. "European Marriage Patterns in Perspective," in *Population in History,* ed. D. V. Glass and D. E. C. Eversley. London.

—— 1983. "Two Kinds of Pre-Industrial Household Formation Systems," in Wall, ed., 1983, pp. 65–104.

Hammer, Carl I., Jr. 1983. "Family and *Familia* in Early Medieval Bavaria," in Wall, ed., 1983, pp. 217–48.

Hanawalt, Barbara A. 1985. *The Late Medieval Peasant Family.* New York and London.

Heers, Jacques. 1977. *Family Clans in the Middle Ages. A Study of Political and Social Structures in Urban Areas,* trans. Barry Herbert. Europe in the Middle Ages, 4. Amsterdam and New York.

Helmolz, R. H. 1974. *Marriage Litigation in Medieval England.* London and New York.

Herlihy, David. 1958. "The Agrarian Revolution in Southern France and Italy, 801–1150," *Speculum* 33: 23–41.

—— 1960. "The Carolingian *Mansus,*" *Economic History Review* 13: 79–89.

—— 1962. "Land, Family and Women in Continental Europe, 701–1200," *Traditio* 18: 89–120.

—— 1967. *Medieval and Renaissance Pistoia. The Social History of an Italian Town.* New Haven.

—— 1969. "Family Solidarity in Medieval Italian History," pp. 173–84, in *Economy, Society and Government in Medieval Italy,* ed. D. Herlihy, R. S. Lopez, and V. Slessarev. Kent, Ohio.

———— 1973. "The Population of Verona in the First Century of Venetian Rule," pp. 91–120, in *Renaissance Venice*, ed. J. R. Hale. London.

———— 1978a. *The Social History of Italy and Western Europe. Collected Studies*. London.

———— 1978b. "Medieval Children," pp. 109–42, in *The Walter Prescott Webb Memorial Lectures. Essays on Medieval Civilization*. Austin and London.

———— 1983. "The Making of the Medieval Family: Symmetry, Structure and Sentiment." *The Journal of Family History* 8: 116–30.

———— 1984. "Households in the Early Middle Ages: Symmetry and Sainthood," in *Households: Comparative and Historical Studies of the Domestic Group*, ed. Robert McC. Netting, Richard R. Wilk, and Eric J. Arnould. Berkeley, Los Angeles, and London.

Herlihy, David, and Klapisch-Zuber, Christiane. 1978. *Les Toscans et leurs familles. Une étude du catasto florentin de 1427*. Paris.

———— 1985. *Tuscans and Their Families. A Study of the Florentine Catasto of 1427*. New Haven and London.

Hilaire, J. 1973. "Vie en commune, famille et esprit communautaire," *RHDFE* 51: 8–53.

Holdsworth, Sir William. 1936. *A History of English Law*. 4th ed. London.

Homans, G. C. 1960. *English Villagers of the Thirteenth Century*. New York.

Hopkins, M. K. 1965. "The Age of Roman Girls at Marriage," *Population Studies* 18: 309–27.

Hughes, Diane Owen. 1975. "Domestic Ideals and Social Behavior: Evidence from Medieval Genoa," in *The Family in History*, ed. Charles E. Rosenberg, pp. 115–44. Philadelphia.

———— 1978. "From Brideprice to Dowry in Mediterranean Europe," *Journal of Family History* 3:262–96.

———— 1977. "Kinsmen and Neighbors in Medieval Genoa," in *The Medieval City*, ed. Harry A. Miskimin, David Herlihy and A. L. Udovitch, pp. 95–112. New Haven.

Hughes, Kathleen. 1972. *Early Christian Ireland. Introduction to the Sources*. Ithaca, New York.

Humbert, Michel. 1972. *Le remariage à Rome. Etude d'histoire juridique et sociale*. Milan.

Hyams, Paul R. 1980. *King, Lords and Peasants in Medieval England*. Oxford.

Imberciadori, I. 1951. *Mezzadria classica toscana con documentazione inedita dal sec. 9 al sec. 14*. Florence.

Jacquin, A. M. 1931. "La prédestination d'après St. Augustin," *Micellanea Agostiniana* 2:853–78. Rome.

Jochens, Jenny M. 1980. "The Church and Sexuality in Medieval Iceland," *Journal of Medieval History* 6: 377–92.

Kalifa, S. 1970. "Singularités matrimoniales chez les anciens Germains. Le rapt et le droit de la femme à disposer d'elle-même," *RHDFE* 48: 199–225.

Kantorowicz, Hermann. 1938. *Studies in the Glossators of the Roman Law. Newly Discovered Writings of the Twelfth Century.* Cambridge.

Kaser, Max. 1968. *Roman Private Law*, trans. R. Dannenbring. Durban.

—— 1971. *Das romische Privatrecht*, 2 vols. Handbuch der Altertumswissenschaft, X, 3, 3, 1. 2nd ed. Munich.

Kelly, Henry Ansgar. 1975. *Love and Marriage in the Age of Chaucer.* Ithaca and London.

Kenney, James F. 1927. *Sources for the Early History of Ireland*, I: *Ecclesiastical.* New York.

Kent, Francis W. 1977. *Household and Lineage in Florence: The Family Life of the Capponi, Ginori and Rucellai.* Princeton.

King, P. D. 1972. *Law and Society in the Visigothic Kingdom.* Cambridge Studies in Medieval Life and Thought, 3rd ser. 5. Cambridge.

Kirshner, Julius. 1978. *Pursuing Honor While Avoiding Sin: The Monte delle Doti of Florence.* Quaderni di "Studi Senesi," 41. Milan.

Kirshner, Julius, and Molho, Anthony. 1978. "The Dowry Fund and the Marriage Market in Early *Quattrocento* Florence," *Journal of Modern History* 50: 403–38.

Kelso, Ruth. 1978. *Doctrine for the Lady of the Renaissance.* Urbana.

Koch, Gottfried. 1962. *Frauenfrage und Ketzertum im Mittelalter. Die Frauenbewegung im Rahmen des Catharismus und des Waldensertums und ihre sozialen Würzeln (12.–14. Jahrhundert).* Forschungen zur mittelalterlichen Geschichte, 9. Berlin.

Klapisch, Christiane. 1983. "La 'mère cruelle.' Maternité, veuvage et dot dans la Florence des XIVe–XVe siècles," *AESC* 38: 1097–1107.

Koebner, Richard. 1911. "Die Eheauffassung des ausgehenden deutschen Mittelalters," *Archiv für Kulturgeschichte* 9: 136–98; 279–318.

Krieger, Karl Friedrich. 1974. *Die Lehnshoheit der deutschen Könige im Spätmittelalter.* Aalen.

Kroeschell, K. 1968. *Haus und Herrschaft in frühen deutschen Recht.* Göttinger Rechtswissenschaftliche Studien, 70. Göttingen.

Lacey, Walter K. 1968. *The Family in Classical Greece.* London.

Laigle, Mathilde. 1912. *Le Livre des trois vertus de Christine de Pisan et son milieu historique et littéraire.* Paris.

Laribière, G. 1967. "Le mariage à Toulous aux 14e et 15e siècle," *Annales du Midi* 79: 335–62.

Laslett, Peter, and Wall, Richard, eds. 1972. *Household and Family in Past Time.* Cambridge.

—— 1983. "Family and Household as Work Group and Kin Group: Areas of Traditional Europe Compared," in Wall, ed., 1983, pp. 513–64.

Lemaire, André. 1929. "La Dotatio de l'époque mérovingienne au XIIIe siècle," *RHDFE* 4th ser. 8: 569–80.

Levy, E. 1951. *West Roman Vulgar Law.* Philadelphia.

Leyser, K. 1968. "The German Aristocracy from the Ninth to the Early Twelfth Century. A Historical and Cultural Sketch," *Past and Present* 41:25–53.

—— 1970. "Maternal Kin in Early Medieval Germany. A Reply." *Past and Present* 49:126–134.

———— 1980. *Rule and Conflict in Early Medieval Society: Ottonian Saxony.* Bloomington, Indiana.

Longnon, Auguste. 1920–29. *Les noms de lieu de la France. Leur origine, leur signification, leurs transformations.* Paris.

McDonnell, Ernest W. 1954, 1969. *The Beguines and Beghards in Medieval Culture, with Special Emphasis on the Belgian Scene.* New York.

McNamara, Jo Ann. 1983. *A New Song: Celibate Women in the First Three Christian Centuries.* New York.

McNamara, Jo Ann, and Wemple, Suzanne. 1974. "The Power of Women Through the Family in Medieval Europe: 500–1100," *Clio's Consciousness Raised: New Perspectives on the History of Women,* ed. Mary S. Hartman and Lois Banner. New York.

———— 1977. "Marriage and Divorce in the Frankish Kingdom," *Women in Medieval Society,* ed. Susan Mosher Stuard. Philadelphia.

Maine, Henry. 1888. "The Early History of the Settled Property of Married Women," in his *Lectures on the Early History of Institutions.* 7th ed., pp. 306–41. New York.

Manitius, Maximilian. 1911–31. *Geschichte der lateinischen Literatur des Mittelalters.* Handbuch des Altertumswissenschaft, 9 abt. 3 vols. Munich.

Marius, Richard. 1984. *Thomas More. A Biography.* New York.

Martines, Lauro. 1974. "A Way of Looking at Women in Renaissance Florence," *The Journal of Medieval and Renaissance Studies* 4: 15–28.

Medieval Women. 1978. *Medieval Women: Dedicated and Presented to Professor Rosalind M. T. Hill,* ed. Derek Baker. Oxford.

Merea, Manuel Paulo. 1952. "O dote nos documentos dos seculos IX–XII," *Estudos de direito hispanico medieval* 1: 59–150.

Merscheberger, Gerda. 1937. *Die Rechtsstellung der germanischen Frau.* Leipzig.

Milden, James Wallace. 1977. *The Family in Past Time.* New York and London.

Milson, S. F. C. 1976. *The Legal Framework of English Feudalism.* Cambridge.

Mitterauer, Michael, and Sieder, Rinhard. 1982. *The European Family. Patriarchy to Partnership from the Middle Ages to the Present,* trans. Karla Oosterveen and Manfred Horzinger, with an Introduction by Peter Laslett. Oxford.

Mols, R. 1954–56. *Introduction à la démographie historique des villes d'Europe du 14e au 18e siècle.* 3 vols. Louvain.

Murray, Alexander Callander. 1983. *Germanic Kinship Structure: Studies in Law and Society.* Pontifical Institute of Medieval Studies, Studies and Texts, 65. Toronto.

Niccolai, F. 1940. "I consorzi nobiliari ed Comune nell'alta e media Italia," *Rivista di Storia del diritto Italiano* 13: 116–17, 292–342; 397–477.

Noonan, John T. 1966. *Contraception. A History of Its Treatment by the Catholic Theologians and Canonists.* Cambridge.

Olms, Georg. 1964. *Scriptorum Historiae Augustae Lexicon,* ed. Georg Olms, 1964.

Ourliac, Paul. 1979a. "Notes sur le mariage à Avignon au XVe siècle," *Etudes d'histoire du droit médiéval.* Paris.

—— 1979b. "La famille pyrénéenne au Moyen Age," *Etudes d'histoire du droit médiéval.* Paris.

Patlagean, Evelyne. 1977. *Pauvreté économique et pauvreté sociale à Byzance 4e-7e siècles.* Civilisations et Sociétés, 48. Paris and the Hague.

Perrin, C. E. 1945. "Observations sur le manse dans la région parisienne au début du IXe siècle," *Annales d'histoire sociale* 2: 39–52.

Pertile, Antonio. 1892–1902. *Storia del diritto italiano dalla caduta dell'Impero romano alla codificazione.* 2nd ed. 6 vols. Turin.

Phillpotts, Bertha. 1913. *Kindred and Clan.* Cambridge.

Pieri, G. 1968. *L'histoire du cens jusqu'à la fin de la république romaine.* Paris.

Plochl, Willibald. 1935. *Das Eherecht des Magisters Gratianus.* Weiner Staats—und Rechtswissenschaftliche Studien, 24. Leipzig and Vienna.

Plummer, C. 1925. *Miscellanea Hagiographica Hibernica . . . accedit Catalogus Hagiographicus Hiberniae.* Subsidia Hagiographica, 18. Brussels.

Pollock, Sir Frederick, and Maitland, F. W. 1952. *The History of English Law Before the Time of Edward I.* 2nd ed. Cambridge.

Portmann, Marie-Louise. 1958. *Die Darstellung der Frau in der Geschichtsschreibung der frühern Mittelalters.* Basel.

Power, Eileen. 1975. *Medieval Women,* ed. M. M. Postan, Cambridge, London, New York.

Power, Patrick C. 1977. *Sex and Marriage in Early Ireland.* Dublin.

Raftis, J. A. 1964. *Tenure and Mobility: Studies in the Social History of the Medieval English Village.* Toronto.

—— 1974. *Warboys: Two Hundred Years in the Life of a Medieval English Village.* Toronto.

Razi, Zvi. 1980. *Life, Death and Marriage in a Medieval Parish. Economy Society and Demography in Halesowen, 1270–1400.* Past and Present Publications. Cambridge.

RHDFE. Revue historique de droit français et étranger.

Riché, Pierre. 1962. *Education et culture dans l'Occident barbare, VIe–VIIIe siècles.* Patristica sorbonensia, 4. Paris.

—— 1968. *De l'éducation antique à l'éducation chevaleresque.* Questions d'histoire. Paris.

Ring, Richard. 1979. "Early Medieval Peasant Households in Central Italy," *Journal of Family History* 2:2–25.

Ritzer, Korbinian. 1962. *Formen, Riten und religiöses Brauchtum der Eheschliessung in den christlichen Kirchen des ersten Jahrtausends. Litugiewissensschaftliche Quellen und Forschungen,* 38. Münster im Westfallen.

—— 1970. *Le mariage dans les églises chrétiennes du I au XI siècle.* Paris.

Robleda, Olis, S.J. 1970. *El matrimonio en derecho romano.* Rome.

Ross, J. B. 1905. "The Middle Class Child in Urban Italy, Fourteenth to Early Sixteenth Centuries," in *The History of Childhood,* ed. L. de Mause, pp. 183–228. New York.

Ruether, Rosemary and McLaughlin, Eleanor. 1979. *Women of Spirit. Female Leadership in the Jewish and Christian Traditions.* New York.

Russell, Josiah Cox. 1948. *British Medieval Population.* Albuquerque.

—— 1958. *Late Ancient and Medieval Population.* American Philosphical Society, Transactions, n.s. 48, pt. 2. Philadelphia.

Santini, P. 1887. "Società delle torri in Firenze," *Archivio Storico Italiano* 1887: 25–58; 178–204.

Sapori, Armando. 1926. *La crisi delle compagnie mercantili dei Bardi e dei Peruzzi.* Biblioteca Storica Toscanan, 3. Florence.

Sawyer. P. H. 1982. *Kings and Vikings: Scandinavia and Europe, AD 700–1100.* London and New York.

Schmid, Karl. 1978. "The Structure of the Nobility in the Earlier Middle Ages," trans. Timothy Reuter, in *The Medieval Nobility: Studies on the Ruling Classes of France and Germany from the Sixth to the Twelfth Century.* Europe in the Middle Ages, Selected Studies, 14, pp. 37–59. Amsterdam.

Schmitt, Charles B. 1971. "Theophrastus in the Middle Ages," *Viator* 2: 251–70.

Schmitz, Philibert. 1942–56. *Histoire de l'ordre de Saint Benoît.* 7 vols. Paris.

Schulenberg, Jane T. 1978. "Sexism and the Celestial Gynaeceum," *The Journal of Medieval History* 4:117–33.

Seitz, Joseph. 1908. *Die Verehrung des hl. Joseph in ihrer geschichtlichen Entwicklung bis zum Konzil von Trient dargestellt.* Freiburg im Breisgau.

Sheehan, Michael, and Scardellato, Kathy. 1976. *Family and Marriage in Medieval Europe: A Working Bibliography.* Vancouver.

Smith, Richard. 1983. "Hypothèses sur la nuptialité en Angleterre au XIIe–XIVe siècle," *AESC* 38: 107–24.

Smyth, Alfred P. 1982. *Celtic Leinster: Toward an Historical Geography of Early Irish Civilization, A.D. 500–1000.* Dublin.

Soliday, G. L. 1980. *History of Family and Kinship: A Select Bibliography.* New York.

Stoeckle, Maria. 1957. *Studien über Ideale in Frauenvita des VII–XI Jahrhunderts.* Munich.

Stone, Lawrence. 1977. *The Family, Sex and Marriage in England, 1500–1800.* New York.

Tamassia, Nino. 1910. *La famiglia italiana nei secoli decimoquinto e decimosesto.* Milan.

Thurneysen, R. et al., eds. 1936. *Studies in Early Irish Law.* Dublin.

TLL. 1900– *Thesaurus linguae latinae editus auctoritate et consilio academiarum quinque Germanicarum.* Leipzig.

Todd, Malcolm. 1972. *Everyday Life of the Barbarians.* London.

—— 1975. *The Northern Barbarians 100 B. C.–A. D. 300.* London.

Toubert, Pierre. 1973. *Les structures du Latium médiéval. Le Latium méridional et la Sabine du 9e siècle à la fin du 12e siècle.* 2 vols. Bibliothèque des Ecoles Françaises d'Athènes et de Rome, 221. Rome.

Vauchez, André. 1981. *La sainteté en Occident aux derniers siècles du*

Moyen Age d'après les procès de canonisation et les documents ha-giographiques. Bibliothèque des Ecoles françaises d'Athènes et de Rome, fasc. 241. Rome.

Villers, R. 1982. "Le mariage envisagé comme institution d'Etat dans le droit classique de Rome," in *Augstieg und Niedergang der romischen Welt im Spiegel der neueren Forschung,* ed. Hildegard Temporani and Wolfgang Haase, II: *Principät,* 14: 285–301. Berlin and New York.

Violante, Cinzio. 1977. "Quelques caractéristiques des structures familiales en Lombardie, Emile et Toscane aux XIe et XIIe siècles," *Famille et parenté dans l'occident médiéval,* ed. Georges Duby and Jacques Le Goff. Rome.

Wall, Richard, ed. 1983. *Family Forms in Historic Europe,* with Jean Robin and Peter Laslett. Cambridge and New York.

Wemple, Suzanne Fonay. 1981. *Women in Frankish Society. Marriage and the Cloister, 500–900.* Philadelphia.

Westphal, Alexandre. 1935. "Recensement," *Dictionnaire encyclopédique de la Bible,* 2:531–32. Valence-sur-Rhone.

Wrigley, E. A. and Scofield, R. S. 1981. *The Population History of England.* Cambridge, Mass.

Yver, Jean. 1966. *Egalité entre héritiers et exclusion des enfants dotés; essai de géographie coutumière.* Paris.

Ziegler, Josef. 1956. *Die Ehelehre der Ponitentialsummen von 1200–1350.* Regensburg.

NOTES

1. THE HOUSEHOLD IN LATE CLASSICAL ANTIQUITY

1. *CI*, 1954. There is an English translation in *Civil Law*, 1932.

2. Thus, the standard dictionary of classical Latin, the *TLL*, 199–, VI, 1, cols. 234–45 defines the word's original meaning as property or persons subject to authority (*potestas*) and, later, all members of an agnate descent group. In antiquity it apparently never took on the meaning of the small, coresidential descent group, the *Kleinfamilie*.

3. See, for example, Xenophon's *Oeconomicus* (Xenophon, 1970), in which Socrates is presented as the principal speaker. Plato expounds his famous critique of marriage, the family and the private household in the fourth book of the *Republic*, to which Aristotle replies in the *Politica* (Aristotle, 1946). See also pseudo-Aristotle, *Oeconomica*, ed. E. S. Forster, in Aristotle, 1921–28, 1343–1353.

4. *Oeconomicus*, vi.4 (Xenophon, 1970, p. 26).

5. Aristotle, 1946, i.3: "a complete household consists of slaves and free-men." *Ibid.*, i.4: "Property is a part of the household."

6. Gai Inst. ii.102 (*Syntagma*, 1880, p. 93): "familiam suam, id est, patrimonium suum." See the equivalent use of *familia* and *hereditas* in an early saint's life: "et omnes qui pertinebant ad familiam et hereditatem eorum," from the Acta Martyrii S. Calisti, *ASS*, II Maii, p. 615.

7. Dig. 50.16.195, cited in *TLL*, 1900–, VI, 1, col. 237: "iure proprio familiam dicimus plures personas quae sub unius potestate aut natura aut iure subiectae, ut puta patremfamiliam."

8. *Ibid.*, "servitium quoque solemus appellare familias . . . non omnes servi, sed corpus quodam servorum."

9. Isidore, 1911, ix.4.4: "Nam familia est liberi ex liberis legibus suscepti, a femore."

10. Cf. *ASS*, I Januarii, p. 106, Life of Adelhard of Corbie, in which the word signifies household servants: "familiam quoque satis illaesam a juogo servitutis conservans." On this complex life, written in the eleventh century on the basis of ninth century materials, see Manitius, 1911–31, II, 465–66.

11. Tertullian, adv. Marc. 4.36, "distincta . . . Iudaea gens per tribus et populos et familias et domus," cited in the *TLL*, VI, 1, col. 241.

12. Rendering Numbers 2.2, the Itala has "per domus familiarum suarum"; the Vulgate uses "cognationum" for "familiarum." Compare the use of *familia* in the sense of lineage in the fourth-century *Scriptores Historiae Augustae*. The lexicon compiled by Olms, 1964, p. 200, cites "vir antiquae familiae."

13. Tacitus, 1911, cap. 25.

14. See the uses of the word cited in the *TLL*, 1900–, IV, 1, cols. 987–91. "Hearth" is rarely used as a metaphor for "household."

15. *ASS*, II Maii, p. 496, Pope Calixtus baptizes the entire household of the Roman senator Simplicius, "omnem domum Simplicii, et uxorem et filios et familiam, animas promiscui sexus sexaginta octo." See also *ASS*, II Aprilis, p. 416. The members of the household of the Gallo-Roman Gaianus, baptized with their master, numbered 412.

16. Listed in Westphal, 1935.

17. Numbers 1.2–3. David's efforts to number the people of Israel provokes God's wrath in Kings 2.24.

18. On Roman censuses and the many problems regarding the units actually counted, see Brunt, 1971; Pieri, 1968.

19. For a recent reexamination of the problem, see Goffart, 1974.

20. Livy, 32.29.4 (1967, IX, 242): "trecenae familiae in singulas colonias iubebantur mitti"; 37.46.10 (X, 428), "sex milia familiarum conscriberet quae in eas colonias iubebantur dividerentur."

21. *Scriptores Historiae Augustae*, 48.2 (1960, III, 289).

22. On ancient and medieval ways of reckoning degrees of kinship, see Champeaux, 1933; Bouchard, 1981a.

23. Edited in Ausonius, 1919–21, pp. 57–95. See Russell, 1958, p. 30, Table 31, for a tabulation of Ausonius' relatives with slightly different totals from those presented here.

24. Esmein, 1929–35, I, 335. See *CI*, 5.6.19, for a statement of the prohibited degrees in the late empire; and *CI*, 5.4.17 for a prohibition of marriage in the direct line. Emperors Arcadius and Honorius allowed first cousins to marry, *CI*, 5.6.19 (a. 405), but Theodosius reinstated the prohibition.

25. Esmein, 1929–35, I, 337.

26. "Nuptiae autem sive matrimonium est viri et mulieris coniuctio individuam consuetudinem vitae continens," Inst. 1.9.1. *CI*, 1954, I, 4. See its use in Bracton, 1968–77, III, 363.

27. "Liberorum quaerendorum causa." Census takers asked citizens if they were living with a woman for that purpose; they thus distinguished legal wives from concubines.

28. Soldiers on active service were not allowed to marry until the reign of Septimus Severus (193–211). The law allowing senators to marry actresses is in *CI* 5.6.23.

29. On the marital gifts in the late empire, see Anné, 1941.

30. The kiss is first mentioned in a constitution of Constantine the Great. *Theodosian Code*, 3.5.6 (a. 336) (1952, p. 67); *CI*, 5.3.16. If the engaged couple has exchanged a kiss, and if one subsequently died before the marriage, then the surviving spouse could keep one-half of the gifts received; if no kiss had been exchanged, all the gifts had to be returned. See *CI*, 5.3.16.

31. Dig. 50.17.30.

32. The following summary is taken from Corbett, 1930; Carcopino, 1940; Buckland, 1966; Robleda, 1970; and Villers, 1982.

33. Cicero *top.* 23, cited in *TLL*, 1900–, V, 1, col. 2043, "cum mulier viro in manum convenit, omnia, quae mulieris fuerunt, viri fiunt dotis nomine."

34. Juvenal, Satura, VI, lines 229–30 (1965, p. 100) in which one woman is said to have had eight husbands in five "autumns" (Juvenal, 1965, p. 227).

35. Csillag, 1976, reviews the Augustan marriage legislation. See also Astolfi, 1976.

36. Gaudemet, 1952, examines the rather restricted influence of Christianity on the late ancient family. Humbert, 1972, pp. 459–63, systematically summarizes the legislation of the Christian emperors on remarriage, and says much on marriage too. Esmein, 1929–35, I, 3, distinguishes three phases in the development of the canon law of marriage. In the first, lasting up to the twelfth century, canon law exerted a "parallel action" to that of civil law, and the two laws were very different; from the twelfth to the sixteenth century, canon law dominated; and since that time its influence has greatly receded.

37. *CI*, 5.17.8 (a. 449) for the law on divorce.

38. Gaudemet, 1952, p. 62, emphasizes the equality of the spouses and the reciprocity of their obligations in Christian teachings: "una lex de mulieribus et viris." See also Esmein, 1929–35, I, 91.

39. His treatises on marriage are collected and translated in Augustine, 1955.

40. A point emphasized by Esmein, 1929–35, I, 68.

41. *De genesi ad litteram,* Augustine, 1894, viiii.7 (p. 275); "hoc autem tripartitum est: fides, proles, sacramentum. In fide attenditur, ne praeter vinculum coniugale cum altero vel altera concumbatur; in prole, ut amanter suscipiatur, benigne nutriatur, religiose educeretur; in sacramento, ut coniugium non separetur et dimissus aut dimissa ne causa prolis alteri coniugatur."

42. Noonan, 1965, pp. 119–39.

43. Gaudemet, 1952, p. 66, notes that the phrase is borrowed from Cicero, *De officiis.*

44. Goody, 1983.

45. Ibid., pp. 48–82.

46. Ibid., p. 215.

47. See below, chapter 3, "Commensurable Units."

48. The basic study of Christian marital rituals is Ritzer, 1962 and 1970.

49. *ASS*, I Maii, p. 54. The blessing given *in thalamo* was a Gallican ritual that disappears as the Roman liturgy comes to predominate in France from the Carolingian period. See Ritzer, 1962, pp. 325–26.

50. On the dowry and its development in Roman law, see Kaser, 1971, I, 284–90. There is an English translation of an earlier edition of this survey, Kaser, 1968.

51. "Dos est donatio, quae a muliere vel eius parte marito vel eius parti ea destinatione datur seu promittitur, ut perpetuo apud eum sit propter onera matrimonii" (Dig. 23.3.1).

52. Dig. 24.1.1 (*CI*, 1954, I, 347). See also *Theodosian Code*, 5.1.9 (1952, p. 106): "the ancients did not concede to husbands and wives the right which is granted to extraneous persons, and often to those who are even unknown, in respect to gifts and successions, for they judged that as married persons are in an unstable position, mutual favor ought to be restrained in their case rather than encouraged."

53. Aulularia, 191. *Plautus*, 1916, I, 254.

54. "Filius hunc miles, te filia nubilis angat." Remediorum amoris, 571 (Ovid, 1962, p. 216).

55. *Memorabilia* 4.4.10 (1888, p. 192): "quo non solum humanitas patrum conscriptorum sed etiam habitus veterum patrimoniorum cognosci potest."

56. Ibid., "Dotatae cognomen invenerit [Megullia]."

57. Varro, 1974, no. 38 (II, 144): "dotis dato insulam Chrysam, agrum Caecubum, Seplasia Capuae, macellum Romuli."

58. *Naturales Questiones* (Seneca, 1971, p. 94). "Iam libertinorum virgunculis in unum speculum non sufficit illa dos quam dedit populus Romanus."

59. Juvenal, Satura, VI, 11. 139 (1965, p. 94): "inde faces ardent, veniunt a dote sagittae."

60. Anné, 1941, pp. 450 ff. The first mention of the *donatio* is at the end of the second and beginning of the third century.

61. Cento nuptualis, Ausonius, 1967–68, I, 382, "Oblatio munerum."

62. In cant. I, 89, "sponsa quaedam, quae susceperit quaedam sponsaliorum et dotis titulo ab sponso nobilissimo." Ibid., p. 90, "ecclesia . . . dicat . . . 'repleta sum muneribus, quae sponsaliorum vel dotis titulo ante nuptias sumpsi'." Cited in *TLL*, sub verbo *dos*.

63. NMaj 6.10. *Theodosian Code*, 1955, p. 556.

64. Csillag, 1976, p. 208, for Justinian's title as *legislator uxoris*.

65. *CI*, 5.3.20.

66. *CI*, Nov. 97.

67. Life of St. Euphraxia from the *Vitae patrum*, PL 73, col. 629: "Ecce omnem substantiam meam et patris tui dedi in manus tuas."

68. Ibid.

69. On marriage in ancient Greece, see Lacey, 1968. He concludes (pp. 106–9) that men normally married at age 30, and girls at 16. Much information on Roman ages at first marriage is given in Friedlaender, 1968, I, 232–34. "As a rule" Roman girls married between 13 and 17 years of age.

70. *Works and Days*, lines 695 ff. (Hesiod, 1967). *Politics*, vii.16 (Aristotle, 1964, p. 1334): "Women should marry when they are about eighteen years of age, and men at seven and thirty; then they are in the prime of life, and the decline in the powers of both will coincide."

71. *Oeconomicus*, vii.5 (Xenophon, 1970, p. 29).

72. Ulpian, Liber singularis regularum, 16.1 (*The Civil Law*, 1932). The ages during which "lex liberos exigit" are 20 to 50 for women and 25 to 60 for men.

73. The Augustan marriage laws have not survived in their original form,

but must be reconstructed from later citations. Csillag, 1976, pp. 36–73.

74. *PL* 74, col. 333: "Nupta igitur viro est cum tredecim esset annorum."

75. *PL* 73, col. 625. "Et factum est ut arrhas Euphraxia acciperet. Susceptis arrhis, puellae aetas expectabatur. Erat enim nimis infantula, quasi annorum quinque."

76. According to the *Confessions*, vi.13 (Augustine, 1963, p. 131).

77. Passio Perpetuae et Felicitatis, cap. 2 (1972, p. 108): "erat autem ipsa circiter annorum viginti duo."

78. See above, n. 70.

79. Valerius Maximus, 1888, 4.3.1: "Quartum et vicesimum annum agens Scipio . . . et iuvenis et coelebs."

80. Hopkins, 1965, pp. 309–27, calculates on the basis of inscriptions that pagan girls married at age 12 to 15, and Christian girls between 15 and 18.

81. See above, n. 72.

82. One of the purposes of the reforms attempted by the Gracchi brothers was to encourage a higher birth rate. See Plutarch, Tiberius Gracchus, cap. 8 (1965, p. 160): "The poor, when they found themselves forced off the land, became more and more unwilling to volunteer for military service or even to raise a family." On government subsidies for population increase, see Duncan-Jones, 1982, pp. 288–319.

83. Dio, liv.16.2 (1960, VI, 323). "And since there were far more males than females, he allowed all who wished, except the senators, to marry freedwomen and ordered that their offspring should be held legitimate."

84. Ibid., lvi.13.3 (1960, VII, 25).

85. See discussion of sex ratios in Brunt, 1971, pp. 151–52.

86. An English translation is given in *Ancient Roman Statutes*, 1961, p. 3, n. 4.

87. See above, n. 83.

88. *ILCV*, n. 2159 (1961, I, 423), "dilectissimo marito anime dulcissime Alexio lectori de fullonices, qui uixit mecum ann. xv, iunctus mihi ann. xvi uirgo and uirgine, cuius numquam amaritudinem habui." (Vita Melaniae, 1886, p. 22.) "Juncta autem beatissimo Piniano decem et septem annos agenti." Melany was "about 14."

89. *PL* 74, col. 258. "Cum esset . . . puer a parentibus derelictus, et ad viginti duorum pervenisset numerum annorum, invitus ab avunculo suo matrimonio vinculis illigatus est."

90. *ASS*, I Januarii, p. 243: "alter [frater] sub annum vigesimum quintum destinatus thamalis a parentibus, et tabulis de more compositis, et aliis omnibus rebus ad nuptias preparatis." But the boy died before the marriage.

91. *ASS*, I Januarii, p. 576. "Ad haec parentes responderunt: 'Annorum es circum decem et octo, quomodo te excusare poteris ne conjugio socieris?' "

92. Parentelia, ix (Ausonius, 1967–68, I, 72).

93. Parentelia, vi and xxvi (Ausonius, 1967–68, I, 66 and 90).

94. Epigrammata, xxxiv (Ausonius, 1967–68, II, 276): "Ad Gallam puellam iam senescentem." "Galla, senescimus; effugit tempus . . . obrepsit non

intellecta senectus / nec revocare potes." But he also writes an epitaph for a married woman dead at age 16, Epitapha, xxxv (Ausonius, 1967–68, I, 160).

95. *PL* 73, col. 283. "Parentes valde loculpetes . . . desponsaverunt ei puellam adhuc in pueritia constituto."

96. *ASS*, II Martii, 213. "Annorum factus duodecim, puellae despondetur, et cum ea annis octo vitam agit socialiter. Erant ambo opibus locupletissimi . . . cogebat socer, ut nuptiarum legitima impleret. Ergo dum constituta dies advenisset, ponitur thalamus, Hymenaeus occinitur, reliquaque nuptiarum solemnia peraguntur." See Patlagean, 1977.

97. Csillag, 1976, p. 23.

98. NMaj. 7.9. *Theodosian Code*, 1952, p. 556.

99. NMaj. 6.1 and 6.5. *Theodosian Code*, pp. 553–54.

100. Anné, 1941, for example, gives this as the principal reason for the triumph of the *donatio*.

101. Parentalia, vi (Ausonius, 1967–68, I, 66). "Aemilia Hilaria matertera virgo devota."

102. *ILCV*, n. 2031 (I, 401), "Castula puella ann. xlviii." Ibid., n. 2797a (II, 56), "puella defuncta nomine Axungiosa que uixit annus plus minus xxiii." Ibid., n. 2851b (II, 72), "Aurelia Leontis uixit annos xxiii uirgo."

103. Ibid., n. 615 (I, 121), "Scantia Redempta . . . antistis disciplinae in medicina fuit . . . haec vixit annos xxii." Ibid., n. 681 (I, 121), "Valeria . . . filia obsetricis." Among other occupations held by women are, n. 619, "Novica nutrix"; n. 632, "Masumilla aurifex"; n. 633, "Vincentia . . . filia auri netrix."

104. *PL* 74, col. 295. "Piamon nomine virgo quaedam fuit quae omnes aetatis suae annos cum matre sua vixit, jugiter faciens opus lini."

105. NMaj. 6.5 *Theodosian Code*, 1955, p. 555.

106. *ASS*, I Aprilis, p. 1204 (*Historia lausiaca*;cp. "In civitate Ancyra sunt multae quidam aliae virgines, nempe ad decem milia."

107. On the influence of these philosophies, see Csillag, 1976, p. 52; Humbert, 1972, p. 327.

108. Reviewed in Humbert, 1972, pp. 327 ff.

109. *Epistolae* 22.20, cited in Humbert, 1972, p. 321.

110. St. Jerome, cited in Humbert, 1972: "Laudo nuptias, laudo coniugium, sed quia mihi virgines generant."

111. One of the most influential of these tracts was the *Liber aureolus*, composed by the Athenian philosopher and student of Aristotle, Theophrastes. It has not survived, but lengthy passages were incorporated in St. Jerome into his Contra Jovinianum, *PL* 33, col. 211 ff. Juvenal's sixth satire is written in an equivalent spirit (Juvenal, 1965).

112. Ep. 123.10, cited in Humbert, 1972, p. 329: "Occasio liberatatis, ut sui corporis habeat potestatem, ne rursus ancilla fiat hominis."

113. *PL* 72, col. 879: "simulque cum pudicitia libertatem perdunt."

114. *ASS*, III Maii, p. 7. See also *ASS*, I Januarii, p. 254, for an extended comparison between spiritual and corporal marriages. McNamara, 1983, argues that Christian women who spontaneously embraced a life of virginity were so many as to restructure the whole social order.

115. Muratori, 1739–42, III, 1123–36, "affectus parentum erga liberos"; IV, 1237–86, "affectus liberorum erga parentes"; IV, 1287–1428, "affectus conjugum"; IV, 1429–1514, "affectus fratrum, cognatorum et amicorum."

116. Cf. *ILCV*, n. 4121 (II, 352), "Aeliae sextae, filiae dulcissimae, quae uixit annis xxi, m. v, d. xxii, h. v."

117. *De civitate dei*, 21.14: "Quis autem exhorreat, et mori eligat, si ei proponatur, aut mors perpetienda, aut rursus infantia?"

118. *De rerum natura*, lines 1157–74 (Lucretius, 1965).

119. Tertullian, 1954, p. 827.

120. Ibid.

121. See, for example, his sermon in Augustine, 1837, col. 628: "Miraris quia deficit mundus? mirare quia senuit mundus."

121. Augustine, 1955, pp. 21–22 (from the *De bono coniugali*): "in the earliest times of the human race, especially to propagate the people of God . . . the saints were obliged to make use of the good of marriage . . . But now . . . even those who wish to contract marriage only to have children are to be admonished that they practice the greater good of continence." Ibid., p. 2: "there is not the need for procreation that there once was"; ibid., p. 34: these changes came about through "the mystery of time."

123. Ibid., p. 159, from the tract *Contra Jovinianum*.

124. Ibid., p. 166.

125. Sermo 250 (Augustine, 1837, V, 1506): "Nemo minus, nemo plus erit, integer numerus erit."

126. See, for example, Anselm of Canterbury (d. 1109), Cur Deus Homo? 1.16, *PL* 158, col. 531: "Ratio cur numerus angelorum, qui ceciderunt, restituendus sit de hominibus."

127. Polybius, xxxvi.17 (1960, p. 383).

128. Brunt, 1971, pp. 131–33.

129. Commemoratio professorum Burdigalensium (Ausonius, 167–68, I, 96–139).

130. *Confessions*, 13.119.

131. Ibid.

132. "Sancte, sis dux, Rex puerorum intactorum." Cited in Herlihy, 1978, p. 134, n. 31.

133. From Leo's Sermon on the Epiphany, cited in Riche, 168, p. 31.

134. Jacquin, 1931, p. 868.

135. Ibid. "Ecce exposuit tibi quod sit regnum, et quid sit ignis aeternus, ut quando confitearis parvulum non futurum in regno, fatearis futurum in igne aeterno."

136. *Confessions*, i.7 (*Confessions*, 1963, p. 7).

137. *De civitate dei*, 22.22. "Nam quis ignorat cum quanta ignorantia veritatis, quae iam in fantibus manifesta est, et cum quanta abundantia vanae cupiditatis, quae in pueris incipit apparere, homo veniat in hanc vitam, ita ut, si dimittatur vivere ut velit et facere quidquid velit, in haec facinora et flagitia . . . vel cuncta vel multa perveniat."

138. Isidore, 1911, xiv.4.4

139. Paul the Deacon, 1878, i.1 (p. 52). "Multae quoque ex ea, pro eo quod tantos mortalium germinat, quantos alere vix sufficit, saepe gentes

egressae sunt, quae nihilominus et partes Asiae, sec maxime sibi contiguam Europeam adflixerunt."

2. THE HOUSEHOLD IN LATE BARBARIAN ANTIQUITY

1. For a bibliography of Irish lives, see Plummer, 1925. On the use of these lives as historical sources, see the observations of Hughes, 1972, pp. 217–48, and Doherty, 1982.

2. *CS*, 1966, p. 256. "In occidentali plaga orbis est insula quaedam . . . insula sanctorum nomine appropriater dicebatur."

3. See the comments of Heist in his introduction to *CS*.

4. Discussed in ibid.

5. Ibid., p. 1. "Sed postquam Anglia dominos cepit habere Normannos."

6. See the comments of Heist on the "conservatism" of the Salamanca Codex, ibid., p. xi, and the remarks of Kenney, 1927, I, 294. Plummer, in his introduction to the *Vitae sanctorum*, 1910, I, cxxix–clxxxviii, points out numerous survivals from "heathen folk-lore and mythology" in the lives of Celtic saints generally.

7. Chadwick, 1970, p. 255, calls it "the oldest vernacular literature north of the Alps," although, like the Latin lives, it was not put in writing until comparatively late.

8. It is given a fine edition with commentary by Heist in *CS*, 1966.

9. Ibid., p. 132. "Alio die, quidam vir senex, de filiis Coilboth, caput suum in sinum pueri Lugidi reclinavit, ut puer a capite senis vermes colligeret."

10. Ibid., p. 348. "Tunc vir Dei, zelo iustitie ductus, viperium semen animari nolens, impresso ventri eius signo crucis, fecit illud exinaniri."

11. See Plummer's comments in the preface to *Vitae sanctorum*, 1910, I, clxxiii–clxxiv.

12. Power, 1977, pp. 33 and 55.

13. The Latin version in the *Vitae sanctorum*, 1910, I, 221, simply says "partus in utero evanuit." Other allusions to the annihilation of fetuses, though not to abortions, are: Vita s. Aidi killariensis, *CS*, 1966, p. 172: "Intuens autem sanctus Aidus virginem que sibi ministrabat, vidit quod uterus illius, partum gestans, intumescebat . . . Sanctus autem Aidus benedixit uterum eius, et statim infans in utero eius evanuit quasi non esset." Vita s. Cainnechi, ibid., p. 197: "Quedam virgo in vicino sibi loco habitans occulte fornicavit, et uterus eius partu intumuit. Que a sancto Kannecho postulavit ut uterum suum, quasi aliquo dolore tumescentem, benediceret. Cumque ille benedixisset eam, statim infans in utero eius non apparens evanuit." For the Old-Irish version, see *Bethada Náem nÉrenn*, 1922, II, 101: "Ciaran then made the sign of the Divine Cross over her and it (the foetus) vanished immediately without being perceived."

14. See, for example, its use in Cogitosus' life of Brigid, *PL*, 72, col. 786. On the problem of early Irish "tribes" and social organization, see Byrne, 1971.

15. *Bethada Náem nÉrenn*, 1922, II, 11: "Now my Bairre was of Connaught by race, of the descendants of Brian son of Eochaid, to speak precisely

[geneology follows]." For Mochua, see *ASS*, I Januarii, p. 45: "Clarus genere vir erat, nomine Mochua filius Lonani; ex Lugne trahens originem."

16. *Bethada Náem nÉrenn*, 1922, II, 161, gives a geneology of St. Coemgen extending over seventeen generations, and adds an "etc." at the end.

17. *ASS*, I Januarii, p. 47 (translated from the Irish): "abavo Lugo (qui Lugici generis apud Ibernos haud obscuri fuit auctor)."

18. The abundant literature is reviewed in Murray, 1982, pp. 11–38.

19. Life of St. Patrick by Jocelin of Furness, *ASS*, II Martii, p. 553: "Deliberavi et statui ex corpore natae, nepotum procreatione, prosapiam meam ad robur regni et solatium meum dilatare: sed succisa est successio . . . Sed ergo pro tantae stirpis amissione [I hope to win eternal life]."

20. Vita B. Aengussio Keledeo . . . vita a Joanne Colgano, ibid., p. 87: "Quartus libellus continet maternam ducentorum decem circiter Sanctorum Hiberniae geneologiam: quod indicio est paternam Sanctorum geneologiam vel ab eodem, vel ab aliquo antiquiore auctore fuisse ante contextam." But no paternal genealogy is known.

21. *CS*, 1966, p. 87. "Post haec virgo Christi ad aquilonalem plagam Hybernie deveniens, cognatos suos . . . visitavit. Finito quoque itinere ad campum nomine Murthenne, qui sue genti praecipua fuit habitatio, tandem pervenit."

22. Ibid., p. 130. "Quodam autem tempore, gens Arad, congregati in unum, consilium fecerunt ut lupos sibi nocentes a suis finibus repellerent."

23. *PL*, 72, col. 786: "per cognationes et familias . . . diviserunt viam illam, quam aedificare debuerunt, in partes proprias, ut unaquaeque cognatio et familia suam sibi creditam construxerit partem."

24. *Vitae sanctorum*, 1910, I, p. 35: "set hoc cognatis suis displicuit."

25. Numerous rich individuals appear in the lives. See n. 27 below for one of many possible examples.

26. *CS*, 1966, p. 87. "Que gens, priscis temporibus artium magicarum pericia pre aliis collateralibus gentibus imbuta, gratia tamen Dei per sanctum Patricium operantem, christinana fuit effecta."

27. *Vitae sanctorum*, 1910, II, 148. "Erat quidem uir ualde diues in finibus Corcumruad, habens duas uxores, secundum legem illius temporis."

28. Ibid. "Et hic homo ambulabat in mandatis Dei, dona et decimas dans in honore eius."

29. *CS*, 1966, p. 2: "sola domus domina."

30. *Cáin Adamnáin*, 1905.

31. Ibid., p. 2. "The work which the best of women had to do was to go to battle and battlefield, encounter and camping, fighting and hosting, wounding and slaying . . . Her husband behind her, carrying a fence stake in his hand, and flogging her on to battle."

32. Ibid., p. 5.

33. *CS*, 1966, p. 15. "Illud refugit ad quod eam Deus fecit, et mente pertinaci sic vivit, et sic vivere disponit, ut nec avum patrem suum, nec avunculos esse velit fratres suos. Institutis Dei vanitatem suam anteponit . . . ad nostrum tam dedecus quam dispendium."

34. *Vitae sanctorum*, 1910, I, 19, Vita sancti Abbani. A man, "senex decrepitus et diues valde," wishes desperately for a son and heir, but his

wife produces a daughter. But St. Abban, in baptizing the baby, changes its sex. In the Old-Irish version, the rich old man is called a king, *Bethada náem nÉrenn*, 1922, II, 8.

35. See, for example, from the life of Maedoc of Ferns, *Bethada náem nÉrenn*, 1922, II, 229: "Now Muirigen son of Duban had a proud and powerful sister named Failenn. She built a royal spacious fort, and a fair and strong city in this territory." Both brother and sister are annoyed that Maedoc occupies "*their* inheritance and land."

36. *Vitae sanctorum*, 1910, I, 185.

37. *Bethada náem nÉrenn*, 1922, II, 15. Fourteen women "offered their churches to God and to Bairre in perpetuity." Other examples of women holding and giving land are on pp. 105 and 117.

38. Vita s. Mochtei, *CS*, 1966, p. 397. "Brigita vero se suumque dotalem viro Dei tradidit agrum."

39. Miracula s. Fursei, *CS*, 1966, p. 54.

40. *CS*, 1966, p. 177.

41. Miracula s. Fursei, *CS*, 1966, p. 51, "femina nomine Ermenefleda, que videbatur habere multas possessiones et pecunias."

42. Ibid., p. 55. "Erat quedam femina multas habens divicias et possessiones, sed valida infirmitate detinebatur cum suis hominibus."

43. *Bethada náem nÉrenn*, 1922, II, 24. Patrick blesses the descendants of Dobtha: "If it be a warrior . . . pre-eminence of valor on him; if a woman, prosperity of storehouse; if a clerk, pre-eminence in learning and devotion."

44. Vita s. Brigidae, *CS*, 1966, p. 1: "verbis in virum amaris invehitur, de venditione puelle pertinaciter agit, unum iurans futurum ex duobus, aut puelle vendicionem aut suam ab eo separationem."

45. Miracula s. Fursei, *CS*, 1966, p. 54: "Fac me extraneam de tuo coniugio, si sic perseveras ut cepisti."

46. See *Vitae sanctorum*, 1910, I, 65. A "dux" observes a beautiful girl, "quam ipse volebat habere concubinam: et precepit ut nemo assumeret eam in uxorem." On informal marriages, see *Cáin Adamnáin*, 1905, p. 33: "if a woman has been got with child by stealth, without contract, without full rights, without dowry, without betrothal, a full fine for it."

47. *CS*, 1966, pp. 1–37.

48. Ibid., p. 2. "Hiis illa auditis, de stulta protinus efficitur insana, et verecundiam nesciens matronalem, neque maritalem magni faciens reverentiam, inhonestis sermonibus malignam mentem interpretatur . . . Cum que more furentis belue fremeret . . ."

49. Ibid. "Impedimento, ait, michi est uxor mea, ne me liberalem et humanum mea reperiat concubina; quia si ista non venditur, illa amittetur."

50. Vita s. Albei episcopi, *CS*, 1966, p. 119.

51. Vita s. Tigernachi episcopi, *CS*, 1966, p. 107: "Predictus igitur rex Echacus cum tres filias pulcerrimas in palacio suo nutritas haberet, una ex eis, Derfraych, quendam virum nobilem de militibus patris sui, Lagnensem genere, nomine Corbreum, adamavit."

52. *Vitae sanctorum*, 1910, I, 96: "Quadam autem die accidit quod quedam monialis quendam de monachis pro uestimentis lauandis adueniens."

53. Ibid., 65: "Ipse enim commes post ebrietatem deceptus, similitudine Loth, cum sua filia concubuit."

54. Ibid., 183. "Alio tempore quidam infantulus, qui in adulterio natus est, allatus est occulte ad civitatem Rathen, et dimissus est ibi iuxta ecclesiam."

55. Ibid., 32. "Tres filii autem Echach, uidelicet Breas, Nar et Lothar, dormierunt cum una de sororibus suis, Clothra nomine, nesciens unusquisque eorum alterum ex eis cum ea dormiisse. Illa enim eis non indicauit; set postea publicauit."

56. *ASS*, III Maii, pp. 475–95. The life is late medieval, and composed on the Continent, but the legend is consistent with the sexual *mores* described in the properly Irish lives.

57. See above, n. 46, passage from the *Cáin Adamnáin*. On informal marriage among the Germans, see Wemple, 1981, pp. 34–35, and Kalifa, 1970.

58. *CS*, 1966, p. 348. "In una vero domorum dilectus filius regis erat dormiens derelictus. Hunc et alium suum filium." The Old-Irish version explicitly mentions a queen, *Bethada náem nÉrenn*, 1922, II, 112: "And the queen escaped, but forgot her favorite son in the house."

59. See above, n. 27.

60. See, for example, "Vita s. Aidi killariensis," *CS*, 1966, pp. 177–78.

61. Robbers waylay, murder, and behead two women on the highway, *Bethada náem nÉrenn*, 1922, II, 159. Robbers, entrenched on an island in a bog, wreak havoc in the neighborhood. *Vitae sanctorum*, 1910, I, 40: "Erant pessimi latrones in insula in medio stagni, qui multum regioni per circuitum nocebant."

62. *CS*, 1966, pp. 81–83.

63. Ibid.

64. Vita s. Brigidae, *CS*, 1966, p. 10: "nunc coci, nunc pistoris, modo subulci, non nuncquam opilionis, aliquando messoris, sepe textricis officium, et alia atque alia his uiliora, tam domi quam foris . . . laudabiliter consummabat."

65. See the comments of Plummer, *Vitae sanctorum*, 1910, I, ci.

66. *Cáin Adamnáin*, 1905, p. 25.

67. See the "perfidious stepmother" who tries to murder by incantation her stepchildren, *Vitae sanctorum*, 1910, I, 78–79. "Ascendit ergo cum aliis concionatricibus magice artis peritis cuiusdam collis summitatem, ut adorando demones ab eis impetrarent uel filii regis mortem, uel membrorum eius mutilationem."

68. St. Coemghen turns the entire company of witches into stones. *Bethada náem nÉrenn*, 1922, II, 159.

69. *Vitae sanctorum*, 1910, II, 164. "Ducite illum huc; me enim oportet nutrire eum." "Et per uiginti annos beatissima abbatissa Yta in moribus honestis scientiaque literarum nutriuit eum . . . ut sacerdos fieret, et locum Dei edificaret."

70. On the relation of the saints with women, see the comments of Plummer, in *Vitae sanctorum*, 1910, I, cxxi–cxxii.

71. Ibid., 173. "Sanctus silicet Mochutu multum speciosus . . . et in diuersis diebus in iuuentute sua triginta iuuencule uirgines amauerunt eum magno amore carnali, hoc non celantes."

72. Ibid., II, 262.

73. CS, 1966, p. 350. "Considerans vero regina Ethnea egregiam illius Concraidi pulcritudinem, spiculo inordinati amoris vulneratur atque vulneris medelam apud Concradum esse fatetur." According to the Old-Irish version, Kieran purges her of this lust by feeding her blackberries. *Bethada náem nÉrenn*, 1922, II, 114.

74. De s. Columba abbate Hiensi. Vita prolixior auctore S. Adamnano abbate, ASS, II Junii, p. 204.

75. Ibid., p. 204.

76. Ibid., p. 224, "nam quem heri oderam hodie amo."

77. ASS, II Januarii, p. 102.

78. *Vitae sanctorum*, 1910, I, 183. "Et omnes magnificabant propheciam sancti Cathagi, qui genealogiam beati infantis Dimmai, nemine sibi indicante nisi Spirito Sancto, exposuit."

79. Vita s. Albei, *Vitae sanctorum*, 1910, I, 55. "Quadam die quedam mulier que oculte peperit per adulterium . . . Et ait: Ducantur ad me omnes viri qui habitant in una villa cum ea."

80. CS, 1966, p. 31. "Quomodo sanctum episcopum a falso crimine et mulierem a tumore liberavit."

81. ASS, II Martii, p. 558. "Quidam regulus, Brendanus nomine, recenter baptizatus, obnixius deprecabatur S. Patricium ut quandam mulierem gravidam benediceret, quia illius benedictionem ei et soboli profuturam credidit."

82. ASS, II Januarii, p. 98. "Quod enim in ea natum est, de complexu humano suscepit: sed ipse multoties asseruit, et juramento constrinxit, quod a quo, vel quando vel quomodo conceperat, in conscientia non habebat."

83. ASS, II Martii, p. 540: "cum B. Martino Turonensi Archiepiscopo aliquanto tempore demorabatur, qui etiam avunculus matris ejus Conquessae esse dicebatur."

84. Ibid. "cognato suo Patricio monasticum habitum, et ejus instituta tradidit."

85. Ibid., p. 537. "Nutriebatur nempe in Nemphtor oppido puer Domini Patricius in domo materterae suae."

86. Ibid., p. 540. "Vere generatio istarum [sororum] apparet benedicta . . . et haereditas sancta nepotes S. Patricii."

87. CS, 1966, p. 256. "Sanctus ergo Albanus de claro genere Leganiensium ortos est . . . mater vero, dicta est Mella, soror Ybar episcopi fuit."

88. Ibid., p. 269. "Hic latro extitit filius sororis sancti Braccani, abbatis monasterii Cluain Immurchuir."

89. Ibid., p. 275. "Qui itineris comitem . . . virum pudicum et sanctum, Mobai nomine, consobrinum suum, duxit: horum enim duorum et sancti Mochonna matres, tres erant sorores."

90. Ibid., p. 610.

91. *Bethada náem nÉrenn*, 1922, II, 26.

92. *Vitae sanctorum*, 1910, I, 76: "solitus erat, ut matris mamillam, sancti Fregii auriculam sugere destram."

93. *Bethada náem nÉrenn*, 1922, II, 46.

94. *Vitae sanctorum*, 1910, I, p. 100: "faciem sororis aliquando uidebat similem aspectui lune splendentis."

95. Ibid., 162: "et apud eam magnam leticiam inuenit."

96. See the passage quoted in the epigraph to this chapter.

97. *CS*, 1966, p. 2.

98. *Vitae sanctorum*, 1910, I, 78: "uxor regis Lagenie . . . cogitauit arte maligna ut perfida nouerca interimere. Timuit enim quod proli sue preualeret."

99. *CS*, 1966, p. 34.

100. *Vitae sanctorum*, 1910, I, p. 119.

101. Tacitus, 1911.

102. The bibliography is reviewed in Murray, 1983, pp. 11–38; Conrad, 1962, I, 31–44.

103. Adam of Bremen, 1917 and 1959.

104. Jochens, 1980.

105. Phillpotts, 1913, makes much use of the customs of Diethmarsch.

106. Tacitus, 1911, cap. 18. "Intersunt parentes et propinqui ac munera probant."

107. Edictus Rothari, cap. 177, *Leges Langobardorum*, 1962, p. 476. "Si quis liber homo, potestatem habeat intra dominium regni nostri cum fara sua megrare ubi uoluerit."

108. *Leges Burgundionum*, 54.2 (1892, p. 3). "De exartis quoque novam nunc et superfluam faramannorum conpetitionem et calumniam possessorum gravamine et inquietudine hac lege precipimus submoveri."

109. Leo Marsicanus, 1846, p. 603: "Quidam etiam vir nomine Maio de comitatu Teatino obtulit curtem quae dicitur Fara Maionis."

110. Ibid., "quae insimul continet quinque milia octingenta modia de terra." See also ibid., p. 611. "Fara Maionis, et fara que dicitur Biana. Hic Maio fuit consanguineus Poterici praepositi sancti Liberatoris, et obtulit in hoc monasterio eandem faram."

111. Longnon, 1920–29.

112. Murray, 1983, pp. 89–97. Goffart, 1980, p. 131, n. 6, "I understand *fara* . . . to signify 'detachment, expedition'." See also ibid., pp. 252–58.

113. Marius Aventicensis, 1894, 1961, p. 238. "Hoc anno Albuenus rex Langobardorum cum omni suo exercitu reliquens atque incendens Pannoniam suam patriam cum mulieribus vel omni populo suo in fara Italiam occupavit."

114. Ibid. "Hoc anno Albuenus rex Langobardoruma suis, id est, Hilmaegis cum reliquis consentiente uxore sua Verona, interfectus est."

115. See above, n. 107.

116. Paul the Deacon, ii.9 (1878, p. 91). "Qui Gisulfus non prius se regimen eiusdem civitatis et populi suscepturum edixit, nisi ei quas ipse eligere voluisset Langobardorum faras, hoc est generationes vel lineas, tribueret. Factumque est, et . . . quas obtaverat Langobardorum praecipuas prosapias . . . accepit."

117. *MGH Dipl.* IV, 91, no. 72, dated 28 March 1027: "concambio, quod factum est cum Attone comite de ipsa phara filiorum Guarnerii."

118. *Leges Alamannorum*, cap. 81 (1966, p. 145). "Si quis contentio orta fuerit inter duas genealogias de termino terrae eorum, unus dicit: illic is noster terminus."

119. *Freising*, 1905, pp. 30–31, no. 5, dated 3 July 750. See the fine exegesis of this donation by Murray, 1983, pp. 103–6.

120. Ibid., p. 382, no. 446, dated 10 March 821. The lady Hroossuuind gives forest land to the church of Freising. "Illa ipsa pars est in silvis quod XII perticas continet in latitudine inter conmar[canis] et coheredibus meis qui ibidem praesentes fuerunt quando hoc factum fuit." She adds: "Et si aliquis de coheredibus hanc cartulam temptare si frangere possit, . . . a liminibus sanctorum sit extraneus." Thirty witnesses, perhaps her "coheredes," sign the charter. According to ibid., p. 379, no. 442, dated 13 January 821, Friduperht "et coheredes sui" construct a church; they seem equivalent with "multi alii nobiles viri."

121. See the use made of contiguous owners in Herlihy, 1962.

122. On family organization at Amalfi, see Del Treppo and Leone, 1977, pp. 89–120, "la nobiltà dalla memoria lunga," and pp. 257–80.

123. *Amalfi*, 1917, 1951, II, 293, no. 1. "Maru, honesta femina, filia quondam Leonis comitis et relicta quodam Sergii de Vono de Leone comite" sells a vineyard to "domino Lupo comite, filio quondam b.m. domina Drosu de Lupo comite."

124. Herlihy, 1962, pp. 72–93.

125. For examples among the serfs of St. Germain des Prés near Paris, see below, p. 71.

126. Esmein, 1929–35, I, 87–90.

127. Paul the Deacon, iv.37 (1878, pp. 164–66).

128. See the analysis presented by Del Treppo and Leone, 1977, p. 118, Table 5.

129. King, 1972, p. 223, concludes that already in the Visigothic kingdom the *Sippe* had lost its primitive functions and "it was the monagamous family that now constituted the basic social unit."

130. For example, it never exerted collective ownership over developed land, though it apparently did regulate the use of forests. See the classical article refuting the theory of a primitive communism among the German tribes by Foustel de Coulanges, 1885.

131. Wemple, 1981, pp. 27–50, discusses family law and offers helpful bibliographical guidance to the abundant literature in German.

132. Kroeschell, 1968, examines the different types of paternal authority in the Germanic legal codes.

133. Tacitus, 1911, cap. 17.

134. Wemple, 1983, pp. 38–43, "Polygyny and Divorce." McNamara and Wemple, 1977. Merscheberger, 1937.

135. Gregory of Tours, iv.3 (1951, pp. 136–37).

136. Cited in Galy, 1901, p. 29.

137. Adam of Bremen, iv.21 (1959, p. 203).

138. Galy, 1901, pp. 73–76.

139. Edictus Rothari, cap. 167, *Leges Langobardorum*, 1962, p. 43. "Et qui ex ipsis uxorem duxerit et de rebus communes meta data fuerit." On the history of marital conveyances in early medieval Europe, see D. O. Hughes, 1978.

140. Galy, 1901, pp. 21–22.

141. Edictus Rothari, cap. 182, *Leges Langobardorum*, 1962, p. 47, "habeat ipsa mulier et morgingab et, quod de parentes viro adduxit (id est faderfio)."

142. *ASS*, I Januarii, p. 91: "da illum mihi, et ego dabo ei filiam meam Hebrelde, et ditabo eos divitiis affluenter."

143. Tacitus, 1911, cap. 18.

144. *Leges Visigothorum*, 1894, III.1.5. "De quantitate rerum conscribende dotis."

145. Liutprandi Leges, no. 89 (727), *Leges Langobardorum*, 1962, p. 142, "debeat dare, si uoluerit, in solidos quadringentos, amplius non, minus quomodo conuenerit; et reliqui nouilis homenis debeant dare in solidos trecentos, amplius non."

146. On marital conveyances among the Franks, see Galy, 1901, pp. 118–135.

147. Liutprandi Leges, no. 7 (717), *Leges Langobardorum*, p. 102. "Ipsum autem morgingap nolumus ut amplius sit, nisi quarta pars de eius substantia, qui ipsum morgingab fecit."

148. Tacitus, 1911, cap. 18.

149. Gregory of Tours, ix.20 (1951, p. 437), "exemplar pactionis," dated 587.

150. *ASS*, I Januarii, p. 156. "Offerebat [Guthlandus] ergo ipse ememoratus juvenis saepefactae Christi mirabili puellae . . . vestes quam plurimas, auro gemmisque intextas, offerebat praedia multimoda, et mancipia immodica. Quae omnia floccipendens."

151. See above, n. 57.

152. Cited in Galy, 1901, pp. 83–84.

153. Ibid., "ut omnes homines laici publicas nuptias faciant, tam nobiles quam ignobiles."

154. Ibid., pp. 108–9.

155. *Pactus legis salicae*, xliv (1962, pp. 168–73). This obscure text has evoked much comment. See Murray, 1983, pp. 163–76, for a review of the issues.

156. Balon, 1963–74, III, 2, p. 529. He gives a chart showing the order in which matrilineal relatives were called to receive the fine.

157. Murray, 1983, pp. 193–216, systematically reviews the inheritance practices of the Germans.

158. *Leges Visigothorum*, 1894, IIII.2.1 (p. 123). "Ut sorores cum fratribus equaliter in parentum hereditate succedant."

159. *Pactus legis salicae*, lix (1962, pp. 268–73): "de terra nulla in muliere hereditas est, sed ad virilem sexum qui fratres fuerint tota terra pertinet."

160. *MGH Capit.*, 1895–97, I, 8–10, no. 4.

161. See the donation of Thedetrudis or Theodila, daughter of Brodulfo,

to the Basilica of St. Denys, Paradessus, 1843–49, I, 227–28, no. 241, year 627. See also the testament of the Frankish woman Burgundofara, ibid., II, 15–16, no. 257, year 632.

162. *Laws of the Alamans and Bavarians*, 1979, cap. XXXII [XXXIII], "Concerning women who are in the duke's service."

163. Ibid., cap. XLVI [XLVII], p. 82.

164. Thus, according to the "De ordine palatii" by the Carolingian scholar Hincmar of Rheims, *MGH Cap.* 1896–97, II, 515–30, "The good management of the palace, and especially the royal dignity, as well as the gifts given annually to the officers (excepting, however, the food and water for the horses) pertained especially to the queen, and under her to the chamberlain."

165. *Vita Liutbirgae*, 1939, p. 13: "ut diversarum artium, quae mulieribus conveniunt operibus." Ibid., p. 26: "multorum muliebrium operum artifex erat."

166. Ibid., p. 15. "Permansit autem venerabilis Liutbirg in domo domini sui et secundum matris suae dispositionem rerumque suarum gubernacula in tantum possidebat, ut domus penes eam regimen constiterit penitus."

167. Ibid., p. 26. "Igniculum vero in ea cella carbonum ardentium propter diversorum tincturam colorum." Ibid., p. 32, she learns "artem texturae," and she also instructs young girls "in artificiosis operibus." She was a busy woman.

168. "Sanctae Radegundis reginae Vita auctore Venantio Fortunato," *PL*, 72, col. 655. "Quae puella inter alia opera, quae sexui ejus congruebant, litteris est erudita."

169. *Passiones vitaeque sanctorum*, 1913–20, I, 66–67. "Nutritur a progenitoribus suis haec cum magno studio totius diligentiae . . . discens etiam litteras in diebus tenerae infantiae . . . laudes discit cantare filio virginis. Fit etiam per divinam clementiam capax memorie audiendo et legendo, exercens se etiam in magisterio doctrinae . . . plena esse eloquentiae, sed multo plus sapientiae."

170. *ASS*, III Martii, p. 384. "In predicto namque monasterio, quo creditae erant beatissimae Virgines erudiendae . . . id est, in legendo, modulatione cantus, psallendo, necnon quod nostris temporibus valde rarum est etiam scribendo atque pingendo . . . Simili modo in universi operis arte, quod manibus foeminarum diversis modis ac varia compositione fieri solet, honestissime fuerant instructae, videlicet nendo et texendo, creando ac suendo, in auro quoque ac margaritis in serico componendis, miris in modis extiterant perfectae opifices."

171. Ibid. "Quatuor Evangelistarum scripto . . . honorifico opere conscripserunt. Nihilminus Psalmorum libellum . . . aliasque quamplures Scripturas."

172. *ASS*, I Aprilis, p. 666. "Comes Eppo . . . librum unde illa sola solebat Psalmos decurrere, ad culinam detulit atque in ignem projecit."

173. Tacitus, 1911, cap. 19.

174. Vita Germani episcopi parisiaci auctore Venantio Fortunato, *Passiones vitaeque sanctorum*, 1913–20, II, 372. "Cujus genetrix, pro eo quod hunc post alterum inter breve spatium concepisset in utero . . . cupiebat

ante partum infantem extinguere: et accepta potione ut abortivum projicerit."

175. Vita Odilae, *Passiones vitaeque sanctorum,* 1913–20, I, 38–39.

176. "Ordinavit etenim, immo per eam dominus, ut et alia pessima et impia cessaret consuetudo, pro qua plures homines sobolem suam interire potius quam nutrire studebant." *ASS,* III Januarii, 354. *MGH, Ss rerum Merovingicarum,* 2:482–508.

177. *ASS,* III Martii, p. 642. "Memorata Liafburg cum nata esset habebat aviam gentilem, matrem videlicet patris sui . . . misit lictores, qui raperent eamdem filiam tunc natam, de sinu matris, ut necarent priusquam lac sugeret: qui sic erat mos Paganorum, ut si filium aut filiam necare voluissent, absque cibo terreno necarentur."

178. Tacitus, 1911, cap. 20. "The lord and slave are in no way to be distinguished by the delicacy of their upbringing."

179. Gregory of Tours, viii.9 (1951, p. 376).

180. Ibid., "sed, ut credo, alicuius ex leudibus nostris sit filius."

181. Tacitus, 1911, cap. 20. "An uncle shows the same regard for his sister's children as does their own father. Some tribes consider this relationship more binding than any other."

182. *Passiones vitaeque sanctorum,* 1913–20, II, 160–75.

183. *ASS,* III Februarii, pp. 514, "quae ab ipsa genitrice sua tradita fuerat beatae ac sacratae Virgini Aldegundi Abbatissae germanae praefata Waldetrudis, matertae suae, ad erudiendum ac sanctam regulam edocendam."

184. *ASS,* VIII Septembris, p. 172. "Amplectabatur amoris privilegio avunculum suum, sanctum videlicet Basinum."

185. See above, n. 128.

3. THE EMERGENCE OF THE EARLY MEDIEVAL HOUSEHOLD

1. *St. Germain,* 1844, 1886–95.

2. Herlihy, 1960, p. 82.

3. Ibid.

4. *MGH Capit.* 1893–97, no. 273, 25 June 864.

5. Herlihy, 1960, p. 79. The term may appear on the Continent as early as 632 in the testament of Burgundofara, Pardessus, 1843–49, no. 257 (II, 15–16), but the phrase "cum terris, domibus, mansis" may be a transcription error for "cum terris, domibus, mancipiis." It is certainly used in charters from about 690.

6. Bede, 1971, i.25 (I, 108). See the epigraph to this chapter. See also ibid., iii.24 (I, 452), in regard to estates: "Singulae vero possessiones decem erant familiarum . . . possessione decem familiarum"; and Bede, I, 454, "regnum australium Merciorum, qui sunt, ut dicunt, familiarum quinque milia."

7. *Corvey,* 1843, no. 30 (p. 17). "Tradidit Folcberth pro anima Gherberghe I familiam in Altungunhus nomine Unuan, et xxx jugera." See the interesting comments of Kroeschell, 1968.

8. Ibid., no. 450 (p. 99). "Tradiderunt Albmer, Pumi, Magenhard et sorores Adallog, Fastred atque Hildiburg mansum unum in Aldberteshusen cum familia Weinwed et alterum mansum in Boffeshusen cum familia Hun."

9. Vita alia auctore Luidolpho presbytero, *ASS*, I Februarii, pp. 88–91.

10. Ibid., p. 88: "cum quibus opera muliebria, victum quaeritans, oper-abatur. Nam lanam nere, more faeminarum atque texere solebat, unde vulgo lanarius vocabatur."

11. Ibid., p. 89: "ut qui in hoc seculo communiter viximus, etiam com-muni sepultura utamur."

12. The following figures are based on a count of the relatives mentioned in donations listed in *Corvey*, 1843.

13. In 334 Constantine ordered that the families of married slaves were not to be separated, "since it is unjust that children be separated from parents, or wives from husbands." *Theodosian Code*, 2.25.1 (1952, p. 56).

14. See the use of "peculium" in *Theodosian Code*, 5.19.1 (1952, p. 117): "A colonus shall not alienate his peculium"; "There is no doubt that coloni do not have the right to alienate the fields that they cultivate."

15. See Herlihy, 1960.

16. Emperor Constantine in 332 decreed that all fugitive "coloni, tenants and slaves" be returned to their place of origin and, if free, that they be reduced to servile status: *Theodosian Code*, 5.17.1 (1952, p. 115). Valentin-ian and Valens in 365 forbade coloni from instituting civil suits without their patrons' permission: ibid., 5.19.1 (1952, p. 117).

17. *Tablettes Albertini*, 1952.

18. Herlihy, 1960, p. 86.

19. On the customary or "vulgar" law of the late empire, see Levy, 1951, pp. 194–97.

20. See above, p. 12, and the decree of Honorius and Theodosius in 409 on the settlement of the barbarian Scyrae within the empire. *Theodosian Code*, 5.6.2 (1952, pp. 107–08).

21. Tacitus, 1911, cap. 25, already mentions "housed" slaves among the Germans. "Each has his own domicile and rules his own house." See *Freis-ing*, 1905, p. 448, no. 524, 20 April 825, when free men, called "barscalci," accept ecclesiastical land, apparently forests, in return for rents and services. See also the life of Rupert duke of Bingen, a contemporary of Louis the Pious, by St. Hildegard. The life was written in the twelfth century but certainly based on older materials. Rupert "in praedio suo, quod latissimum fuit, villas et ecclesias in quibus locis non erant, aedificari fecit, et homi-nibus suis ea distribuit, quatenus inibi manentes et matri suae, quamdiu viverent, ministrarent." *ASS*, V Maii, p. 504.

22. Echternach, 1929–30, no. 8, 1 May 704, "cum omni peculio vel la-boratu eorum quod habent vel habere noscuntur." This is the oldest such usage I have noticed. Fulda, 1956, no. 39, 762–63, "quantum nobis genitores nostri dimiserunt et nos ipsi conlaborati habemus."

23. *Canones Theodori*, 1929, 13.3, p. 33: "non licet homini a servo sub-tollere pecuniam quam ipse labore suo adquesierit."

24. Esmein, 1929–35, I, 87–90 and 335–56, explains the Church's very complex rules on close marriages. See also, for Merovingian marriages, Galy, 1901, pp. 26–29.

25. *MGH Ep.*, III, 275. "Dicimus, quod oportuerit quidem, quamdiu se

agnoscunt affinitate propinquos, ad hujus copulae non accedere societatem."

26. On the Germanic method of reckoning kinship, see Champeaux, 1933.

27. Esmein, 1929–35, I, 357–62.

28. See the equivalent prohibition in the Edictus Rothari, cap. 185, *Leges Langobardorum*, 1962, p. 49. "Nulli leciat nouercam suam (id est matrinia, qui fuit uxor patris) neque priuignam (quod est filiastra) neque cognatam (qui fuit uxor fratris) uxorem ducere." On early medieval kinship names, see Bullough, 1969. Galy, 1901, pp. 50–57, reviews the provisions of the Merovingian councils against incestuous marriages.

29. Esmein, 1929–35, I, 335, thinks that the prohibition was built on "forced analogies and extreme deductions," forming a *logique outrée*. See more recently Goody, 1983, who seems to consider the incest prohibition the most distinctive rule of marriage in the West. Galy, 1901, 371–72, thinks that the Church's intent was to preserve peace among the kindreds through marital ties.

30. Gregory of Tours, 1951, iv.3.

31. Wemple, 1981, p. 96, argues for the earlier date, but Duby, 1983, believes that the rule was not firmly established until the twelfth century.

32. Pardessus, 1843–49, no. 414 (II, 212–14). In the year 691 Pepin and Plectrudis donate a *mansum indominicatum. St. Germain*, 1886–1895, ii.1 (II, 7).

33. Herlihy and Klapisch-Zuber, 1978.

34. *St. Germain*, 1844, 1886–95.

35. Russell, 1958, p. 94, reviews older studies based on Irminon's polyptych. Ring, 1979, doubts that any Carolingian survey can yield accurate information about sex ratios. See most recently Devroey, 1981, for further comment on the Carolingian surveys as demographic sources.

36. *St. Germain*, 1886–95, I, 9.

37. See, for example, ibid., xxi.81 (II, 294): "Ratbertus colonus, homo sancti Germani, et uxor ejus advena, cujus infantes non sunt sancti Germani." The children's names are not given.

38. Coleman, 1974.

39. See the *Leges Alamannorum*, 1966, p. 150. "Si quis mulieri pregnanti abortivum fecerit, ita ut iam cognoscere possit, utrum vir an femina fuit, si vir debuit esse, cum 12 solidis componat; si autem femina, cum 24."

40. *St. Germain*, 1886–95, II, 311–12.

41. Ibid., i.33 (II, 5). "Ermentildis, colona sancti Germani, tenet de terra arabili antsingam i; facit in unaquaque ebdomada diem i; pullum i, ova v."

42. Ibid., ii.39 (II, 15). "Uldemarus colonus et uxor ejus colona, nomine Ermentildis, homines sancti Germani, habent secum infantes ii."

43. Herlihy and Klapisch-Zuber, 1978, p. 342. Devroey, 1981, p. 77, seems to advocate a similar approach to the analysis of Irminon's polyptych: "La mention d'un étranger n'y est, en règle générale, liée qu'à la possession de terres: l'épouse non liée au *dominus fundi* n'étant pas recensée . . . et son mari apparaissant comme un célibataire." But he seems to limit this category of "strangers" to those expressly called *advena* in the survey. In fact

the number of apparently celebate males exceeds the bounds of credibility. According to Devroey's own count (p. 81), on the estate of Béconcelle celibate males are 47 and account for 11.7 percent of adult males; women celebates are only 3, forming 0.9 percent of all adult females.

44. Herlihy and Klapisch-Zuber, pp. 328–30.
45. *MGH Capit.* 1893–97, I, 83–91.
46. *ASS*, I Januarii, p. 106. "Siquidem viduas hujusce faemiliae destitutas, et caelibes viros per singulas villas constituens, eis stipendia iugiter ministrabat."
47. *Farfa*, 1892, V, 254–63. Ring, 1979, discusses this survey.
48. *St. Germain*, 1886–95, I, 21.
49. See below, chap. 6.
50. Ibid.
51. *St. Germain*, 1886–95, xxiv.85 (II, 332). "Ardoinus extraneus et uxor ejus colona, nomine Gunthildis, homines sancti Germani."
52. See below, chap. 6.
53. Ibid., ii.10 (II, 9–10). See Longnon's long appendix, "Les noms propres de personne au temps de Charlemagne," ibid., I, 254–382.
54. Perrin, 1945.
55. See above, chap. 1, "Husband and Wife."
56. Tacitus, 1911, cap. 20.
57. *PL* 72, col. 874. "Solent ergo qui uxores ducunt dotes tribuere, conferre praemia, et ad vicem perdendi purdoris sua tradere patrimonia."
58. *Corpus iuris canonici*, 1879, Pars II, c. xxx.v, c.3. *MGH Ep.* iv, no. 99, pp. 569–70.
59. Lex Visig. Reccessvindiana sive Liber iudiciorum, iii.5, "De quantitate rerum conscribende dotis," *Leges Visigothorum*, 1894, p. 90. Liutprandi leges, cap. 7 (year 717), *Leges Langobardorum*, 1962, p. 102; see p. 50 above.
60. Decretales Gregorii IX, Lib. IV, Tit. 11, ca. 11 *Corpus iuris canonici*, 1879.
61. Dhuoda, 1975, iii.1.42 (p. 138). "Considerare debet quisquis ille est, fili, si aliquando ad perfectum venerit tempus, ut Deus proles illi concedere dignetur."
62. Aquinas, 1906, XII, 185: "in iuvenile aetate, ad quem terminatur motus crementi et a quo incipit motus decrimenti."
63. See above, chap. 1, n. 76.
64. See, for example, Basil the Great, *PG* 29, col 494. "Sicut autem triginta perfectae aetatis est annus in hominibus."
65. Confessionum libri vi.1. "Iam mortua erat adulescentia mea et ibam in iuventutem, quanto aetate maior tanto vanitate turpior."
66. *ASS*, I Aprilis, p. 550. "Haec aetatem [triginta annorum] Christus super omnia Deus videtur honorare, qui cum triginta esset annorum baptizatus est."
67. Isidore, 1911, xi.2.16. "Sicut enim triginta perfectae aetatis est in hominibus," clearly echoing the judgment of Basil the Great, n. 64 above.
68. *Leges Visigothorum*, 1894, iiii.3 (p. 134): "et aliquis de filiis iam ad perfectam, id est usque ad xx annorum pervenit aetatem." See Codex Euricianus, cap. 321, *Leges Visigothorum*, 1894, p. 15. "Pater autem tam filio

quam filiae, cum xx annos aetatis impleverit, mediam ex eadem, quam unumquemque contingit, de rebus maternis restituat portionem, etiam si nullus fuerit nuptiis copulatus."

69. Liutprandi leges, cap. 117, *Leges Langobardorum,* 1962, p. 155. "Si infans ante decem et octo annos, quod nos instituimus, ut sit legetima etas."

70. *Leges Visigothorum,* 1894, iii.4 (p. 88). "Ne viris minoris etatis maiores femine disponsentur." Liutprandi leges, cap. 129 (year 731), *Leges Langobardorum,* 1962, p. 161, "apparuit modo in his temporibus . . . quoniam adulte et iam mature aetate femine copolabant sibe puerolus paruolus et intra etatem legetimam et dicebant, quod uir eius legetimus esse deuerit, cum adhuc se cum ipsa miscere menime ualerit"

71. *MGH Conc.* 1906, 1979, Concilium Foroiuliense, p. 192: "ut nullus praesumat ante annos pubertatis, id est infra aetatem, puerum vel puellam in matrimonium sociare nec in dissimili aetate, sed coaetaneos sibique consentientes. Multas sepius ex huiusce modi nuptiali contractu ruinas animarum factas audivimus."

72. *ASS,* I Januarii, p. 504. "Praeterea cum esset in anno duodecimo requiritur a quodam Lanfranco nobili genere progenito, qui delates multas secum opes auri et gemmarum ac vestium, tradidit manibus parentum, ut possit Austrudem virginem accipere sibi conjugem."

73. Based on men and women who appear with children but without mention of a spouse.

74. Herlihy and Klapisch-Zuber, 1978, p. 405.

75. *St. Victor,* 1857, II, 633–56.

76. There is a significant number of male bachelors in the families reconstituted by Fossier, 1968, p. 206.

77. See above, chap. 2, n. 149.

78. *ASS,* II Aprilis, p. 34. "Ita cum juvenalis aevi viridante vigore floreret, adoptata sibi coaetanea virgine inter nobilium puellarum agmina, condecretis nuptiarum legibus, uxorem duxit vocabulo Tethe."

79. Ibid., p. 40. "Nam cum aetatis suae vicesimum quartum annum peregisset, abrenuntiatis secularibus pompis."

80. Brandileone, 1931, p. 273.

4. TRANSFORMATIONS OF CENTRAL AND LATE MIDDLE AGES

1. Russell, 1958, pp. 99–113.

2. Russell, 1948, pp. 360–62, proposed an increase from 1.1 to 3.7 million. In the *CEH,* 1964, I, 562, M. M. Postan states that the preplague population may have been nearer 7 million: "to most historians abreast of most recent researches the higher estimates may well appear to be more consistent with the economic and social conditions of rural England at the end of the thirteenth century."

3. Both the late M. M. Postan in England and Emmanuel LeRoy Ladurie in France have been strong supporters of this Malthusian interpretation. See the criticisms of Brenner, 1976, and the long discussion involving many scholars in the pages of *Past and Present,* 78 (1977): 24–55; 79 (1978): 55–69; 80 (1978); 3–65.

4. Benson and Constable, 1982.

5. The fundamental survey of the history of canon law remains that of Esmein, 1929–35. For recent comment on canon law and marriage arrangements in medieval society, see Donahue, 1983.

6. Esmein, 1929–35, I, 108–19 (on Gratian); 119–24 (on Peter Lombard).

7. *CIC*, 1879–81, I, 112. On Gratian's marriage law, see Plöchl, 1935.

8. Esmein, 1929–35, I, 131.

9. See Donahue, 1983, with bibliography, on Alexander's decretals.

10. Ritzer, 1962, 1970, is the standard survey of the rituals of marriage in the early Church (to the year 1000). For the ritual blessing "at the door of the church," see Ritzer, 1962, pp. 315–18.

11. Bracton, 1968–77, II, 372, writing in the thirteenth century, affirms a necessary connection between the endowment of the bride at the door of the church and a legal marriage. "Et ubi ab initio nullum est matrimonium nulla erit dos, et ubi ab initio est matrimonium, ibi erit dos quamdiu steterit matrimonium."

12. Duby, 1973, with bibliography. Duby, 1983, treats these same themes more extensively. For Italy, see Bellomo, 1966. For German lineages, see Leyser, 1968, 1970, and 1980.

13. See for example *Bologna Stat.*, 1937, vii.32 dated 1288, in reference to a man who dies intestate: "si filia seu filie que remanserint fuerit dotata vel fuerint dotate a patre vel a matre, fratre vel fratribus suis, filia seu filie que dotate sunt, sint contente de ipsa dote seu dotibus, et in bonis paternis amplius non petant." See also a Florentine will dated 1308, in which the Father, Lapo di messer Aldobrandesco, wills to his two daughters their dowries and 20 solidi of small Florentine deniers, but "iubens eas inde stare tacitas et contentas et quod nichil amplius in bonis . . . ipsius testatoris petere possint audeant vel presumant." Cited in Herlihy and Klapisch-Zuber, 1978, p. 532, n. 24.

14. Out of many possible examples, see *Tirant lo Blanc*, cap. 29, "How Tirant disclosed his name and lineage" (Martorell and de Galba, 1984, p. 40).

15. For a recent explanation of the complex rules of heraldry, see Dennys, 1982, with a helpful glossary of heraldric terms.

16. Duby, 1983, and in many previous studies, has subjected to close analysis the genealogical literature of northwestern Europe.

17. See Nicholas, "The Domestic Life of a Medieval City: Women, Children, and the Family in Fourteenth-Century Ghent," to be published by the University of Nebraska Press.

18. Goody, 1983, p. 224.

19. For the mutual exclusiveness of the right to marry and the right to inherit, see the eleventh-century tract by Peter Damian: "Quod quibus est jus haereditatis, est et affinitas generis" (Damian, 1853, col. 94).

20. See above, chap. 2, "Polygyny."

21. Wemple, 1981, pp. 75–96, "The Ascent of Monogamy." Although the Church in the ninth century pressed its case for monogamous marriage, it is hard to know how well these standards were maintained in the chaos of the tenth century.

22. Duby, 1983, reiterating a thesis he first advanced in Duby, 1978.

23. Much earlier, St. Adelhard of Corbie (*ASS*, I Januarii, p. 98), a cousin of Charlemagne, objected in vain to his divorce and remarriage to the Lombard princess Disiderata.

24. See, for example, the testament of the Frankish magnate Abbo, in *Novalesa*, 1898, I, 13–38, no. 2, dated 5 May 739, who gives what seems to be his entire patrimony to the monastery of Novalesa. His numerous lands are scattered between Grenoble and Savoy, across the lower Rhone valley and into the Alps, without any clearly defined administrative center. Patrick Geary of Florida State University is preparing a translation and analysis of this remarkable document. The patrimonies of the great Carolingian monasteries are similarly dispersed over vast areas.

25. Herlihy, 1958.

26. See Violante, 1977, for an excellent discussion with bibliography of great Italian families and their relationship with local churches in the high Middle Ages.

27. "Fiebat itaque proptererum (sic) peruriam ut ordines sacros, et ecclesiastica officia, quae pure et absque ulla venalitate solo vitae aeternae intuitu concedi opportet, pro pecuniae acceptione et diversorum munerum acceptione prophanis quibusdam et indignis tribuerent, et quod omnes catholicos detestari et abbominiari opportet, de morte animae vitam corporis sustentarent." *Lucca Mem. e Doc.* no. 1795 (III, 666).

28. *Farfa*, 1892, no 680; see also no. 733, "terra adelmarisca," from 1030 or 1031; *Lucca Reg.* 1910–19, no. 78; *Bobbio*, 1905, 99. See also Herlihy, 1969, p. 177. Toubert, 1973, I, 695–787, discusses family names and structures in central Italy.

29. Herlihy, 1969, p. 177.

30. Bellomo, 1966; Niccolai, 1940; Santini, 1887. The nature of the Italian, especially Florentine, kin organization has been much discussed, but the late medieval centuries have claimed most attention. See Goldthwaite, 1968, and Kent, 1977; the former argues that the *consorterie* were disintegrating into nuclear families in the fourteenth and fifteenth centuries, the latter contends that they retained their cohesiveness.

31. Published in Bongi, 1886.

32. On Genoese families, see Hughes, 1975 and 1977. Heers, 1977, though a general survey, includes much Genoese material.

33. Bongi, 1886, p. 485. "Item, si aliquis de suprascriptis Consortibus vel scribenis emerit vel deganeverit aliquam domum seu casam, turrim aut possessionem aliquam in tribus cappelis seu contratis, quod ipse denuntiabit incontinenti Consuli Domus suprascripte, ut congreget illos Domus quos habere poterit, sine fraude, et denuntiabit suprascriptam emptionem inter eos et offeret eis dare partem inde si voluerint, et dabit si acceptabitur per eos partem velle et cartam venditionis faciet eis inde vero pretio soluto."

34. Villani, 1823, xii.55 (IV, 92).

35. ASF, Manoscritti reg. 544, f. 491, where Ricco appears among the guild members. He was consul in 1234, 1245, 1253, and probably other years.

36. See the will of his son Gualterottus, dated 1278 and copied in ASF, Notarile B1950, f. 102, naming Ricco's other sons, Iacobus, Iulianus, Cambius, Reggetius, Rogerius, Barduccius, and Cionis.

37. ASF, Balia, reg. 1, f. 1, dated September 18, 1342.

38. Herlihy and Klapisch-Zuber, 1978, p. 251. The sixty Bardi households held 2.1 percent of the total wealth of the city.

39. Doffo was the great-grandson of Ricco; his father was Bartolo and his grandfather Iacopo, mentioned in n. 35 above. On the directorship of the Bardi bank, see Sapori, 1926.

40. *Lucca Reg.* p. 1, no. 39, and p. 15. The commentator of the thirteenth century: "Et nota quod de isto Benedicto descenderunt filii Roffredi."

41. Buonaccorso Pitti, 1905, pp. 7–8. Buonnaccorso tried to acquire "i libri e le charte e scritture che Ciore aveva di nostre antichità."

42. Morelli, 1956, p. 85.

43. On emancipations, see Kuehn, 1982; Herlihy and Klapisch-Zuber, 1978, p. 571.

44. Villani, 1823, 12.55: "i quali erano stati i maggiori mercatanti d'Italia."

45. On Boninsegna Angiolino Machiavelli, see Sapori, 1926, p. 245. One Betto di Fenci di messer Ugolino Machiavelli represented the company as a factor on the island of Rhodes. See Sapori, 1926, p. 258.

46. *Grenoble*, 1869, no. 16B.

47. Ibid.

48. For the legal aspects of English feudalism, see Milsom, 1976. On France, in addition to the many studies of Duby, Guilhiermoz, 1902, is still useful for the institutional aspects of French feudal society. On German feudalism, Krieger, 1979, is a recent study.

49. See preceding note.

50. Pertile, 1892–1902, III, p. 304.

51. Bracton, 1968–77, ii.c76.

52. *MGH Capit.*, 1893–97, II, 358. The classic study of this capitulary, recently reprinted, is Bourgeois, 1974.

53. *MGH Const.*, 1893, I, 90.

54. Ibid., cap. 4. "Precipimus etiam, ut cum aliquis miles sive de maioribus sive de minoribus de hoc seculo migraverit, filius eius beneficium habeat." Failing a son, the fief goes to a grandson in the male line. Next called is a brother. The agnatic preference is clear.

55. *MGH Const.*, 1893, I, 247–49, no. 177.

56. Conrad, 1962, I, 414–21.

57. *Coutumiers*, 1896, 26.4.

58. Ibid., 28.1 "And by this manner those born later hold from those born before up to the sixth degree of kinship; in that degree they are obligated to do fealty to the one born earlier; in the seventh degree of kinship he shall be held to do homage and to hold by homage what was formerly held by parage."

59. Excerpts in Stubbs, 1921, pp. 417–506. On inheritance laws in medieval England, see the recent survey of Hyams, 1980.

60. Lambert, 1879.

61. Duby, 1983, pp. 253–84.

62. Manitius, 1911–31, III, 498–502, for comment on his life and sources.

63. Lambert, 1879, p. 583. "Senuit itaque Ghisnensis Comes Manasses . . . Unde et sibi metuens, . . . ne, de corpore suo relicto semine, Ghisnensis terra ab alicuius sororis sue [marito?] . . . quasi ab alieno semine heredem quandoque mendicare debuisset."

64. Duby, 1983, p. 269.

65. Ercole, 1908, p. 39, places the earliest references to the true *dos* in the first years of the twelfth century, but says that its use becomes widespread only after 1150.

66. "Martini de iure dotium tractatus," in Kantorowicz, 1938, p. 261: "equalitas enim dotis et propter nuptias donationis eadem esse debet et in augmentis earum omnino exigitur equalitas tam in quantitate quam in partibus, maioribus pactis ad minora deducendis, ut uterque minorem partem lucretur."

67. See references in Herlihy, 1978, no. XIV, p. 24, n. 19.

68. *Giovanni Scriba*, 1935. Out of thirty marriage agreements in the chartulary, the dowry is higher than the reverse dowry in ten instances; the reverse dowry is higher in four; and the two are equal in sixteen.

69. Reproduced in Caffaro, 1890–1929, I, 31. The text reads: "in isto consulatu tercie ablate fuerunt mulieribus."

70. Brandileone, 1931, p. 273. Ercole, 1908, pp. 92–115. *Volterra Stat.*, 1951, p. 5, enactment dated May 1200, requiring that the *donatio* be no more than "quartam partem dotis." *Florence Stat.*, 1921, II, 98, "ut donatio non excedat libras quinquaginta vel quartam bonorum viri," enacted in 1253.

71. *Milan Cons.*, 1872, cap. 17, p. 245, "quarta tamen, propter eius odium de illis non habetur"; p. 246, " . . . similiter, odio quartae, de nostra consuetudine, quarta non dabitur."

72. The shift in payments from the groom's to the bride's side has frequently been noted. See Bellomo, 1961.

73. *Giovanni di Guiberto*, 1939–40. By my count, out of forty-one marriage agreements, the dowry is higher than the reverse dowry in twenty-five instances; the reverse dowry is higher in one; and the two are equal in fifteen. See, above, n. 67, for the distribution some forty years earlier.

74. Herlihy and Klapisch-Zuber, 1978, pp. 590–91.

75. "Non faceva, nascendo, ancor paura / la figlia al padre; che'l tempo e la dote / non fuggien quinci e quindi la misura," *Paradiso*, 15: 103–105 (Dante, 1960).

76. Villani, 1823, II, 96 (vi.60): "lire cento era comune dota di moglie, e lire dugento o trecento era a quegli tempi tenuta isfalgorata; e le più delle pulcelle avevano venti o più anni, anzi ch'andassano a marito."

77 Kirshner, 1978; Kirshner and Molho, 1978.

78. *ASS*, III Martii, p. 179–250.

79. *ASS*, I Maii, p. 344. The saint includes among his other charities money "pro maritandis filiabus."

80. Pollack and Maitland, 1952, II, 419. "Feudalism destroys the equality between husband and wife."

81. Holdsworth, 1935, III, 524.

82. Lemaire, 1929, p. 602, citing the text: "quod mulier . . . non capiat ibidem medietatem *de adquisitionibus viri sui* . . . sed suo maritagio sit contenta."

83. Merea, 1952–53, I, 78 ff.

84. According to research done by Reuven Avi-Yonah in an unpublished seminar paper at Harvard University.

85. Laigle, 1912, p. 187.

86. The relation of women to the work force in the late medieval towns remains very obscure. See the overly optimistic comments of Power, 1975, pp. 59–69.

87. Macinghi negli Strozzi, 1877; examined by Martines, 1974.

88. Duby, 1983, p. 267.

89. *Rotuli de dominabus*, 1913.

90. *ASS*, III Martii, p. 38: "quia foeminarum religiosarum rara tunc erant monasteria."

91. See Koch, 1964; McDonnell, 1954; Grabmann, 1926.

92. *Corpus Documentorum Inquisitionis*, 1889–1906, I, 176: "terra predicta multum habundat milieribus, quibus secundum conditiones earum et amicorum decentia matrimonia non paterent . . . propter earum multitudinem vel parentum inopiam obtinere de facili non valerent; item quod honestas domicellas et nobiles depauperatas tamen opportet mendicare." "In diversis locis Flandrie quedam spatiosa loca, quae vocantur Beghinarum curie, fundaverunt, in quibus predicte mulieres, filie seu domicelle, reciperentur."

93. *ASS*, III Martii, 179–250. See above, n. 77.

94. *ASS*, II Januarii, p. 681. "Et in regionis pluribus locis multae erant faminae tam religiosae, tam seculares, quae prae animi fragilitate et mobilitate in vitia immaniter corruerunt. Miserae illae neminem habebant, cui prae pudore cordis sui molestissimum dolorem confiteri auderent."

95. *ASS*, III Februarii, p. 821: "quorum in numero erant tenuioris fortunae virgines mulieresque."

96. See above, chap. 1, "Ages at Marriage."

97. Odilo of Cluny. Epitaphium Adalheidae imperatricis, *PL* 142, col. 970: "cum adhuc esset iuvencula et sextum decimum aetatis suae ageret annum."

98. *ASS*, IV Maii, pp. 386–401. "Domina quaedam Humiliana nomine, filia Oliverii Cirki, civis Florentiae, cum esst annorum XVI, tradita est nuptui a parentibus."

99. *ASS*, V Maii, p. 206. St. Humility, whose baptismal name was Rossana, is said then to have entered the convent.

100. *Vita Caterine*, 1.4.

101. *ASS*, II Aprilis, p. 503.

102. *ASS*, II Martii, p. 183.

103. *ASS*, I Aprillis, p. 645.

104. Ibid., p. 644. "Patrem ea habebat rusticum . . . multimodis per totos decem annos exagitavit ad hoc ut maritus consentiret admittere."

105. *Pistoia Stat. pot.*, 1888, p. 120. "De puellis non nubendis . . . ante duodecimum annum sue etatis expletum."

106. Herlihy and Klapisch-Zuber, 1978, p. 205.

107. Ibid., p. 207.

108. See above, n. 74.

109. See above, n. 43.

110. Vida e miracles de sancta Flor, *AB* LXIV (1946), p. 14. She died in 1347.

111. Laribière, 1967.

112. *ASS* I Junii, pp. 362–63. "Quae cum infantiae pueritiaeque transisset annos, jam adolescentili aetate subeunte, nobilis adolescentula, legaliter et honorifice ut condignum, a parentibus in matrimonium coiuncta est." See also ibid., p. 362. "Post obitum vero Roberti . . . quia adhuc juvenis erat."

113. Guibert of Nogent, 1970, p. 63. The Latin text reads: "dum sub marito adhuc juvencula ageret."

114. *ASS*, I Januarii, p. 182: "manebat quaedam mulier, quae a parentibus suis juvencula fuerat maritata . . . Unde factum est, ut dum ipsa juventutis annos decurrerat, et incassaretur digitus, idem impinguatus arctari coepit graviter in annulo."

115. Cited in Laribière, 1967, p. 350.

116. De Navarre, 1889, 5.191.103: "L'an ne devroit ja volantier marier anfant malle tres qu'il ai .xx. anz acomplis . . . Mais les filles doit l'an volentiers marier pui que eles son passé .xiiii. anz."

117. *ASS*, III Martii, p. 735. "Post annos duodecim, parentibus et propinquis de suo coniugio tractantibus."

118. *ASS*, II Novembris, p. 522, "Synopsis vitae B. Franciscae."

119. Christiani matrimonii Institutio, Erasmus, 1703, V, 666. "Nunc rarum exemplum non est, praesertime apud Gallos, puellam vix decem annos natam esse uxorem, undecim anno jam matrem . . . Illud prodigiosum videtur, quod tamen in nonnullis fieri videns, praesertim apud Brittanos et Italos, ut tenera puella nubat septemgenario."

120. *Life of Christina*, 1959. According to C. H. Talbot, Christina was born sometime between 1096 and 1098, and forced into marriage in 1114 or 1115.

121. *Rotuli de dominabus*, 1913.

122. Two scholars who pay particular attention to marriage, but with inconclusive results, are Britton, 1977, and Razi, 1980, pp. 50–63. Razi guesses that among the peasants of Halesowen males married at about age 20, and girls between 16 and 19, but he concedes that the estimates are very rough. Smith, 1983, argues largely from the poll tax returns that women were marrying late in the fourteenth century, but see the comments of Hanawalt, 1985, chap. 6.

123. The cases are printed in Helmholz, 1974, p. 202 ff.

124. *The Canterbury Tales*, "The Wife of Bath's Prologue and Tale," v. 4. Chaucer, 1933, p. 91: "sith I twelf yeer was of age." Kelly, 1975, pp. 182–83, notes that in the tales of both Chaucer and Boccaccio, girls are very young at first marriage.

125. Marius, 1984, pp. 34 and 41.

126. *ASS*, II Julii, pp. 404–10. St. Godelive was born most likely in 1052, married in 1067 and murdered in 1070. On her contemporary life by Drogo of Bergues, see *AB* (1926), pp. 102–37.

127. *ASS*, V Junii, p. 550: "cum esset annorum quatuordecim, eam juveni cuidam matrimonio conjunxerunt."

128. *ASS*, II Januarii, p. 147.

129. *ASS*, II Aprilis, p. 156: "ad bivium Pythagoricae litterae pervenisset."

130. Ibid., p. 272.

131. Erasmus, 1703, III, 290. "Primum adest ipse flos aetatis. Nam, nisi fallor, agis annum iam decimum septimum." Ibid., p. 306. "Est mihi familiaritas cum homine quodam nobili . . . Is duxerat puellam virginem, annos natam decem et septem." Ibid., p. 453: "verum suscipari non potui te puellam vix dum egressam decimum sextum annum tam mature didicisse difficillimam artem gignendi liberos."

132. *ASS*, V Junii, p. 368. "Cum autem esset duodecim annorum, cum eam parentes ipsius matrimonio tradere vellint, . . . perrexit Coloniam."

133. See Vita Hedwegis, 1884, p. 514.

134. Koebner, 1911.

135. *ASS*, XIII Octobris, p. 511: "per fratrem ejus seniorem fuit cuidam manu artifici, viro honesto et maturo, . . . promissa."

136. *ASS*, IV Octobris, p. 384.

137. *ASS*, III Martii, p. 505.

138. Herlihy and Klapisch-Zuber, 1978, p. 400.

139. See above, n. 103.

140. Herlihy and Klapisch-Zuber, 1978, p. 207.

141. Guibert of Nogent, 1970, pp. 63–64.

142. *Life of Christina*, 1959, p. 44.

143. *Rotuli de dominabus*, 1913, pp. 48, 38, and 78.

144. See above, n. 115.

145. Duby, 1964.

146. Ibid., p. 836.

147. *Tristan and Iseult*, 1945, p. 40.

148. *Aymeri de Narbonne*, 1887, pp, 57–58.

149. *Hervis von Metz*, 1903, vv. 635–36. "Vix fu et fraisle, si ot son tans usé / .LX. ans ot li rois en son aé." See also vv. 863–65: "Vix est et frailles, si a ses jours passé / Quatre-vins ans a il moult bien d'aé."

150. Martorell, 1984, p. 259, cap. 148, "Stephanie was fourteen when Diaphebus met her." And Carmesina is described as Stephanie's age.

151. "The Wife of Bath's Prologue," Chaucer, 1933.

152. Marius, 1984, pp. 3 and 34.

153. "Cum autem matrimonia eorum fiebant, erant quasi annorum XXX." Marco Battagli da Rimini, 1913, p. 10.

154. Morelli, 1956, pp. 111–12.

155. Herlihy and Klapisch-Zuber, 1978, p. 205, Table 23.

156. Herlihy, 1973.

157. *ASS*, XIII Octobris, p. 321. "Dilecta soror, quo proponis Joseph ipsum

ducere? Numquid ad fontem juventutis renovantem eum perducere co-neris?"

158. *ASS*, IV Octobris, p. 384.

159. Koebner, 1911.

160. Cited in ibid., p. 140.

161. Guibert of Nogent, 1970, p. 186.

162. *ASS*, I Martii, p. 289. "Contigit quoque annis aliquot decursis, quod iuvenis quidam dum esset desponsatus cuidam puellae nondum nubili; et in domo parentum tamdiu habitaret quousque adolesceret puella."

163. Guibert of Nogent, 1970, p. 51.

164. *ASS*, II Januarii, p. 156. "Qui tamen diu in criminum vitioso mari navigans."

165. Alain de Lille, 1908, p. 55.

166. Ibid., p. 72.

5. DOMESTIC ROLES AND FAMILY SENTIMENTS

1. Ariès, 1973. There is a shortened English translation of the first edition in Ariès, 1965. For a good, critical review of the thesis, see Arnold, 1980.

2. See, for example, Stone, 1977, pp. 5–9. Stone does not see strong affective ties in the English family until the rise of what he calls the "closed domesticated nuclear family," from about 1640. In the "open lineage family," supposedly dominant in the Middle Ages, "affective relations" were "cool" and "widely diffused." The thesis has been attacked from too many quarters to be reviewed here, and today has little life left in it.

3. Kelso, 1978, gives a bibliography of Renaissance writings on manners and household management. The studies collected by Van Hoecke and Welkenhuysen, 1981, are concerned with love and marriage as portrayed in medieval literature.

4. The complete results of this count of saints will be published in my article, "Did Women Have A Renaissance? A Reconsideration," forthcoming in *Mediaevalia et Humanistica*.

5. Vauchez, 1981, p. 243. Weinstein and Bell, 1982, p. 220, also observed this proliferation of female saints from the thirteenth century.

6. Women are numerous among the early martyrs, but their numbers dwindle until a low point right in the middle of the Middle Ages, in the eleventh century, probably as a result of the Gregorian campaign to place women at a distance from the now celibate clergy.

7. *Vita Caterine*, ii.8. "Am I perhaps God," she protests to someone asking for a miracle, "able to free mortals from death?"

8. Many examples of parental efforts to force an unwanted marriage on sons and daughters are given in Weinstein and Bell, 1982, pp. 74–76.

9. Caterina da Siena, 1913, II, 102 (no. 90). Catherine warns Laudomia Strozzi against excessive attachment to "o figliuoli o marito o alcuna crea-tura."

10. "Verum habetur cuiusdam saecularis prudentiae dictum quod omnes socrus oderunt nurus." See *AB* (1926), p. 128.

11. *ASS*, III Februarii, p. 305. "Recordare, quod, tua suggerente noverca, de paterna te pater expulit domo."

12. *ASS*, I Januarii, p. 189. Angela, who dies in 1309, loses her husband and all her children, but thanks God for this "grace," as it allows her to place her heart entirely in His: "magnam consolationem recepi de morte eorum, quamvis eis aliquantenus condolerem." Yvette (d. 1229) also wishes for the death of her husband, *ASS*, II Januarii, p. 147.

13. *ASS*, IV Octrobris, p. 521.

14. *Vita Caterine*, i.4.

15. Schmitt, 1971, traces the use made of Theophrastus and his "little golden book" in the Middle Ages.

16. *Romance of the Rose*, 1971.

17. See Christine de Pizane, 1982. Christine wrote this tract in defense of women; it was in essence a rebuttal to the *Romance of the Rose* and other misogynist literature.

18. On Marbode see Manitius, 1911–31, III, 719–30. Marbode's poems on women are in his *Liber decem capitulorum;* a new edition has appeared, Marbode, 1984.

19. *PL*, 1841–64, 171, col. 1698.

> In cunctis quae, dante Deo, concessa videntur
> Usibus humanis, nil pulchrius esse putamus
> Nil melius muliere bona, quae portio nostri
> Corporis est, sumus atque suae nos portio carnis.
> Multa minora quidem, sed quae tamen exigit usus
> Vitae comunis, tibi femina sola ministrat,
> Nam quis nutricis sumet nisi femina curam,
> Qua sine nemo potest natus producere vitam?
> Quis lanam, linumque trahet? Quis volvere fustum?
> Reddere quis pensum, vel texere quis petietur?
> Usus in nostros fiunt haec, tam commoda fiunt,
> Ut si deficiant, vitae minuatur honestas.

20. For further comment, see Herlihy and Klapisch-Zuber, 1978, pp. 585–88.

21. "L'uomo è animal civile, secondo piace a tutti i Filosofi; la prima congiunzione della qual multiplicata nasce la Città, è marito, e moglie, ne cosa può esser perfetta dove questa non sia, e solo questo amore è naturale, legitimo, e permesso." Cited in ibid. p. 587.

22. Cited in Gies, 1978, p. 34.

23. Barbaro, 1915, pp. 29–30. There is a partial English translation of this tract in Barbaro, 1978.

24. Erasmus, 1969–, I.3, p. 290.

25. Ibid., IV.1, the "Encomium Matrimonii."

26. Ibid., p. 394. "Quorsum haec spectant? eo videlicet, ut intelligamus coniugali societate et constare et contineri omnia, sine ea dissolui, interire, collabi cuncta."

27. Bernardino da Siena, 1950, p. 83. "Ex his omnibus manifeste apparet quod cessat generatio filiorum." "Quod necesse est minui gentes, sicut his temporibus . . . manifeste apparet."

28. *ASS*, II Martii, p. 183.

29. *ASS*, II Januarii, p. 654. "Ut spirituale cum aeterna Sapientia connubium contraxerit."

30. Christina of Stommeln was 10 when she was married to Christ, *ASS*, V Junii, p. 368. Catherine was married to Christ even as her family was celebrating carnival. *Vita Caterine*, i.12.

31. *ASS*, I Januarii, p. 205. "Et ideo prepara te ad recipiendum illum, qui te desponsavit annulo sui amoris, et conjugium jam factum est; et ideo de novo modo vult facere conjugimentum et copulam."

32. *ASS*, II Aprilis, p. 172: "sponso suo Christo Domino . . . firmissime copulans."

33. Cited in Gies, 1978, p. 94.

34. *ASS*, I Aprilis, p. 692: "ecce, respexit in medio choro . . . Virginem inenarrabilis pulchritudinis, regali schemate insignitam: duo iuxta illam juvenes pulcherrimi . . . quos esse Angelos intellexit . . . Oportet, inquit [angelus], ut tibi haec puella clarrisma desponsetur . . . manum ejus dexteram Angelus apprehendit et manui sacratissimae Virginis copulavit et sub his verbis desponsationem perfecit. Ecce, inquit, hanc Virginem tibi trado in sponsam, sicut fuit desponsata Joseph; et nomen sponsi pariter cum sponsa accipias."

35. Ibid., p. 691. "Erat tamen non inhumanus, sicut quosdam e religione videmus, qui omnem sexum femineum execrantur."

36. Ibid., p. 690. "Frequentius illi audivimus accidisse, quod, cum in una abside monasterii orationibus esset ac meditationibus occupatus, vocem Dominae et amicae carissimae, in opposita parte stantis, audivit . . . transivit ad illam et in aliquo secretiori loco pariter considentes, ille Beatae Mariae de statu suo singula requirenti, respondit; et ab ea vicissim, quaecumque voluit, requisivit. Talibus deductionibus nocturnas vigilas solabatur: tali consolatrice quoscumque adversus sustinebat eventus: talis matris consolatoriis uberibus fovebatur: tali magistra multa dubia et incerta se instruente cognovit."

37. Plutarch, On Affection for Offspring, *Moralia*, 496 A (Plutarch, 1920, VI, 349).

38. Barbaro, 1978, p. 221–22 (ii.9).

39. *CS*, 1966, p. 9. "Item enim a natura comparatum est nutricibus, ut quibus prebent lac carnis, prestent etiam semper affectum mentis."

40. *ASS*, II Aprilis, p. 282. "Instante igitur hora Dominicae Nativitatis, vidit haec Virgo omnium illarum virginum ubera, similiter et sua, prae lactis abundantia intumescrere."

41. *ASS*, I Januarii, p. 349. "Nam quadam vice, dum talibus meditationibus operam daret cum magna cordis devotione et dulcedine, delectando in Domino Iesu Christo parvulo nato, coeperunt ipsius Gheertrudïs Virginis ubera tumescere, lacteque manere: sicque per singulos dies a festo Dominicae nativitatis usque ad festum Purificationis non cessavit exitus virginei lactis ex uberis Virginis."

42. *ASS*, III Februarii, p. 333. "Ille autem, qui electorum tristiam vertit in gaudium, statim flavus et parvulus et nive candidior, nudus in praesepio reclinatus apparuit: et postea surgens ad Matris pectus in virginali gremio sedit."

43. Duby, 1964.

44. *Hervis von Metz*, 1903, p. 22.

45. Thomas of Celano, 1904, p. 17.

46. *Les Narbonnais*, 1898, pp. 11–12, and 19.

47. *Hervis von Metz*, 1903, p. 23.

48. Krabbes, 1884, p. 63. "In der aussersten Noth flüchten die Helden sich zu ihrer Mutter bei der sie immer Liebe, Rath und Hülfe finden, und die sie auch gegen den Vater im Schutz nimmt."

49. Thomas of Celano, 1904, pp. 15–16.

50. Catherine of Siena asks God that she be allowed to take the place of the damned in hell: "I would like that hell be destroyed." *Vita Caterine*, Prologue I.

51. Ibid., i.x. "When I heard this, I spoke with her, and with trepidation I said 'O Mamma (for everyone called her by that name) do you not see what danger we are in?' " Catherine in turn calls her followers "O filii."

52. See his letter describing her death to Sister Catherine Petribuoni, in Caterina da Siena, 1943, pp. 335–44.

53. Ibid.

54. *ASS*, III Februarii, p. 317. "Et quis potest numerare Hispanos, Apulos, Romanos et ceteros, venientes ad eam, ut instruerentur salutaribus monitis?"

55. Ibid., p. 342. "Ego enim feci tibi peccatorum matrem."

56. *ASS*, I Januarii, p. 232.

57. *ASS*, II Januarii, p. 157.

58. *ASS*, III Martii, p. 743. "Utrumque sexum, omnem aetatem suis verbis sanctissimis in viam salutis ferventer dirigebat."

59. *ASS*, I Aprilis, p. 444: "quamquam in omni vita sua sublimium personarum moleste sustinuerit."

60. *ASS*, II Septembris, p. 437.

61. *ASS*, III Martii, p. 70. "In convertendis peccatoribus valde sollicita erat."

62. Ibid., p. 70. "Mirandum autem est atque multa veneratione notandum apparebat in verbis ejus, quod mulier idiota de divinis tam ubertim tam prompte, arcana quandoque tam idoneis loqueretur verbis, adeo ut per quemdam Religiosum dicebatur in vita ejus, si meditationes B. Bernardi vel soliloquia B. Augustini attente legisset, non debuisset plus abundare divinorum verborum sententiis."

63. Kempe, 1944.

64. *ASS*, I Januarii, pp. 186–234. The contemporary Franciscan author claims to be repeating the saint's own words.

65. Dominici, 1860. See also Dominici, 1927, for an English translation.

66. No woman, for example, participates in the discussion concerning the family in Alberti, 1960.

67. Maine, 1888, p. 335.

68. "Quia cognovimus per effectum, matres circa filios in exactione dotis et antefacti non maternum affectum sed impietatem habere sepius novercalem." Constitutum legis Pisane civitatis, *Pisa. Stat.* 1870, II, 753.

69. "Hoc fit perraro quippe *genus mulierum avarissimum atque tena-*

cissimum promptius est ad accipiendum quam ad dandum." For the history of the phrase, see Ercole, 1908, p. 95.

70. Cited in Brandileone, 1931, p. 318.

71. *ASS*, I Januarii, p. 350. "Infantes dilexit et pueros haec virgo Gheertrudis. Quapropter diabolus saepe sic transfiguravit non in Angelum lucis, sed in formam pueri plangentis et lugentis et sic occuparet animum Virginis, ut averteret a Deo sive divinis."

72. *ASS*, IV Junii, p. 65. "Non est delectatio, super ista delectatione, qua vir conjungitur mulieri; et non est delectatio, sicut illa quam habet mulier ad puerum."

73. "Jesus at the Age of Twelve," Aelred of Rievaulx, 1971, pp. 1–40. On the basis of his writings, though not specifically this tract, Boswell, 1981, concludes that Aelred was a homosexual.

74. The "Legenda Gregorii" contains a passage, "De presepio, quod fecit in die natalis domini." Thomas of Celano, 1904, p. 67.

75. *ASS*, II Junii, p. 729: "vidit per fenestram amplectentem latenter quemdam puerum, in brachiis S. Antonii, pulcherrimum et jucundum: quem sanctus amplexabatur et osculabatur, indesinenter ejus faciem contemplando."

76. *ASS*, II Januarii, p. 660: "puerum scholasticum tantae venustatis."

77. *ASS*, I Januarii, p. 205.

78. Ibid., p. 206. "Ipsa autem Domina nostra quasi ab itinere fatigata est sedit, et faciebat tam pulchros et delectabiles gestus, et ita honestos, et gratos mores ostendebat." "O dilectrix filii mei, accipe."

79. Ibid. "Dum igitur sic starem subito puer remansit in brachiis totus nudus, et aperuit atque levavit oculos, et respexit, et statim in illorum oculorum sensi et habui tantum amorem, quod vicit me omnino. Exivit enim de illis oculis tantus splendor, et ignis amoris et laetitiae, quod est mihi indicibile. Et tunc subito apparuit una immensa majestas ineffabilis, et dixit mihi: Qui non viderit me parvum, non videbit me magnum . . . et addidit: Ego veni ad te, et obtuli me tibi, ut tu te offeres mihi. Et tunc anima mea modo mirabili et indicibili obtulit semetipsam ei: demum obtuli me totam et filios meos sequentes perfecto et totaliter obtuli."

80. *ASS*, II Januarii, p. 158. "Quam suavis in utero, dulcis in gremio, suave jugum in brachiis, onus leve in humero, matri filius, Mariae Christus."

81. *ASS*, II Aprilis, p. 166. "Ecce puerulus quidam, inaestimabilis . . . elegantiae . . . in lectum ascendens, et sese projiciens super illam, pugnorum ictibus ac pedum tonsionibus ipsam coepit vehementer opprimere."

82. Ibid., p. 177. Ida is given the baby. "Quem illa suscipiens, amplexibus simul et osculis astringebat sibi fortissime, pueri matre super omnia benedicta prope astante . . . Ex alio vero latere beati Praecursoris Domini mater Elisabeth affuit, balneumque quo lavari debuisset infantulus, cum vasis ad hoc praeordinatis applicuit, ipsumque puerum una cum Ida Venerabili balneundum in aquis tepentibus officissime reclinavit. Ubi cum resideret ille puerorum omnium electissimus, ludentium adinstar infantium plausum fecit in aquis ambabus manibus ac infantili more turbans illas et excutiens,

vicina loca sic humectabat, ut illis hac illacque dissilientibus, ipse prius earumdem aspersione per omnem sui corpusculi superficiem humectaretur . . . peracta vero balnectione rursus ex aqua puerum elevavit, et suis iterum panniculis involutum in sinu suo recondit, ipsique materno more familiariter alludendo, supra quam dici vel excogitari posset, in Deo salutari suo mirabiliter exultavit."

83. Ibid., "jucundissima disceptatio supraque modum gratiosa altercatio."

84. *ASS*, I Aprilis, p. 692. On the history of the cult of St. Joseph in the West, see Seitz, 1908.

85. See, for example, among the visions of Angela of Foligno, the token appearance of "Joseph senex," *ASS*, I Januarii, p. 218. *ASS*, III Februarii, p. 333, "pro honore Joseph senis," in reference to the prayers offered by Margaret of Cortona.

86. Bernardino da Feltre, 1964, I, 395. "Sed non conoscitur quia pingitur cossi un vechiarello, par cossi un tal christianello."

87. Praise of St. Joseph is scattered throughout the works of Gerson, 1962.

88. Gerson, 1962, VII, 75. "Si est bien à penser que Joseph attendit jusques environ cest aage."

89. Gerson, 1962, IV, 34, from the "Josephina." "Virgo . . . nova tunc iuvensque puerpera, pauper / simplex, sueta domi, regionum nescia."

90. Gerson, 1962, VII, 75: "ne fust point viel, lait, déffecteux et febble et comme impotent au labeur."

91. "Ioseph portat, Ioseph tractat, Ioseph mulcet osculis." Cited in *ASS*, III Martii, p. 6, attributed to Pierre d'Ailly.

92. Bernardino da Feltre, 1964, I, 400. "O, che fragrantia, quando tenebat in brachijs el Re del Paradiso! Pensa che ogni cor mancha etc. Quando regressi sunt de Egypto, erat Puer septem annorum, non poterat ita portari in brachiis, lo menava per mane, quando era straco lo dolore Yesu se sedeva e lo toleva in brachiis, stringebat ad pectus, deosculabatur, li liquefaceva el core de devotione, se gli dormentavi in brachiis. Oymi, che non posso più. etc."

93. Bernardino da Feltre, 1964, I, 401: "in Paradiso servatur ordo charitatis et propinquitatis, quia gratia non destruit naturam."

94. Listed in *ASS*, II Martii, pp. 2–6.

95. Bernardino da Feltre, 1964, I, 400. "Monarchia totius mundi de iure pertinebat Joseph." See also Gerson, 1962, IV, 97. He is "chief et seigneur de la mère du chief et du seigneur de tout le monde."

96. This is one of the twelve honors of Joseph, according to Pierre d'Ailly, "Mariam et Iesum sibi subditos habuerat." *ASS*, II Martii, p. 6.

97. Gerson, 1962, IV, 97. "Espers terroris, labor anxietas procul absunt; / Quaesumus intende nobis miserosque benignis / Inspice nos oculis, quos tanta pericula turbant . . . nos heu retinet tenebrosa / Torquet et Aegyptus."

98. Bernardino da Feltre, 1964, I, 402.

99. These names represent people considered eligible for office over the period mentioned; the collection is intended eventually to serve as the basis of prosopographical studies of the Florentine office-holding class.

100. For further comment, see Herlihy, 1978.

6. THE HOUSEHOLD SYSTEM IN THE LATE MIDDLE AGES

1. On the Catasto, see Herlihy and Klapisch-Zuber, 1978.

2. See, for example, Bernardino da Siena, 1950–, III, 307: "Filio non des potestatem super te in vita sua."

3. "Come de' figlioli, così della villa: una éne poco, due sono assai, tre sono troppi." From *Villa*, Alberti, 1960, I, 360.

4. Surveyed in Berges, 1938.

5. Vincent of Beauvais, 1624. He says that the "economic art" consists of four parts: education of children, selection of a wife, the management of the household (especially servants), and the cultivation of friends. The humanist Alberti, 1960, follows exactly the same outline in his "Four Books on the Family."

6. See Colonna, 1858.

7. Alberti, 1960.

8. Ibid., I, 92.

9. Ibid., I, 234: "sotto uno tetto si riducano le famiglie, e se, cresciuta la famiglia, una stanza non può riceverle, assettinsi almeno sotto una ombra tutti d'uno volere."

10. See further comments in Herlihy and Klapisch-Zuber, 1978, pp. 509–11.

11. Ibid., pp. 470–79.

12. The turmoil often created by a departing widow is emphasized by Klapisch, 1983.

13. Damian, 1853, col. 194. "Quod quibus est jus haereditatis, est et affinitas generis."

14. For a critical evaluation of Le Play's thesis, a little too severe in tone, see Mitterauer and Sieder, 1982, pp. 24–26.

15. Hilaire, 1973, and, on the general relationship between inheritance rules and family structures, Goody, Thirsk, and Thompson, 1976.

16. Homans, 1941, 1960.

17. Razi, 1980, p. 50. See most recently Hanawalt, 1985, chap. 4: "peasants might try to honor local inheritance rules, but they certainly did not feel bound by them."

18. Herlihy and Klapisch-Zuber, 1978, p. 78. Most of the calculations given here are based on a fresh analysis of the machine-readable file. Totals differ slightly from those previously presented. They reflect whether or not the count includes marginal entries, such as households with an inheritance but no persons. The differences are tiny and have no statistical significance.

19. See Imberciadori, 1951.

20. Herlihy and Klapisch-Zuber, 1978, p. 486.

21. Ibid., p. 389.

22. Britton, 1977.

23. Herlihy and Klapisch-Zuber, 1978, pp. 512–22.

24. Ibid., p. 400.

25. The estimate comes from Enrico Fiumi, cited in Herlihy, 1967, p. 114, n. 33. In 1738 Tuscany had only 890,608 inhabitants, and 1,565,751 in 1846.

26. Examples are given in Herlihy, 1967. For example, Joseph R. Strayer concludes that the French county of Beaumont-le-Roger was not greatly inferior in its population size in 1313 to what it is today.

27. Wrigley and Scofield, 1981.

28. Surveyed in Noonan, 1966.

29. Duby, 1983, p. 268.

30. Bernardino da Siena, 1888, I, 95.

31. Bernardino da Siena, 1950–, I, 210. "O quot indicibilibus modis et quot incredibilibus modis viri abutuntur uxoribus suis! Quis umquam honeste exprimere potest?"

32. Lorenza, wife of Matteo Corsini, gave birth to 20 babies in 24 years, from 1365 to 1389. Cited in Herlihy and Klapisch-Zuber, 1978, p. 196. Mme Klapisch, from her studies of the largely unpublished Florentine *ricordi*, concludes that there is no evidence of a limitation of births among these women.

33. The nature of the Catasto is extensively discussed in Herlihy and Klapisch-Zuber, 1978.

34. See ibid., p. 421.

35. Ibid., pp. 360–70.

36. Klapisch, 1983.

37. Herlihy and Klapisch-Zuber, 1978, pp. 59–62.

38. Ibid., p. 331.

39. Ibid., pp. 417–19.

40. Britton, 1977.

41. Hajnal, 1983.

INDEX

Abban, Irish saint, 32–33, 187, 188

Abduction, 31, 38, 40, 43, 50, 52, 55, 78, 157

Abortion: among Alamanni, 65; among Merovingians, 53, 146, 195; in ancient world, 25; in early Ireland, 31–32, 186

Acta sanctorum, collection of saints' lives, 113

Adalbert, husband of Dorothea of Montau, 107, 109, 115

Adalheid, German empress, 103, 204

Adam, first man, 7, 24, 26, 132

Adam of Bremen, medieval chronicler, 44, 49, 191, 192

Adamnan, Irish saint, 29, 34–35, 190

Adelhard of Corbie, Carolingian abbot, 67, 179, 201

Adoption, 2, 6, 132

Adultery, 37, 40

Aedh, Irish saint, 34, 36

Aelred of Rievaulx, English Cistercian, 126, 211

Aemilia Hilaria, Gallo-Roman woman, 20–21, 184

Aeneas, Roman epic hero, 15

Aetas perfecta, 74–75

Affinity, 6, 7, 11, 84–85, 135

Agde, council of, 61

Age at marriage: at Florence, 109; at St. Germain, 69; in ancient Rome, 17–23; in central Middle Ages, 103–10, 157–58, 182–83; in early Middle Ages, 74–79

Age differences between spouses, 76, 120–21, 124, 129, 144, 154

Agri deserti (deserted fields), 59

Ailbe, Irish saint, 37, 40

Ailly: *see* Pierre d'

Alain of Lille, French poet, 110, 207

Alamanni, Germanic people, 45; laws of 46, 50, 52, 106

Alban, Irish saint, 41, 190

Alberghi, Genoese houses, 89

Alberti, Giannozzo, Florentine sage, 134, 135

Alberti, Leon Battista, Florentine author, 131, 134–35, 210, 213

Alboinus, Lombard king, 45

Aldetrude, Merovingian saint, 55

Alexander II, pope, 87

Alexander III, pope, 81, 200

Alexandria, Egyptian city: *see* Clement of

Alexandria, Italian city, 98

Algeria, 59–60

Alps, 5, 81, 201

Amalfi, Italian city, 47, 192

Amator of Autun, Merovingian saint, 13–14

Ambrogio Sansedoni, Sienese saint, 99, 103

Ambroise: *see* Françoise d'

Ancillae, women slaves, 67, 69, 184